DIVINE HEARTBEAT

DIVINE HEARTBEAT:
LISTENING TO GOD'S HEARTBEAT FOR PREBORN CHILDREN

Timothy L. Fan

Published by
God-centered Universe Press
Aurora, Colorado
www.gcupress.com

Copyright © 2014 by Timothy L. Fan
All rights reserved.

ISBN-10: 069226065X
ISBN-13: 978-0-692-26065-4

Library of Congress Control Number: 2014916636

All Scripture quotations, unless otherwise indicated, are taken from the World English Bible® (WEB), a modern, public domain translation based on the American Standard Version 1901 Bible, Biblia Hebraica Stuttgartensia Old Testament, and Byzantine Majority Text New Testament. However, the (WEB) Scripture quotations have been adapted in the following manner: (i) the use of the divine name, Yahweh, has been quoted in its traditional English rendering, "the LORD"; (ii) contracted English words have been expanded into their formal equivalents (e.g. "don't" is quoted as "do not"); and (iii) pronouns representing God have been capitalized (e.g. "him," when referring to God, is quoted as "Him").

Scripture quotations marked (KJV) are taken from the King James Version of the Bible.

Scripture quotations marked (NKJV) are taken from the New King James Version®. Copyright © 1982 by Thomas Nelson. Used by permission. All rights reserved.

Scripture quotations marked (NASB) are taken from the New American Standard Bible®, Copyright © 1960, 1962, 1963, 1968, 1971, 1972, 1973, 1975, 1977, 1995 by The Lockman Foundation. Used by permission. (www.Lockman.org)

Scripture quotations marked (ESV) are taken from The Holy Bible, English Standard Version® (ESV®), copyright © 2001 by Crossway, a publishing ministry of Good News Publishers. Used by permission. All rights reserved.

Scripture quotations marked (NIV) are taken from the Holy Bible, New International Version®, NIV®. Copyright © 1973, 1978, 1984, 2011 by Biblica, Inc.™ Used by permission of Zondervan. All rights reserved worldwide. (www.zondervan.com) The "NIV" and "New International Version" are trademarks registered in the United States Patent and Trademark Office by Biblica, Inc.™

Scripture quotations marked (RSV) are taken from the Revised Standard Version of the Bible, copyright 1952 [2nd edition, 1971] by the Division of Christian Education of the National Council of the Churches of Christ in the United States of America. Used by permission. All rights reserved.

"Wash yourselves, make [yourselves] clean. Put away the evil of your doings from before My eyes. Cease to do evil. Learn to do [good]. Seek justice. Relieve the oppressed. Judge the fatherless. Plead for the widow." (Isaiah 1:16-17, WEB)

CONTENTS

Acknowledgments — i

"Years of Darkness": A Poem for the Preborn — iii

Foreword: Craig Houghton — v

Preface: A Prayer for the Reader — vii

Introduction: The Need for a Scripture-based Approach — ix

PART ONE
BIBLICAL FOUNDATIONS IN GENESIS 1-3

1 God's Littlest Image Bearers: — 3
The Image of God and Preborn Children

2 God's Great Blessings: — 25
Procreation and Preborn Children

3 Eve's Children: — 45
The Doctrine of Sin and Preborn Children

4 Adam's Guilt: — 67
Male Responsibility and Preborn Children

PART TWO
THE OLD TESTAMENT HEARTBEAT

5 Baby Moses in the Nile: — 89
Motherhood and Preborn Children

6 The Deathblow of Abortion: 111
Political Law and Preborn Children

7 David's Little Boy: 131
Bereavement and Preborn Children

8 Woven in the Womb: 155
God's Omniscience and Preborn Children

9 She Did Not Remember: 177
God's Fatherhood and Preborn Children

PART THREE
THE NEW TESTAMENT HEARTBEAT

10 The Baby Leaped: 195
Elizabeth, Mary, and Preborn Children

11 Christ's Temple: 219
The Physical Body and Preborn Children

12 The Heavenly War: 243
Spiritual Conquest and Preborn Children

Conclusion: They are "Still Speaking" 267

Appendix: Abortion Condemned by the Church Fathers 275

Select Person Index 277

ACKNOWLEDGMENTS

The glory of God is the current author's aim. Without the shed blood of Jesus Christ and the power of His resurrection, there would be no grace available for any good work, much less for an effort to reform the current Protestant Church in the Western World both in its doctrine and in its views on abortion. Therefore, let "God's Glory!" be the cry in all things.

It is, however, quite Christian to give thanks to those who have been an immeasurable comfort along the way of this book-writing journey. First, and foremost, I am grateful to my wife, Sarah, who, throughout the writing of this book, wept beside me and prayed with me on behalf of the preborn children. Your wisdom, my Beloved, is a gift from the Holy Spirit. Your wounds are His wounds. You are my best friend. Your radiance is like a lily among thorns. The Spirit of glory and of God rests upon you.

I would also like to express my deep, deep love and admiration for my children, who teach me daily how much God loves "the little ones." My Beloved Children, may Isaiah 66:2 be a treasure of promise bound continually to your hearts and worn always around your necks. Your Daddy loves you "all the way to the Cross."

My parents—Dad and Mom—have been my guides from infancy in the paths of Christian integrity and Christian justice. Along with my beloved sisters, they have stood beside me through recent years of hardship and ecclesiastical persecutions. It is sheer grace, Dad and Mom, to be your son. You wear the crowns of wisdom and of glory upon your heads.

My father- and mother-in-law are immovable in their defense of the babies in the womb. Your encouragement has meant the world to me.

Dr. and Mrs. Y.K. Chen have comforted my family in our darkest hours. Your love for God's Word is exemplary. The love of Christ that you have shown to us has humbled us in very deep ways. My family's debt of love to you shall continue on, with great joy, into eternity.

Our precious family members at Genesis Family Church in Denver, Colorado, have prayed me (every Monday) through the writing of this book. They have joined with other friends around the country who have faithfully prayed with much persistence and grace on my behalf. They have also been "strong and courageous" in their own efforts to defend the little ones in the womb—the precious little ones for whom this book is written.

TO MY BELOVED WIFE

Whose heart beats for God, and for the little ones in the womb.
Her children shall rise up and call her blessed. Her husband also.

AND TO MY MOTHER

Who prayed over me when I was in the womb, and who first convinced me
that babies in the womb are worthy of our protective, Christian love.

Years of Darkness[1]

We were not to speak about the "choice,"
Forbidden to say out loud what "choice" had chosen
(The tearing of the soft, silken skin
From its nurturing cradle in the womb).
No one dared discuss the deadly act—
Even the act-ors found *that* in poor taste.
The evil euphemisms of the day
Were weak and twisted into false positives:
"Pro" (that's for) and "choice" (that's death): *for death*.
The courtroom placed its hands on eyes, ears, mouth.
Physicians, sworn to do no harm, instead
Washed their blood-stained hands of any guilt.
In Mississippi, they once said black men have no souls.
In Auschwitz, they once said that Jews were not human.

Then, one by one, young people—boys, girls—
Stood up and cried, "Enough! This is insane!"
Doesn't she see the baby is alive?
A doctor helps her take her own child's life!
With surgical precision he invades
The holy sanctuary of the womb.
(They lied when they told her it was really nothing.)

---

[1] "Years of Darkness" by Anne Manning Fan, © 2014 by God-centered Universe Press. May not be reproduced, in any form, without the express written consent of God-centered Universe Press. All rights reserved.

Divine Heartbeat

That's why, at night, she shuddered at the deed
The horror of her tiny baby, dead
Herself broken, bleeding, a living nightmare.
Then, at last, she understands, repents,
Knowing the peace of complete forgiveness
Through Christ, her Lord, broken and bleeding for her.
God lets her have a single glimpse of him:
He with the mop of dark curls, rosy cheeks;
She of the grey-eyed smile;
He, barefooted at the edge of a pebbly stream;
She, with a ponytail and a baseball glove.

Then, like a mighty army, young and old
Rose up like the tide rolling in, breaking
And crashing on the changing shore,
Moving the continent that moves the world.
All the vague suggestions, glib instructions
Would have to stop. "This is a *baby* here.
This baby has a future, has a name."
So ended the deceitful, murderous game.

-Anne Manning Fan

FOREWORD

Timothy Fan has undertaken to challenge all of us to consider a distinctly Christian view of preborn children. Most of us would certainly join ourselves to the Anti-abortion camp, and our hearts grieve to think of the murder of the truly innocent amongst us. Some would venture into the Pro-life movement to the extent that we are not just against abortion, but we are in favor of life and truly feel that children are a blessing. But Timothy has called us to something further and deeper, and uses the pages of *Divine Heartbeat* to convince us that we should support and participate in what he refers to as "Abortion Abolitionism." We may be comfortable speaking out against abortion. We may quietly suggest that God's blessings may include lots of children and a large family, but do we see the need for something more? Is the "divine heartbeat" calling us to the kind of Abortion Abolitionism that includes both committed prayer for the preborn and the Sword of Scripture, with which to cut away the vain philosophies and pagan understanding that have crept in unawares and corrupted our thinking on the preborn? Are we prepared to follow the example and passion of that great slave-trade abolitionist, William Wilberforce, and to persevere in this battle for the minds and hearts of men to see that the killing of the preborn is abolished in the civilized world?

Timothy claims to be unconcerned with scholarly approval in this work, however he has shown himself to be a gifted and compelling writer, and he has produced a book that will stand up under any scholarly scrutiny. He references many Christian writers from every era, with a special love for John Chrysostom, but most importantly weaves Scripture through each section of his book and lays a solid foundation with the truth of God's Word. Timothy shares my heart when he writes that the "crisis over the lack of sound Abolitionist thinking in the Church is a crisis over Scripture."

Christians have been given God's inerrant, sufficient, and authoritative Word to be used to defend truth and defeat our enemies. We must be convinced by studying and meditating on the Bible that God's heartbeat for the preborn is not in doubt, nor a matter for dispute; but rather clearly establishes that all humans are created in His image, that all in the womb are constantly the object of

His love and care, and that our heart should break with His over the Abortion Holocaust.

Timothy consistently reminds readers throughout this book that God's love, forgiveness, and grace is extended to those who may have been deceived by our enemy and have been party to abortion in the past. Timothy presents a Scriptural foundation to take us from wishful thinking to confident assurance that the millions of aborted babies have been translated into the loving arms of our Savior.

Chapter 2, "God's Great Blessings," is especially dear to my heart and compliments *Family UNplanning*, which I was privileged to write several years ago. There is a direct connect between procreation and preborn children. As Timothy rightly observes, "There is, therefore, a great hypocrisy afoot in the modern Church, and it is crippling Her Abortion-Abolitionist efforts.…They are anti-abortion, to be sure. But they are simultaneously pro-contraception." Timothy is not afraid to speak truth to the Church, pulls no punches, and has the backing of Holy Scripture to convince the honest reader that God has spoken definitively: His desire for believers is to continue to fulfill the command to "be fruitful and multiply."

My study of Scripture compels me to ask: If we can trust God with our eternal destiny, can't we trust Him to plan our families? If we can live as His servants here on earth, can't we be a voice for the innocent amongst us that have no voice? If we can use our talents and resources in Christian ministry, can't we minister to those that fill Protestant pews near and far by using the Sword of Scripture to wake us from our slumber and join a great cause? If we love God and study His Word, can't we discover His divine heartbeat for preborn children? Timothy has addressed all of these questions with a resounding, "Yes!"

Some of the information in this book will break your heart as it breaks His heart. It may, then, be exactly the spark that we need to give us hope, courage, and exhortation to have a vision, centered on the Gospel of Jesus, to win this war through the power of the Holy Spirit, and to the glory of our Heavenly Father.

In His Glad Service,

CRAIG HOUGHTON
Author of *Family UNplanning*

PREFACE

Dear Reader,

To search the Scriptures in order to hear God's heartbeat for preborn children is not a safe endeavor. There is much potential spiritual peril involved. For, to speak wrongly on God's behalf regarding the colossal crisis of global abortion is to commit calumny against the King of kings and Lord of lords. One cannot emerge from such a search of the Scriptures unchanged. Either the author and reader will come away from it convicted, brought to repentance, and sanctified by it, or else the author and reader will finish the search with an inflated sinful pride, a stronger resistance to the Law of Christ, and, therefore, a much higher culpability than when they first began.

It is thus with a tremendous amount of fear and trembling before the throne of our thrice-holy God that the present author invites you to join him on this search through the Holy Bible. Accordingly, he invites you to pray with him for large, generous, and overly-abundant measures of grace as you seek to listen to the divine heartbeat for the little ones in the womb:

> "O, Sovereign Lord, You, alone, are holy. It is You, alone, who have created the heavens and the earth, the sky, the sea, the mountains, the valleys, and all that are in them. By Your will they have existed and were created. Righteous Father, keep us from searching the Scriptures in vain, thinking that in them, alone, we have eternal life, while at the same time being blind to how they testify of Your Son, Jesus Christ. Rather, Holy Father, allow our hearts to burn within us as Your Spirit expounds to us in all the Scriptures the things concerning Your Son. Open our understanding, that we might comprehend the Scriptures rightly. Let us behold wonderful things in Your Law. Holy Father, keep us in the Name of Jesus Christ, and sanctify us by Your truth—Your Word is truth. Guard us from vile sins of commission, and also from grave sins of omission. Protect us from the evil one. And gather Your Church from the four winds of the earth. As we labor, O Lord, on behalf of the preborn child, may Yours be the Kingdom, the power, and the glory, forever. Amen."

God's speed to you as you seek your place in the holy calling of distinctly Christian Abortion Abolitionism.

In Christ's Covenantal Love,

Timothy L. Fan
Aurora, Colorado
February 2014

"This one thing indeed the Church can do: it can distinguish the Word of God from the words of men."

- Martin Luther

INTRODUCTION:
The Need for a Scripture-based Approach

THERE is no lack of logical artillery in defense of preborn life within the current Abortion Abolitionist cause.[1] The combined forces of ultrasound technology and high-powered evidential and philosophical reasoning have inflicted many wounds on the pro-abortion consensus that still dominates the "liberal" wings of our world's political parties and university faculties. The rational fight for the sanctity of human life in the womb has been a valiant one.[2]

Nevertheless, there is a foreboding sense amongst the most passionate and longsuffering of Christian Abortion Abolitionists that the purely rational case against abortion is not sufficient to win the war. Rational spokesmen for the preborn have demonstrated a wonderful ability to make converts to the Abolitionist cause. However, they have not had the firepower to penetrate the enemy's deepest defenses. To put this in biblical terms, the rationalists have not sufficiently proved *"mighty before God to the throwing down of strongholds"* (2 Corinthians 10:4). The strongholds of false (religious) doctrine, regarding abortion, are still yet to be thrown down by Christians.

What is primarily needed is neither new political strategies, nor more grassroots Abolitionist organizations. These things are needed, to be sure, but not in a primary sense. They are necessary, but not sufficient to win the war for the defense of the preborn. In

---

[1] The author here, and afterwards refers to our movement as the "Abortion Abolitionist" one, rather than the "Pro-life" one, in order to attempt to reshape the language of the conflict at hand. This, he believes, is closer to the kind of language that William Wilberforce (1759-1833) would employ, were he to be immersed in our modern Christian cause on behalf of the preborn children of the world.

[2] In this regard, we must not forget Francis Schaeffer's reminder to the Church in *A Christian Manifesto* (First trade paperback ed.; Wheaton: Crossway Books, 2005), 73-74, that the battle over abortion is ultimately a battle of competing worldviews: "Certainly every Christian ought to be praying and working to nullify the abominable abortion law. But as we work and pray, we should have in mind not only this important issue as though it stood alone. Rather, we should be struggling and praying that this whole other total entity—the material-energy, chance worldview—can be rolled back with all its results across all of life."

themselves, they, too, lack the spiritual muscle to conquer the Canaanite giants of pro-abortion thought and political domination.

The Christian, then, immediately thinks of prayer. It is prayer, no doubt, that alone has the power to slay the beast. Over a century ago, E.M. Bounds (1835-1913) reminded us that "the Gospel cannot live, fight, or conquer without prayer—prayer that is unceasing, instant, and ardent."[3] Therefore, the first and primary task of the *distinctly Christian* Abortion Abolitionist is prayer. In our homes and in our churches, we must call ourselves to pray—and teach our children how to pray—in God-centered fashion, for the abolition of abortion.

Still, there is a Sword that has been far too neglected in this long, horrific war. It is the *"Sword of the Spirit"* (Ephesians 6:17), the one that has the power to split open the pro-abortion citadel with such force that it can expose it as *"naked and laid open before the eyes of Him to whom we must give an account"* (Hebrews 4:13). This is the Sword concerning which David—after asking Ahimelech the priest for a sword and being given *"the sword of Goliath the Philistine, whom you killed in the valley of Elah"*—would say, *"There is none like [it]. Give it to me"* (1 Samuel 21:9).

This is none other than the Sword of Sacred Scripture. It is the Word of God. It is the Book on which Martin Luther took his stand, and by our use of it, as Luther taught us to sing, Satan shall fall. For, even just "one little Word shall fell him."

The current book is written for, and presented to the Church as a means of training the current and future generations of Christian Abortion Abolitionists in the use of this Sword. It is the conviction of the present author that the Word of God, and no other weapon, shall prove to be the decisive factor in this war against Satan, sin, and the unthinkable slaughter of countless children in their mothers' wombs. The Bible, and nothing less than the Bible, will be sufficient to win the war.

A Disillusioned Seminary Student

The present author knows a man in Christ who fourteen years ago sat in a large, crowded room filled with orange-fabric-padded seats during his first full-semester seminary class, restless with

---

[3] E.M. Bounds, *E.M. Bounds on Prayer* (New Kensington, PA: Whitaker House, 1997), 56.

Introduction: The Need for a Scripture-based Approach

excitement. The class was entitled, "Biblical Interpretation," and he was chomping at the bit to learn *"the deep things of God"* (1 Corinthians 2:10) from his seemingly wise instructor. The high privilege and spiritual enormity of a seminary education made him expect even angels to look upon the opening lecture with a sense of wonder and awe.

However, these great expectations all came crashing down before the first night of class had ended. Towards the end of his lecture, which was clearly building a thesis for a thoroughly modern, rationalistic, and academically head-strong approach to biblical interpretation (he only mentioned the Church Fathers in order to make sport of them), the professor brought up the issue of abortion. Already grieved over the professor's evolutionary view of knowledge—wherein "current scholarship" holds authority over ancient wisdom—the young man straightened his back against his orange-padded chair, bracing himself for what might come next.

It was a heartbreaking moment for the newly drafted seminarian. Out of the mouth of the professor came the following words, "I, personally, am against abortion, but the Bible, itself, including Psalm 139, is silent on the issue of abortion." Immediately, for the young man, the room became blurry. His stomach sank, like a ship that had just been blasted with missiles. In front of a room packed and overflowing with future pastors, this professor, this "Doctor of New Testament" had taken the Sword of Scripture out of the hands of God's Abolitionist soldiers.

Several years later, the same young man found himself sitting, on the Lord's Day, in the sanctuary of one of the most influential multicultural churches in the American South. The pastor of the church, an otherwise godly man, preached that morning on the entirety of Psalm 139. Yet in working through the Psalm, verse by verse, he failed to mention abortion even once.

The young man, churning with grief and anguish in the pew while the pastor concluded his sermon, began asking himself direct questions concerning how such a travesty could occur. Could it be that the pastor was scared of offending various sectors of his greatly diverse church? Or, even more importantly, could it be that the pastor had once been a seminary student, himself, and had, during his seminary days, been intimidated by the lecturer in his own "Biblical Interpretation" class into thinking that, for Christians, the abortion debate is solely a matter of Christian logic and common sense moral reasoning, and not an arena in which a Christian Abolitionist is allowed to employ the Sword of the Spirit as his primary weapon?

The Demonstration of a Scripture-based Approach

C.S. Lewis (1898-1963) once said, with his usual, lucid wit, "Good philosophy must exist, if for no other reason, because bad philosophy needs to be answered."[4] Yet, despite all of the good that Lewis did in the defense of the historic Christian faith, he also made a fantastic blunder in his apologetic for Christian philosophy. That is, Lewis made it sound as if high-level and strongly academic Christian thought is a sharper sword than Scripture, itself:

> If all the world were Christian, it might not matter if all the world were uneducated. But, as it is, a cultural life will exist outside the Church whether it exists inside or not. To be ignorant and simple now—not to be able to meet the enemies on their own ground—would be to throw down our weapons, and to *betray our uneducated brethren* who have, under God, *no defense but us* against the intellectual attacks of the heathen.[5]

But what does this say about Lewis' view of the Bible? Does he not realize that the "fishermen" of Acts 4:13 were *"uneducated,"* and yet were anything but defenseless? Was not Peter's use of *"the Word of God"* (1 Peter 1:23) a much more powerful weapon to pierce the hearts of men (Acts 2:37) than all of the philosophizing of all of the scholars of Athens and Corinth, combined? Did not Paul, who was one of the greatest of intellects of all time, consider *"the foolishness of God"* as being *"wiser than men"* (1 Corinthians 1:25)? It is certainly not, therefore, the "uneducated" who are defenseless against the intellectual attacks of the heathen. It is, rather, those who have willingly laid aside the Sword of Scripture in order to "meet the enemies on their own ground," who have become defenseless.

The crisis within the Church concerning its negligence, apathy, and great sins (both of commission and of omission) regarding the

---

[4] C.S. Lewis, *The Weight of Glory and Other Addresses* (ed. Walter Hooper; New York: Touchstone, 1996), 48.
[5] Ibid., 48, emphases added.

Introduction: The Need for a Scripture-based Approach

Abortion Holocaust, then, is one of biblical doctrine. Unhealthy doctrine produces unfit Christian Abolitionists. Scripturally-ignorant soldiers (and how many pastors today have become quite ignorant of Scripture?) are fighters without discipline, and swordsmen without swords. The primary battle is not Christian philosophy versus Secular Humanist philosophy. It is, rather, God's voice of revelation in Scripture versus Satan's voice of biblical distortion in a nominally Christian society. The real quip, therefore, ought to be, "Sound preaching must exist, if for no other reason, because bad preaching needs to be answered."

Therefore, this is not a book that makes any intentional effort to shy away from the costly spiritual rigors of whole-Bible reading and whole-Bible doctrine. It is, rather, founded upon seven important convictions. Firstly, whenever and wherever *a Spirit-reborn, God-centered heartbeat* is wanting, it is impossible to have a God-pleasing Abortion Abolitionist effort. Secondly, *the Word of God* ought to be the dominant voice in Christian Abortion Abolitionist proclamation, for it, alone, has the supernatural power required to reform society. Thirdly, *the fear of the Lord*, as practiced in and through the Gospel of Jesus Christ, is the key that unlocks a sound understanding of whole-Bible doctrine. Fourthly, *truly historic Christianity* requires the teachings of the great pastors and martyrs throughout the history of the Church as necessary guides for correct biblical interpretation. Fifthly, Protestant Christians during the modern Abortion Holocaust have hurt the Abolitionist cause by failing to submit to the biblical commandment (and thus to appropriate the biblical blessing) of *Christ-exalting procreation*. Sixthly, *the inter-connectedness of Christian doctrine* requires that a truly whole-Bible proclamation of God's heartbeat for preborn children will necessarily address the controversial doctrinal issues of our day, including the current invasion of feminism, pro-homosexual thought, and Darwinian dogma into the Church. And seventhly, *the preborn children* of the Abortion Holocaust are not merely to be seen as victims, but also as *valiant martyrs*, whose crowns of glory shall be revealed on the great Day when Jesus Christ is revealed to the world, in all of His glory.

It would be an exercise in prolixity to expound on each of these seven convictions, especially in an Introduction. Let them, rather, be shown, by way of demonstration throughout the course of the book, to have the ability, in their combined forces, to pull down the strongholds of pro-abortion thought. If they are a true alliance of solidly biblical principles, then let them come forth *"in demonstration of the Spirit and of power"* (1 Corinthians 2:4). And if they are not merely the present author's convictions, but also patterned (albeit imperfectly) after the Apostolic tradition, then let them prove, at the final reckoning, to consist of *"gold, silver, [and] costly stones,"* rather than *"wood, hay, [and] stubble"* (1 Corinthians 3:12).

Along the way, of course, the reader will discover the present author's dependencies and idiosyncrasies. The author leans, intentionally, on the sturdy pillars of several of his own Christian heroes, including John Chrysostom (347-407), Richard Baxter (1615-1691), and the great champion of Slave-trade Abolition, Wilberforce, himself. His dependency upon them is more than evident.

Also, the shape and format of the book is somewhat idiosyncratic. It is not a "topical" study of God's heartbeat for the preborn. Rather, it surveys the Bible, allowing Scripture to interpret Scripture, seeking a whole-Bible understanding of specific Christian doctrines, and especially as they relate to the preborn child in the womb. It intentionally ignores many modern commentators, in favor of ancient ones. Its repetitious underlining (literally, within the very formatting of the pages) of biblical phrases will, no doubt, be criticized as non-scholarly. Yet this is a book unconcerned with "scholarly" approval or disapproval. Rather, it seeks to reform the Church's thinking and approach on abortion, and thus is written for the Church, not the Academy.

As such, the author has attempted to recognize and honor the many Christian Abolitionists of today's Church who have labored tirelessly and risked much for the sake of the preborn. Wherever he has not had space to acknowledge specific Christian heroes and heroines in this battle for life and justice in the womb, he nevertheless is deeply grateful for their valiant faith, and for all that they have taught him concerning Christian obedience to Isaiah 1:17; Amos 5:24; Micah 6:8; etc. He thus follows them, even as one untimely born into the Gospel, in praying for a truly Christian Abolitionism, for the glory of God and the saving of many lives.

Part One:

Biblical Foundations in Genesis 1-3

Divine Heartbeat

1

GOD'S LITTLEST IMAGE BEARERS:
The Image of God and Preborn Children

(Genesis 1:26-28, Part 1)

GOD is the Ruler over all things. By His own divine nature, He has the divine right, power, and authority to reign over the heavens and the earth. He created all things, and, therefore, has dominion over all things. He governs the flight pattern of every sparrow in the air, and He plans the formalwear of every lily in the field.

This God, to whom we are to give an account at the end of the age, has unrivaled power and authority. No one can challenge Him to an arm wrestling match and win. Nothing can undermine or usurp His sovereign control over the universe. He is the unrivaled God.

And yet this God of Scripture, whose power to rule is incomparable, is unrivaled, also, in compassion and covenantal love. He describes Himself as *"the LORD, the LORD God, compassionate and gracious, slow to anger, and abundant in covenantal love and faithfulness"* (Exodus 34:6).[1] He shows mercy to sinners. He goes out, Himself, in search of the lost sheep. As the Good Shepherd, He binds up the injured of the flock, protects them from the bullies of the fold, lifts the little lambs into His lap, and gently leads the nursing ones. He, the Good Shepherd, lays down His life for the sheep. As a Ruler, God exercises holy, protective love over His subjects.

This means that most human rulers are very unlike God. The human king, premier, prime minister, or president thinks that he has the divine right to rule—whether by way of succession, appointment, military takeover, democratic election, or some other means of rising to power. And yet, historically speaking, he typically rules with an unjust rule. He most often exalts his own word above the Word of God, and in doing so he oppresses and brutalizes his subjects.

---

[1] The present author's translation.

The history of human rulership is, for the most part, a history of tyranny.[2] It begins with Cain, the son of Adam, who chose to crush his brother, Abel, in an act of murder. It includes Pharaoh, king of Egypt, who, in his rule over his Hebrew slaves, demanded the drowning of all Hebrew baby boys in the Nile River, and who introduced unreachable quotas for the slaves in their brick-making labors. It climaxes, in many ways, in the Old Testament with the wickedness of King Manasseh, who mandated pagan idols in the Temple and who sacrificed his own sons in the fire.[3]

Horrific things have been done throughout history in the name of human rulership. For example, sometime in the eighth century BC, the ruler of the people of Ammon thought that it was wise and expedient warfare to slaughter pregnant women as part of his conquest of portions of Israel; his men *"ripped open the pregnant women of Gilead, that they may enlarge their border"* (Amos 1:13). In the third century BC, China's first emperor, Qin Shi Huang, whom Mao Zedong later came to admire, murdered over a thousand scholars, seeing them as a threat to his power, and over four hundred of them he buried alive. Much later in history, during the age of the Reformation, Thomas More (AD 1478-1535), Chancellor of England, developed an addiction to torturing and burning Evangelicals, and he oftentimes quoted the Bible in order to justify and feed this addiction.[4] And in post-World War I Germany, a charismatic man named Adolf Hitler rose to power, promising economic recovery and prosperity to his nation, but instead immersing it in mass brutality and bloodshed.

---

[2] This cursory survey of the history of human tyranny is not meant to neglect the bright spots of rulership in world history. There have been great rulers in history; these great rulers practiced justice and righteousness for the glory of God and for the benefit of their people. King Josiah, for example, was a just king in Judah who served his subjects best by honoring God the most (see, for example, 2 Kings 23:1-3).

[3] And yet the grace of God is displayed all the more in the fact that Manasseh, at the end of his life, repented before God, and God accepted his repentance/faith and brought him, personally, into salvation (see 2 Chronicles 33:10-13).

[4] Despite the Roman Catholic historical apologetics that are exercised on More's behalf, whose arguments are designed to downplay More's bloodthirsty violence, there is overwhelming evidence of tyranny found in More's own writings (especially his personal letters); this evidence is documented throughout Brian Moynahan's *God's Bestseller: William Tyndale, Thomas More, and the Writing of the English Bible—A Story of Martyrdom and Betrayal* (New York: St. Martin's Press, 2002).

Yet the greatest of all abuses of human rulership, the greatest of all tyrannical acts, happened in between ancient warfare and Enlightenment-age genocides. It happened when a Roman governor named Pilate threatened an impoverished Jew from Nazareth with the prospect of crucifixion, as an attempt to compel the Jew to cooperate with him: *"Are You not speaking to me? Do You not know that I have power to release You, and have power to crucify You?"* (John 19:10). Of course, Pilate did not use his power to release Jesus of Nazareth; he released Barabbas, the murderer, instead. This act of Pilate was the epitome of tyranny.

What, then, of the horror of abortion, as it relates to human rulers? How should human rulers view abortion? How should the king of Saudi Arabia, the Parliament of the United Kingdom, the Standing Committee of China, and the Supreme Court of the United States understand the practice of abortion? This is *the greatest* ethical question of our time. It cries out for much more than scientific, philosophical, or political debate. It pleads for the Sovereign LORD to speak His own sovereign decree concerning it. For, the question of how human rulers ought to face the prevailing practice of abortion in our world is a question that will lead us into the heart of what it actually means to be human.

__HUMAN BEING AND THE IMAGE OF GOD__

The Bible has a very specific definition of humanity. It is vastly different, even worlds apart, from the modern scientific and psychological definitions of human being. The modern definitions are, in essence, atheistic ones. They define humanity according to evolutionary processes, predictable social behaviors, and (merely physical) genetic heredity. The Bible, in stark contrast to these cold, anti-supernatural definitions of human being, says that to be human is to be created in the "image of God":

> *God said, "Let Us make man __in Our image__, __after Our likeness__: and let them have dominion over the fish of the sea, and over the birds of the sky, and over the livestock, and over all the earth, and over every creeping thing that creeps on the earth." God created man __in His own image__. __In God's image__ He created him; male and female He created them.* (Genesis 1:26–27)

What does this mean? If we want to understand who we are—what it means for us to be human beings—we must seek out what God means when He says, *"...in Our image."* What kind of marvelous language is this, that we, frail creatures of dust, should be said to be God's image bearers?

The language of "image" in the Bible is the language of family resemblance. When little boys burst into their father's home office, interrupting his work with their joyful laughter and childhood play, the father delights in the scene primarily because he sees, in their little faces, the resemblances of their mother, and of himself. Similarly, when certain orphans, whose parents died when they were still infants, long to recapture, in their minds, the visages of their parents (but lack photographs or images to help them to remember them), they simply need to look at themselves in the mirror. When they see themselves, they see the "images" of their parents:

> *Adam lived one hundred thirty years, and became the father of a son <u>in his own likeness, after his image</u>, and named him Seth.* (Genesis 5:3)

To be human, then, is to be created "in" God's image.[5] We are not God's image, itself. Still, we are created "in" His image. We are created to resemble our Creator, just as a son resembles his father. And we are created to mimic God's holiness, just as a son mimics his father's character.

The Image of God versus the Image of Idolatry

Here a grave danger emerges in the realm of human temptations. All is well when we accept our status as creatures made in the image of God. The Lord God created us as image bearers. Yet what if human beings decide to craft their own images? What if we turn the created (hierarchical) order upside-down? What happens when we

---

[5] Notice that we are created in the image of God, not in the image of ape or monkey. This shows, from a theological perspective, the absurdity of Darwin's view of human evolution. We are made in the "likeness" of God, not in the "likeness" of ape. Moses says that the "father-son resemblance" of the image of God is a God-human resemblance; modern pseudo-science, especially in the field of biology, exercises both hubris and foolishness in claiming that humanity's "image" is, in essence, an ape-human resemblance. Jesus became incarnate as Man, not as ape.

ignore God's right to create us in His own image, and decide, ourselves, to try to create "gods" in our own image?

Idolatry is the product of the human decision to create "gods" in our own image. This is why the Israelites were to destroy the Canaanite peoples. The Canaanites were masters at the skill of idol-craft:

> ...then you shall drive out all the inhabitants of the land from before you, destroy all their stone idols, destroy all their <u>molten images</u>, and demolish all their high places. (Numbers 33:52)

Humans are created in God's image, but God will have no rivals. He will not allow the creation of other "gods" in His likeness:

> To whom then will you <u>liken</u> God? Or what <u>likeness</u> will you compare to Him? (Isaiah 40:18)

Again, God creates human beings in His image, in His likeness. However, as human beings who have inherited a sinful nature from Adam, we are ever prone to seek to create our own "gods" in our own likeness. God made us for His own glory, but we make idols for our own glory:

> You also carried the tent of your king and the shrine of your images, the star of your god, <u>which you made for yourselves</u>. (Amos 5:26)

Making idols in our image is tantamount to blasphemy. It defames the glory of God by reducing our very concept of God to the created realm. We pretend to be creators, ourselves, when we make our own "gods" out of the stuff of creation:

> [They] traded the glory of the incorruptible God for <u>the likeness of an image of corruptible man, and of birds, and four-footed animals, and creeping things</u>. (Romans 1:23)

Ultimately, this great sin of idolatry will result in the whole world being handed over to the deception of Antichrist. In the last days, says the Bible, a great "beast" will arise who will lead people into deception through the creation of an "image." Instead of "the image of God," people will now commit themselves, wholeheartedly, to "the image of the beast":

> *He [the false prophet] deceives my own people who dwell on the earth because of the signs he was granted to do in front of the beast; saying to those who dwell on the earth, that they should <u>make an image to the beast</u> who had the sword wound and lived. It was given to him to give breath to it, <u>to the image of the beast</u>, that <u>the image of the beast</u> should both speak, and <u>cause as many as would not worship the image of the beast to be killed</u>.*
> (Revelation 13:14–15)

Idolatry, then, is insidious for the very reason that it twists and mangles our understanding of the image of God. We bear God's image, having been created in His image, but idolatry is the destruction of that image. When we craft idols, pretending to be creators, ourselves, we actually mar and tear the portrait of the image of God that the Spirit of God has painted within us.[6] Our sin tempts us to believe that we, like Oscar Wilde's character, Dorian Gray, whose portrait never aged, can have perpetual youth and beauty, all the while living in frivolity and licentiousness. In the end, if we do not repent of our wickedness and call upon the Lord for salvation, the portrait of our souls will become more and more like a hideous image of Satan, himself. The Father of Lies, the Devil, wants to replace the image of God in us with his own image.

Jesus Christ is the Image of God

Why, then, is the voice of Genesis 1:26 a plural voice? God says, *"Let <u>Us</u> make man in <u>Our</u> image, after <u>Our</u> likeness..."* and thus He speaks in the plural voice. He does not say, in the singular voice, "Let Me make...in My image, according to My likeness." Rather, He says, *"Us...Our...Our...."* Why does God speak here in the plural voice?

Modern scholars, in the name of "biblical scholarship," have tried to avoid any reference to the Triune nature of God in this verse. These scholars have called for esoteric theories involving Hebrew

---

[6] Athanasius (c. AD 298-373), the courageous bishop of Alexandria, says in his masterful book, *On the Incarnation of the Word* 14.1 (NPNF[2] 4:43), that the effects of idolatry and sin on the image of God in us are comparable to "when the likeness painted on a panel has been effaced by stains from without."

grammar[7] that try to avoid hearing the Father, Son, and Spirit speaking, in the plural, in Genesis 1:26. However, we do well here to listen, instead, to the wisdom of the early Church Fathers.

John Chrysostom was one of the greatest pastors and preachers of early church history. In one of his sermons on Genesis 1:26, he says that God cannot be speaking to angels (which is another theory that seeks to avoid hearing the Triune nature of God in the verse). Chrysostom brings to our attention that when God says, *"Let Us make man in Our image, after Our likeness..."* He does not say, "Your [singular] and My image," nor does He say, "Your [plural] and My image," but rather He says, *"Our image."*[8] This, says Chrysostom, shows the unity of the image. There are not two images (one of God and one of angels). Rather, there is only one image (God's own image). So the *"Our image"* must refer to the one image of God, and thus belong to all "Persons" contained within the "Our." This means that Genesis 1:26 is a record of God the Father speaking to God the Son, Jesus Christ, and to God the Holy Spirit.

Why does this matter? It matters a great deal because the source of "the image of God" in the Bible is not found in human beings themselves. Humans are created "in" God's image, but they are not, themselves, the very image of God. Rather, in the Bible it is God's only begotten Son[9] who, Himself, *is* the very Image of God:

[He] is the image of the invisible God, the firstborn of all creation. (Colossians 1:15)

---

[7] For example, there is the "plural of majesty" theory, which says that God speaks in the plural in the same way that an ancient king might speak in the plural. The king does not say, "I decree that..." but rather "We decree that..." as a way of using grammar to assert his royal majesty. But this kind of speculation (which stems from a historical-critical bias against the traditional reading of the early Church Fathers) about Hebrew grammar ignores the theological connection that the Bible is making between the Triune nature of God and the image of God, itself. It also lacks biblical support.

[8] St. John Chrysostom, *Eight Sermons on the Book of Genesis* (trans. Robert Charles Hill; Boston, Mass.: Holy Cross Orthodox Press, 2004), 47; for the Greek text of Chrysostom's sermon, which alone is able to bring out the nuances of the second-person singular and second-person plural pronouns that he uses in his argument, see St. John Chrysostom, *Sermons sur la Genèse: sources chrétiennes no. 433* (trans. Laurence Brottier; Paris, France: *Les Éditions du Cerf*, 1998), 190.

[9] Here it is good to recall the concept of father-son resemblance in the "image."

The "image" belongs to God alone. It belongs to Jesus Christ alone. We have been made in His image, but we are not the image itself. Our Lord Jesus is the very image of God. He alone perfectly resembles the Father in Heaven. When we see the Son, we also see the Father, for the Son is the Father's perfect image.

Therefore, committing sins against the image of God, in which we are created, is tantamount to belittling and assaulting Christ Himself. To curse the image of God, which is stamped upon our human identity, is to hurl curses at the Lord Jesus, who is *the Image* of God. Thus, when we speak of all humans as being created in the image of God, we must speak reverently and cautiously, with fear and trembling. For in so speaking, we are describing the handiwork and resemblance of Jesus Christ, Himself.

Gloriously, this path of thought turns out to be the one that leads us to the knowledge of true humanity. Jesus Christ is fully God, yes, but also fully *human*. At the incarnation, Jesus assumes a full human nature. He does not merely "seem" to be human, like a divine apparition, lacking physicality. Nor does He merely possess a human body, while lacking a human mind or will. Rather, everything that human nature possesses, He possesses. He is, as the Creed of Chalcedon (AD 451) states, "to be acknowledged in two natures [divine and human], inconfusedly, unchangeably, indivisibly, inseparably." As fully God, He reveals God to us. As fully human, he reveals to us what it means to be truly human. Our sin nature has distorted our humanity. But Jesus' humanity is perfect, and thus untainted by the distortions of sin.

What does it mean to be human? The only way to answer this foundational question of our existence is to know Jesus Christ. He, alone, is the embodiment of what a spiritually spotless and morally flawless human being ought to be. How does a true human speak? To know this, we must listen to how Jesus Christ speaks in the Scriptures. How does a true human pray? To answer this, we must study how our Lord prays in the Bible. In what ways does a true human honor and relate to his mother? To learn this, we must carefully follow the ways in which Jesus honors and relates to His mother, Mary, in the Gospels. He is true humanity.

Contemplation of Jesus' true humanity leads inexorably to the beginning of His humanity: His conception. True humanity is revealed in Jesus Christ, and Jesus' incarnation begins not outside of the womb, but *in the womb*. The very definition of humanity begins with the miracle of the virgin conception. That is, prior to the virgin birth, there is a supernatural conception. The Holy Spirit overshadows Mary, and Isaiah's prophecy is fulfilled, *"Behold, the virgin will conceive, and bear a son, and shall call his name Immanuel"* (7:14). Jesus' first nine months of humanity are spent in the womb. He shows us true humanity by starting with His own true humanity in the womb, from the very moment of conception.

The Image of God and Bloodshed

Abortion is bloodshed in the womb. For example, a typical "Dilation and Evacuation" (commonly known as a D & E) abortion involves "the crushing, slicing, and dismembering of the unborn."[10] During these abortions, which take place between 12 and 24 weeks of pregnancy, the baby feels physical pain.[11] And there is much bleeding during the little baby's murder. Or, in the case of a saline abortion, in which solutions of high salt concentrations are injected into the womb, the baby experiences immense pain. Medical doctors have documented that an "aborting mother can feel her baby thrashing in the uterus during the approximately two hours it usually takes for the saline solution to kill the [baby]."[12]

This is murder. It is the taking of the life and blood of a human being, who is created in the image of God. Remember, Jesus, in the womb, is fully human, right from the moment of conception. Jesus is *the Image of God* in Mary's womb. Therefore, according to God's Word, this means that to be a baby in the womb, at any stage of physical development, from conception onwards, is to be fully human, and already (conception is a past event) created in the image of God. Therefore, all abortions involve the shedding of the blood of fellow human beings, who are fellow image bearers.

Biblically, then, this raises the stakes on the abortion debate to a level that is exceedingly high. It is the "image of God" doctrine that

---

[10] Francis J. Beckwith, *Politically Correct Death: Answering Arguments for Abortion Rights* (Grand Rapids: Baker Books, 1993), 48.
[11] Ibid., 48.
[12] Vincent J. Collins, M.D., Steven R. Zielinski, M.D. and Thomas J. Marzen, Esq., "Fetal Pain and Abortion: The Medical Evidence," *Studies in Law and Medicine, no. 18* (Chicago: Americans United for Life Legal Defense Fund, 1984), 8; qtd. in Beckwith, *Politically Correct Death*, 48.

makes abortion the greatest wickedness of our time. Babies in the womb, who bear God's image, are to be protected by divine law:

Whoever sheds man's blood, his blood will be shed by man, <u>for God made man in His own image</u>. (Genesis 9:6)

Once we realize Jesus' own humanity in the womb, from conception onwards, as the embodiment of the image of God, and once we hear God's Word say to us that *all* babies in the womb, from conception onwards (no matter what sufferings brought about the conception),[13] are created in His image, then we realize the gravity of abortion. In abortion, human beings, bearing God's own image—and we dare not forget that He is a holy, holy, holy God—are slain. Their blood is spilled. And thus, with Abel's blood, their blood *"cries out to Me from the ground"* (Genesis 4:10).

In Judeo-Christian societies,[14] children are taught from a very early age the Sixth Commandment, *"You shall not murder"* (Exodus 20:13; Deuteronomy 5:17). Either the fear of God (for Christians) or the fear of judicial law (for unbelievers) warns us, from childhood onwards, not to murder. Whenever we are tempted, through hatred, selfishness, coveting, plotting, or feelings of rage, to strike someone so as to murder him, our fear of law (either divine or human) keeps us from doing so.

---

[13] The sufferings of rape and incest, in particular, are not to be downplayed in the slightest. The Old Testament calls for the death penalty for the perpetrators of such crimes (for rape, see Deuteronomy 22:25-27; for incest, see Leviticus 18:6ff., 29) precisely because they are so evil and horrific. Nevertheless, a preborn child who is conceived as a result of these evils is not to be murdered, in the same way as it would be a crime to murder a three-year old child who was conceived as a result of rape or incest. There is no difference in the divine-legal protection rights of the preborn child, as compared with those of the three-year old child. Both are equally protected by Genesis 9:6 from the horror of murder.

[14] It must be noted that nations that have traditionally been seen as representing Judeo-Christian societies—nations such as the United Kingdom and the United States—are currently eroding, morally, at an alarming rate. The knowledge of the Sixth Commandment, for example, can no longer be taken for granted amongst the youth of England, or the youth of America. And a strong case may be made for the proposition that our legal-political acceptance of abortion (along with our intellectual embrace of Darwinian thought) has done more to undermine our Judeo-Christian ethics than any other cultural, political, or social development in the history of our nations. If this is true, time will bear it out.

Still, what undergirds the Sixth Commandment (and our human laws that are based upon it) is the doctrine of the image of God. God says to Noah, *"Whoever sheds man's blood, his blood will be shed by man, <u>for God made man in His own image</u>"* (Genesis 9:6). That is, the ultimate reason why a person ought to flee the thought of ever raising a knife to murder someone is that every "someone" is created in the image of God. Seeing the image of God in him, he must fear the thought of unjustly harming him. The infinitely bright light of the glory of God, reflected in finite ways through the image of God in us,[15] makes the very idea of murder a terrifying one. For, the wrath of God is poured out against those who would slay His image bearers.

But this same truth applies to *all* preborn babies. From conception onwards, all preborn children have been created in the image of God. Therefore, seeing God's glory being reflected through these little image bearers, the thought of raising a suction tube, a curette, a knife, a needle, a bottle of saline solution, or a pair of forceps over a preborn baby ought to be a most terrifying one. We ought to shudder, with horror, at such a thought. In light of God's holy wrath against the shedding of innocent blood, since *"God made man in His own image,"* abortion is a most hideous and most terrifying practice.

A word must be said here to the contemporary Evangelical Church in the Western world. The spiritual decline of the contemporary Evangelical Church in the Western world, which is taking place before our very eyes and is so obvious now that it cannot be ignored,[16] may well be a judgment from God (at least partially—for our spiritual idolatry is also an enormous factor) against our passivity and practical indifference towards the Abortion Holocaust.

---

[15] Athanasius, in *Against the Heathen* 8.2 (NPNF[2] 4:8), describes the image of God as "the mirror which, as it were, is in [the human soul], by which alone [the human soul] ha[s] the power of seeing the Image of the Father."

[16] To see this, one only needs to compare the popular sermons being preached by the average contemporary Evangelical preachers in the Western world—but there are, of course, bright and hopeful exceptions to this norm—with the sermons of our Puritan forefathers. The chasm between the two, in both doctrine and holiness, is so large as to call into question, with alarming bewilderment, our current methods of exposition and discipleship. Or, to see how alarming the spiritual decline really is, one only needs to point to the glaring moral laxity of the contemporary Evangelical Church in the Western world and its trajectory towards the apostasy of licentiousness, of which we are told, in the book of Jude, to beware.

So obsessed with "missional contextualization" (the idea of adapting the Gospel to its host culture, in a missions-minded way) and issues of what it calls "reading the culture," the Neo-Evangelical movement, which may have reached its zenith in the late twentieth century, has become a slave to its surrounding culture. It has sold itself into slavery under the cultural fads and trends of this present world.

In specific, the current Evangelicals of the early twenty-first century have discovered a zeal for what is broadly termed by the secular world as "social justice." Awakening to the teachings of Carl Henry (1913-2003),[17] who helped launch the Neo-Evangelical movement in the late 1940's, young Evangelicals are now following rock-and-roll stars, such as Paul David Hewson (commonly known as "Bono," the lead singer of the rock group U2), and even their own worship-music pop stars, in a quest for meaning in life through social action. Much of this is biblical (e.g. Amos 5:24). Adopting orphans, caring for the poor and the needy (especially widows), developing prison ministries, fighting against global sex trafficking, coming to the aid of earthquake victims, and working towards ethnic reconciliation[18] in the Church, are all things of monumental significance, and things that God lovingly demands of His people (for the divine "demand" of biblical social action, see, among many other New Testament passages, Matthew 25:32-46).

However, there is something very amiss in all of this. The fact is that social justice is trendy and modish, both in the Evangelical Church *and in the non-Christian world.* This is not a bad thing, per se,[19] and a genuine, sacrificial (as opposed to Marxist) concern for the needy should be welcomed by all as a great development in the realm of social concern. Nonetheless, it is telling that while Evangelicals wax bold on the very issues that are in harmony with their

---

[17] In many ways, the work of Carl F.H. Henry, *The Uneasy Conscience of Modern Fundamentalism* (Grand Rapids: Eerdmans, 1947), marks the beginning of the Neo-Evangelical Movement in America.

[18] The present author has purposefully avoided using the phrase "racial reconciliation," as there is, in the Bible, only one true "race," which is the human one. Also, there are not different "colors" of people in the Bible. There are, however, *ethnic* groups, all of whom God loves. He is indebted to the preaching of Ken Ham, president of Answers in Genesis, for this insight.

[19] However, let us who treasure passages such as Isaiah 1:16-17 not forget that the "Social Gospel" of the early twentieth century was, indeed, heretical, and ultimately led many professing Christians (who were not regenerate believers) to Hell.

unbelieving peers, they are culpably silent on matters that would draw the hatred of their unbelieving peers.[20]

For example, contemporary Evangelicals may give lip service to a traditional view on sexuality and marriage, but they are too quick to claim (erroneously) that homosexuality is no greater sin than heterosexual fornication (while, in reality, both are horrible sins, but homosexuality is, biblically speaking, the greater sin).[21] They are forever speaking against any kind of "fire and brimstone" type of evangelism (while Ezekiel, for example, preaches, evangelistically, both *"fire"* and *"brimstone"*; see Ezekiel 38:22), preferring, instead, to proclaim a very placid, non-threatening version of "Jesus." In response, it must be said that while we are to preach "judgment" in a charitable and humble way, there is no avoiding the biblical evidence that the proclamation of *"the judgment to come"* (Acts 24:25; note that Felix, the unbeliever, becomes "afraid" of Paul's evangelism) is a big part of the preaching of the Gospel, itself.[22]

There are degrees of sin. All sins are worthy of everlasting condemnation in Hell.[23] But some sins are much worse than others.[24] Lust is Satanic, and just as condemning as adultery (so out the window goes Pharisaical righteousness), but lust is not as evil as the actual act of adultery, which is unconscionable. Hatred condemns a

---

[20] This is not to imply that it would be a bad thing for the non-Christian world to embrace the idea of the abolition of abortion, or that Christians should not welcome the global (non-Christian) popularity of things that are in line with biblical justice. Nor is this to say that if the abolition of abortion were to gain the approval of many unbelievers that we should, therefore, cease to be as passionate about it as we were when it was a minority view. This is simply to say that contemporary Evangelicals tend to gravitate towards social causes that cost them little in the way of persecution, whereas they tend to shy away from social causes that draw persecution.

[21] Why is it, for example, that many Evangelicals seem to be ashamed of the intensity of the word "abomination," which was chosen by God for a specific purpose in Leviticus 18:22 (KJV, NKJV, ESV, NASB)? Is this not reflective of how both the lies of "genetics/psychology," on the one hand, and the pressures of the surrounding culture, on the other, have blunted their view on what is, in truth, the shocking and abhorrent nature of homosexuality?

[22] See especially: John 16:8; Acts 17:31; Hebrews 6:2; 10:27; Revelation 14:9-11.

[23] Thus James 2:10 is rightly understood as speaking about the ability of all sins, including a single sin, to bring condemnation. It is not, however, teaching that "all sins are equal," in the sense of having equal degrees to them.

[24] Consider the following: Exodus 21:14-19; Leviticus 10:2, 19-20; Matthew 26:24; Mark 9:42; Luke 12:47-48; John 19:11.

soul to Hell, but murder is much worse. Hoarding wealth and multiplying vacation homes in a world of starving people is wicked—even deserving of a Sodom-like judgment (see Ezekiel 16:49). But abortion is even worse. It is the worst of all of the social sins because it is the slaughter of the weakest of the weak. It attacks and murders *the most vulnerable of image bearers in all of God's creation*. It brings bloodshed into the sanctuary of the womb.

What is needed, then, within the contemporary Evangelical Church, is a deep, somber, heart-tearing repentance over the issue of priorities. For example, most American Evangelicals are at least nominally pro-life. But many American Evangelicals recently voted, at least once and some of them twice, for the most aggressively pro-abortion president in the history of America. These Evangelicals failed to uphold *the top priority of the defense of preborn life* on God's scales of justice. They elevated what they called "economic justice"[25] above the Abortion Holocaust.

We must see justice as God sees it. Genesis 9:6 elevates the murdering of preborn children, who are created in the image of God, decisively above other issues of justice in our world.[26] The sheer numbers of preborn children slaughtered in the Abortion Holocaust should cause us to rethink our priorities. The numbers are beyond staggering. Since the *Roe v. Wade* decision in America, which took place on January 22, 1973, there have been considerably more than 50,000,000 abortions perpetrated on American soil.[27] Also, since the implementation of the one-child policy in China, there have been

---

[25] "Economic justice" is a matter that, itself, must be worked out biblically, and not Socialistically, but this debate is beyond the scope of this book.

[26] This is not to say that other issues, such as the horror of human sex trafficking, are not important. They are immensely important, and ought to receive enormous amounts of attention from Christians. It is to say, however, that abortion is the greatest issue of our day, and that no one claiming to love God's justice can do so truthfully without making the abolition of abortion their *highest* priority in the realm of societal justice.

[27] The usual statistics on the number of children murdered by abortion in America since 1973 do not take into account all of the children who have been slaughtered via: (i) the murderous discarding of embryos during the in vitro fertilization (IVF) process; (ii) the widespread use of the birth control pill, which sometimes causes abortions (see, especially, Randy Alcorn, *Does the Birth Control Pill Cause Abortions?* [10th ed., rev.; Sandy, OR: Eternal Perspective Ministries, 2011], 52); (iii) the rise in popularity of "the morning after pill"; and (iv) other "contraceptive" means that cause abortions.

upwards of 336,000,000 recorded abortions in China,[28] not counting those abortions that have been caused by the mass employment of intrauterine devices (commonly called IUD's, which produce abortions)[29] in China.

The numbers are vastly appalling, but there is more. The high-resolution ultrasound machines that have come to us through modern technology are lifesavers (literally), and they have given pregnant mothers a window into the grandeur of God's artistic design of babies in the womb. The ultrasound images, too, summon us to action. Any compassionate consideration of the sheer beauty and vulnerability of these little image bearers, who suck their thumbs, adorably, and who love the rhythms of their mothers' heartbeats echoing in the womb, should compel us to rethink our rhetoric about abortion. Therefore, instead of always speaking in the language of "a positive alternative to expectant mothers," and couching our arguments in blunted fashion, as a way of cowering before the criticisms of the advocates of abortion, we need to start speaking much more firmly, openly, and boldly about what abortion actually is in the eyes of God. We need to speak of bloodshed as bloodshed. Such radiant image bearers deserve our courageous and unwavering (though still full of grace, seasoned with salt) speech in their defense.

Preborn children, all of them, from conception onwards, are little image bearers. They are precious to God because in their tiny and marvelous beauty, they are children who are vulnerable, weak, dependent, trusting, and very much attached to their mothers' love. Abortion, in all cases, is the act of spilling the blood of these image bearers. It is a most murderous practice. And we, who claim to worship the God of Scripture, and by worshipping Him also claim to *"practice justice"* (Micah 6:8, the present author's translation), ought to be in tears for the preborn. We should find ourselves weeping and sobbing for them. We must tear our clothes, rend our hearts, and wail

---

[28] Malcolm Moore, "336 Million Abortions Under China's One Child Policy," *The [London] Telegraph*, March 15, 2013. Cited 18 March 18, 2013. Online: http://www.telegraph.co.uk/news/worldnews/asia/china/9933468/336-million-abortions-under-Chinas-one-child-policy.html.

[29] After surveying the detailed medical evidence that IUDs can prevent implantation, J. Collins and P.G. Crosignani et al., "Intrauterine Devices and Intrauterine Systems," *Human Reproductive Update* [an Oxford Journal] Volume 14, Issue 3 (2008), 197-208, conclude that "both clinical and experimental evidence suggests that IUDs can prevent and disrupt implantation."

over our sins of omission in not doing more to protect them. And, afterwards, we must commit ourselves to place the defense of the preborn, which includes the total abolition of abortion, *at the very top* of our list of objectives when it comes to praying for, and fighting for God's justice in the world.

THE IMAGE OF GOD AND HUMAN RULERSHIP

To be human is to be created in the image of God. How, then, should human rulers view the practice of abortion? The two concepts of "the image of God" and of "rulership" are intimately connected. Part of God's image in us involves the capacity to rule.

> *God said, "Let Us make man in Our image, after Our likeness: and let them have [rulership] over the fish of the sea, and over the birds of the sky, and over the livestock, and over all the earth, and over every creeping thing that creeps on the earth." God created man in His own image. In God's image He created him; male and female He created them. God blessed them. God said to them, "Be fruitful, multiply, fill the earth, and subdue it. Have [rulership] over the fish of the sea, over the birds of the sky, and over every living thing that moves on the earth."* (Genesis 1:26-28)

What does it mean to be created in God's image? Part of the answer to this question involves human rulership *"over the fish of the sea, over the birds of the sky, and over every living thing that moves on the earth"* (v. 28). God made us to organize and govern His creation, as His under-rulers. He is the Ruler over all. In His likeness, we are made to be sub-rulers, rulers under His sovereign rule, and we are to imitate Him in ruling our little domains with holiness, justice, mercy, and love.[30]

Of course, the history of human rulership is not an upright one. Adam forfeited his rule over the Garden through his sin. Ever since then, all humans—save Christ Himself—have been conceived with a sin nature, and are naturally bent towards a sinful or tyrannical form

---

[30] Tertullian (c. 145-220), in *Against Marcion* 2.8 (*ANF* 3.304), speaks of the image of God in the language of human rulership: "[Man] being the image and likeness of God, was stronger than any angel…[God] would not have made all things subject to man, if he had been too weak for the dominion, and inferior to the angels, to whom He assigned no such subjects…."

of rulership. This sinful rulership is not just something that exists in the pagan nations that surround Israel. Even the Israelites, those who are called by God's own name, participate in a very sinful kind of rulership over their own people:

An astonishing and horrible thing has happened in the land. The prophets prophesy falsely, and <u>the priests rule by their own authority</u>; and My people love to have it so. What will you do in the end of it? (Jeremiah 5:30–31)

God is the Good Shepherd. He rules His people with perfect righteousness and unblemished justice. However, in Ezekiel 34, the Good Shepherd is quite angry. He is angry because His under-shepherds, the rulers of Israel, are abusing their power and oppressing their subjects:

You have not strengthened the diseased, neither have you healed that which was sick, neither have you bound up that which was broken, neither have you brought back that which was driven away, neither have you sought that which was lost; but <u>with force and with rigor you have ruled over them</u>. (Ezekiel 34:4)

There is, then, the cry in Israel for a Messianic King, who will rule Israel with perfect righteousness and complete justice. Only the Messiah will rule with a sinless rule:

God, give the king Your justice; Your righteousness to the royal son. He will judge Your people with righteousness, and Your poor with justice....<u>He shall have [rulership] also from sea to sea</u>, from the River to the ends of the earth. (Psalm 72:1-2, 8)

Jesus is the Messiah. King of kings and Lord of lords, He has inaugurated His Kingdom on earth through His death, burial, resurrection, and ascension. His rule shall be, in the future, first a millennial rule (see Revelation 20:1-6),[31] and then an everlasting rule. Still, in the time between His first and second comings, He has delegated His rulership to His bondservants. And, in the parable of Matthew 24:45-51, Jesus makes it clear that those church rulers who abuse their rulership in the interval between His first and second advents will be judged severely. Rulership in the Church is always a delegated rulership. It is to be handled with fear and trembling before Christ, the King.

Much of biblical rulership, to be sure, is sacrificial in nature. A true ruler becomes the slave of all. He washes the feet of his subjects. He exercises mercy and compassion in abundance. He learns from Christ Jesus to serve others, not for selfish agendas or for gaining influence over others, but simply out of sacrificial love. He governs with the rod and staff of the under-shepherd, and he lays down his life for the sheep.

Still, rulership in the Bible also involves the act of subduing. Image bearers are those who, in Genesis 1:28, *"fill the earth and subdue it."* They exercise rulership by bringing the whole of creation into submission to Christ's holy government. To be truly human is to be someone who desires to subdue the earth under the Lordship of Christ Jesus.

In our fallen world, this involves the conquest of evil, for the increase of Christ's dominion on earth:

> *The whole congregation of the children of Israel assembled themselves together at Shiloh, and set up the Tent of Meeting there. The land was subdued before them.* (Joshua 18:1)

---

[31] The Millennial Kingdom of Christ is the perfect fulfillment of the image of God as it entails human rulership. Christ, the Image of God, shall be the perfect Ruler on earth during His thousand-year reign that precedes the second resurrection of the dead, and the final judgment. Amillennialists, who deny a literal and future thousand-year reign, ought not too quickly dismiss the weight of Justin Martyr's words in his *Dialogue with Trypho* 81, 82 (*ANF* 1:239, 240), on this doctrine, "But I and others, who are right-minded Christians on all points, are assured that there will be a resurrection of the dead, and a thousand years in Jerusalem, which will then be built, adorned, and enlarged, [as] the prophets Ezekiel and Isaiah and others declare…And further, there was a certain man with us, whose name was John, one of the apostles of Christ, who prophesied, by a revelation that was made to him, that those who believed in our Christ would dwell a thousand years in Jerusalem; and that thereafter the general, and, in short, the eternal resurrection and judgment of all men would likewise take place."

In Scripture, King David is a warrior. He exercises his status as God's image bearer and sub-ruler by subduing lands and peoples under the reign of the Kingdom of Israel:

David also commanded all the princes of Israel to help Solomon his son, saying, "Is not the LORD your God with you? Has He not given you rest on every side? For He has delivered the inhabitants of the land into my hand; and the land is subdued before the LORD, and before His people."
(1 Chronicles 22:17–18)

Jesus, however, is greater than David. He is a greater warrior than David. Not with sword and spear, but rather with His own suffering and weakness on the Cross, Jesus conquers vast territories for God, His Father. He subdues our sin and wins our souls through His blood:

He will again have compassion on us. He will [subdue] our iniquities under foot; and You will cast all their sins into the depths of the sea. (Micah 7:19)

Yes, but Jesus still has a war to fight. He came to earth, the first time, gentle and humble, peaceful and riding on a donkey. But He shall come, a second time, in war. He will subdue the earth with a warrior's shout and a soldier's sword. And we, His people, shall fight with Him to subdue the earth beneath His righteous authority:

The LORD will be seen over them; and His arrow will [go forth] like lightning; and the Lord GOD will blow the trumpet, and will go with whirlwinds of the south. The LORD of Hosts will defend them; and they will destroy and [subdue] with sling stones; and they will drink, and roar as through wine; and they will be filled like bowls, like the corners of the altar.
(Zechariah 9:14–15)

The cry of every truly Christian prayer, then, is a cry for the increase of the rulership and dominion of Christ on earth: *"Let Your Kingdom come. Let Your will be done, as in heaven, so on earth"* (Matthew 6:10). We are God's image bearers. We are, therefore, charged with rulership over the earth. Yes, but this rulership is an under-rulership. Like Christ, we subdue the earth, in this present age, not with Christian violence, but by way of our own sufferings and persecutions. And like Christ's rulership, our own under-rulership must be executed with protective love for the weak, the downtrodden, the injured, and the vulnerable. It must subdue the forces of evil that war against God's holy name, so that all lands and all peoples may be brought into submission to the Lordship of Christ Jesus.[32]

Human rulers, therefore, must exercise power and authority only as under the rule of Christ.[33] They are not permitted to write laws which are contrary to God's law. They do not have the right to use their own political philosophies or national self-interests in order to exalt themselves above God. Most importantly, they are not allowed to oppress, injure, and murder the weak in the name of "the common good" or "women's rights" or "national prosperity." They are, rather, charged by God with the promotion of holiness and mercy in the world. And they shall answer to God for how they have exercised their power, whether for good or for evil.

How then, should human rulers, whether the Parliament of the United Kingdom or the Standing Committee of China, view abortion? What laws should they establish in relation to abortion? The answer should now be obvious. If human rulership is viewed through the lens of the doctrine of human beings as created in the image of God, then all human rulership is to be practiced *as under God's sovereign Rulership*. It is God, and not man, who must decide the matter. It is man's job to enforce the rule of God on earth in a way that pleases God: by loving Him, first, and then by loving one's neighbor as one's very self. When it comes to abortion, then, the total and complete abolition of abortion, in all nations and at all times, is the responsibility of all human rulers. To bear God's image is to

---

[32] The Bible, however, makes it clear that Christians, this side of Christ's Second Coming, will not be victorious in bringing all nations into submission to the Lordship of Christ Jesus. It is true that throughout history, Christians will be the harbingers of salvation to people from every tribe, every tongue, and every nation. Nevertheless, Revelation 11:10 and 13:7 seem to indicate that there will be a mass persecution and slaughtering of Christians just prior to the return of Christ, and that Christian influence in the world will wane in the final days before His return.

[33] To be sure, unbelievers who rule over nations do not recognize the rule of Christ, and, therefore, they wickedly deny their limited status as sub-rulers who, themselves, are subject to the rule of Christ. However, the rule of Christ remains the unchanging truth, even for them. It remains the standard of rulership and justice, even for them. And at the resurrection of the just and the unjust, they shall be judged by Christ, Himself, on how they responded to this standard of rulership.

subdue the evil of abortion by ruling in such a way that will protect and treasure all human life in the womb, under all circumstances.

William Wilberforce was not the king of England, but he was, by God's gracious providence, one of the most powerful rulers in England in his day. His sharp wit and selfless love for others made him powerful as a Member of Parliament (MP). Yet it was, more fundamentally, his strong commitment to the fear of God and Lordship of Christ Jesus that made him powerful. He was unwavering in his moral convictions. He would not vote along party lines when his conscience was being pricked. He exercised his status as God's image bearer by ruling with justice, compassion, and Christian piety.[34]

It was not so for all MP's in Wilberforce's day. There was a time, for example, when Wilberforce's voice in Parliament was so strong that the abolition of the slave trade looked imminent, even as early as the year 1796. However, on March 15 of that year, when Wilberforce's Abolition Bill came up for vote on a Third Reading, the cause was lost by four votes (70 in favor, 74 opposed). This was a crushing defeat for Wilberforce, especially because he had personal knowledge that at least five or six MP's who would have otherwise voted on his side had, instead of attending the vote, decided to go to the Opera House to hear the new Italian opera that had come to town.[35] It would be another 11 years (the decisive vote in Parliament took place on February 23, 1807) before the abolition of the slave trade. In those 11 years, many Africans, who were equally created in God's image, lost their families, their freedom, and their lives.

Most Christians are not political rulers. In America, for example, most Christians lack the money and influence to become United States congressmen or senators. Still, all Christians are created in the image of God. That means that God has given to us, each and all, a certain amount of rulership. Pastors have a certain amount of

---

[34] Many admirers of Wilberforce who nevertheless do not know the details of his life's story might be surprised to learn just how vocal he was about his faith in the God of Scripture, and how much he quoted the Bible in public. He was, first and foremost, committed to Christian piety, which one of his best friends, Hannah More, described as "a religion of the heart." But for both Wilberforce and More, this religion of the heart is dead if it lacks feeling for the weakest and most vulnerable members of society.

[35] For the details of this historical event, see John Pollock, *William Wilberforce* (Sandy Lane West, Oxford: Lion Publishing 1977), 143.

dominion in their churches. Doctors have a certain degree of authority in their hospitals and clinics. Fathers and mothers have a large amount of dominion in their homes. Every web blog, every Christmas letter, and every financial gift to a Christian ministry, is an expression of the image of God through the exercise of sub-rulership in the world. God has given us talents to use in order to rule over His created order—in the fear of Him—and in order to subdue the earth under His Lordship.

Therefore, beloved Reader, when it comes to the Abortion Holocaust, the legalized slaughtering of the weakest of the weak, you have an obligation to act, courageously, in their defense. Jesus Christ, your Creator and your Lord, demands it of you. How, then, are you exercising your domains of sub-rulership on their behalf? Are you willing to speak up for them, who are unable to speak up for themselves? Are you willing to be persecuted for them, or to die for them? Will you commit yourself to the work of the abolition of abortion, in a holy and distinctly Christian manner, no matter what it may cost you? Should not the evil of abortion be subdued in our world, against all odds, so that the goodness and glory of God may be on display for all the world to see? Dear and precious Reader, exercise your realms of rulership for the sake of the preborn. Do not let the Sovereign Lord find you at the Opera House on the Day of Decision.

2

GOD'S GREAT BLESSINGS:
Procreation and Preborn Children

(Genesis 1:26-28, Part 2)

THAT Johann Sebastian Bach (1685-1750) was one of the greatest musicians of all time is a matter that is beyond dispute. However, what is often missed in the retelling of Bach's life is the recognition of his colossal achievements in the realm of Christian fatherhood. Trained as a boy by his God-fearing father, Ambrosius, who was an extraordinary musician, and being descended from a long line of great musicians who also happened to be mighty men of faith, Sebastian Bach knew the spiritual power of family-based Christian discipleship. He, therefore, took upon himself the weighty responsibilities of both the musical training and the spiritual instruction of his own children.

Sebastian Bach loved children. He also knew the sorrows of the Cross of Christ. He was married twice. His first wife, Maria Barbara, died at the young age of 36, having given birth to seven children, three of whom died in infancy. Bach's second wife, Anna Magdalena, was sixteen years his junior, but was, despite her youthfulness, a very beloved wife and mother. She gave birth to thirteen children, seven of whom died at early ages.[1] Therefore, Sebastian Bach had a total of twenty children, ten of whom died in infancy or early childhood. He loved a multitude of children; he suffered through the loss of many of them.

Is it not, then, wonderful and awe-inspiring to think of Bach as the father of such a large number of children? Are we not

---

[1] Hans Conrad Fisher, *Johann Sebastian Bach: His Life in Pictures and Documents* (eds. Christopher Pipe and Tim Dowley; trans. Silvia Lutz; redesigned ed.; Holzgerlinger, Germany: Hänssler Verlag, 2000), 115-116, documents the mournfully short lifespans of Anna Magdalena's seven children who died at early ages. Two examples suffice to remind us of Sebastian and Anna's tears: (i) "Christiana Sophia Henrietta, born and baptized in the spring of 1723 at Cöthen, died July 1, 1726, in Leipzig"; and (ii) "Christiana Benedicta, baptized on January 1, 1730, died January 4, 1730, in Leipzig."

mesmerized by his mention, in a letter that he sent to an old friend, of his family making music together, with Anna Magdalena and his daughters doing the singing?[2] With what vivacious music did Bach, his wife, and his children fill his composing room—which was attached to their home in Leipzig? Can we not picture, in our minds, the family gathering in the evening time for a festive hour of doxological music playing? And would not the Bach family's worship of God have been filled with the instrumental sounds of such virtuoso musicians that it could move a listener to tears of gladness and joy?

Here, then, is one of the critical ways in which the Christian piety of Johann Sebastian Bach indicts the modern Church. Namely, Bach asked God, through the Lord Jesus Christ, to bless him with an overflowing number of children, and, as a wise and pious man, he craved such a blessing. However, the modern Church, in stark contrast to Bach, has, quite capriciously, turned Her back upon the wonderful, worshipful, and even "musical" blessings of bountiful Christian procreation.

The great guilt of the modern Church regarding Her shunning of the blessing of God in procreation can thus be illustrated by Bach's own family. For, it is the modern Church that says, "Smaller families are better." It is, to Her shame, the modern Church that so audaciously claims that Christian parents have the right, if not the responsibility, to take willful and intentional measures to prevent the conception of children. Yet this attitudinal posture towards Christian procreation is the very antithesis of what brought so much life and joy into the Bach family music room.

Where, then, are today's Christian proponents of contraception when the opportunity arises to peer, historically, into the family life of Johann Sebastian Bach? What Christian will have the cold-heartedness to claim that one or more of the children in the Bach family music room should never have been conceived?[3] Which child should not have been allowed to exist? Is it that shy teenage boy,

---

[2] Gregory Wilbur, *Glory and Honor: The Musical and Artistic Legacy of Johann Sebastian Bach* (Nashville, Tennessee: Cumberland House Publishing, 2005), 193.
[3] This argument is strengthened by the fact that Anna Magdalena and her surviving children faced poverty and hardship after Bach's death. Should these extreme financial hardships of Bach's youngest children have warranted a denial of their right to be conceived?

playing the violin next to his beloved father? Is it that beaming young girl, sitting at the harpsichord next to her affectionate mother? Would the Bach "family orchestra" be better off with fewer members? Would the Lord God really think the music better if several of the players had been denied existence through contraception? Or, is not God *delighted* by the *multitude* of instruments sounding in the Bach family music room, and especially by the instruments of the youngest players—those with the smallest fingers and the squeakiest violins?

There is, therefore, a great hypocrisy afoot in the modern Church, and it is crippling Her Abortion-Abolitionist efforts. This hypocrisy is seen, in glaring fashion, in the case of a "pro-life" married couple who attend church regularly, and who enthusiastically support their local crisis pregnancy center, but who, simultaneously, have only four pairs of hiking boots (one pair for each of them, and one pair for each of their two children) stored away in the garage of their large, extravagant house. They have, through contraception, traded the opportunity to have an over-sized shoe bin filled with ten, fifteen, or even twenty pairs of shoes (the pairs of shoes, of course, represent a large, overflowing number of children), for the greedy prospect of being able to afford their largely self-indulgent lifestyle. They are anti-abortion, to be sure. But they are simultaneously pro-contraception. And in the light of Holy Scripture, this is a great hypocrisy.

Evangelical Christians, in particular, have inherited the sinful practice of contraception from their immediate forefathers. This is now a generational sin, since it is being passed down from one generation of Christians to the next via common practice and bankrupt theological reasoning. Evangelicals have thus *inherited* the sinful culture of contraception that pervades their churches, and so are quite shocked to hear it exposed as sinful, rather than viewed as acceptable and normative. Therefore, the current generation of Evangelicals, if it desires to please God in this matter, must become like Gideon. It must be courageous enough to tear down the "family altar" of contraceptive ideals and practice. And, in order to do so, it must come to understand the intimate relationship between the doctrine of man—especially as man is created in the image of God—and the Lord's blessing of bountiful procreation in Christian marriage.

The Image of God and Fruitfulness of the Womb

It is most remarkable to note the very special way in which God ties the doctrine of human beings *as created in the image of God* to His love for *a multitude of children*. We have seen, in the previous chapter, that the "image of God" doctrine prohibits abortion, in all cases, on account of Genesis 9:6 (which prohibits the shedding of blood of all image bearers). We have also seen that to be created in the image of God means to possess a sub-rulership in the world (under the divine rulership of Christ), and that this sub-rulership ought to be exercised in defense of preborn children, in order to abolish abortion, and thus work to subdue nations under the good and merciful law of Christ. But there remains one more very important reflection on how the image of God in humanity speaks to the Abortion Holocaust in our world. It involves the inseparable connection between the image of God and the fruitfulness of the womb.

There is, indeed, a very special way in which the image of God in us speaks directly to God's love for a multitude of children. Positively, the image of God in husbands and wives creates a yearning in their hearts for the maximum fruitfulness of the womb. Negatively, the doctrine of the image of God in Scripture, and especially in Genesis 1:26-28, creates an inseparable link between *the sin of abortion* and *the sin of contraception*.[4] It affirms God's love for a multitude of children, and thus commands human fruitfulness—a fruitfulness which both the sin of abortion and the sin of contraception violently destroy.

---

[4] The present author writes the following as one who, himself, has had to repent of the sin of employing contraception (in marriage). His journey from seeing non-abortifacient (that is, non-abortion-causing) contraceptives as morally acceptable to seeing them as unbiblical and sinful has been a long and painful one. By God's loving discipline and grace, he has repented of this sin of contraception. He confesses this sin, publicly, as a way of encouraging his fellow Protestants to consider, with humility and prayer, that freedom from the modern culture of contraception—which we, as Protestants, have recklessly immersed ourselves in— is both freedom from sinful bondage and freedom to live life much more abundantly.

The Bible is *Contra* Contraception

The image of God is inextricably linked to procreation (the bringing of children into the world). This is the first imperative (i.e. grammatical form of command) in the Hebrew Old Testament, and it is *the first command that God gives to humanity in the Bible*. The image of God and procreation go together. They are not to be divided from one another:

God created man in His own image. In God's image He created him; male and female He created them. God blessed them. God said to them, "Be fruitful, multiply, fill the earth, and subdue it. Have dominion over the fish of the sea, over the birds of the sky, and over every living thing that moves on the earth." (Genesis 1:27–28)

This command of procreation is repeated to Noah after the global flood has decimated the global human population and reduced it to eight people. Noah, his wife, their sons, and their wives, are commanded to be fruitful and multiply:

God blessed Noah and his sons, and said to them, "Be fruitful, and multiply, and [fill] the earth." (Genesis 9:1)

The procreative command is thus a timeless, trans-cultural one. It is given to Adam and Eve. It is reaffirmed and reapplied to Noah, well before the time of the Mosaic Law. It is thus a command that is given to all of humanity, at all times in human history.

Furthermore, it must be observed that the command to be fruitful and multiply, through childbearing, is *never rescinded in the Bible*. It is always upheld in Scripture, from Genesis through Revelation. The Bible, from cover to cover, views all children as blessings from God. It never once suggests that large families, with a dozen or more children, are a burden to society or a hindrance to mission work. To the contrary, the Bible describes large families, the ones with many children, as those who have received the special blessing of God.[5] It also describes nations that have vast multitudes of youngsters as nations whom God has blessed:

> *I will make you <u>exceedingly fruitful</u>, and I will make nations of you. Kings will come out of you.* (Genesis 17:6)

And,

> *The children of Israel were <u>fruitful</u>, and <u>increased abundantly</u>, and <u>multiplied</u>, and <u>grew exceedingly mighty</u>; and <u>the land was filled with them</u>.* (Exodus 1:7)

Two consecutive Psalms, 127 and 128, speak loudly about this truth of an increase of blessings that comes with an increase of the number of one's own children:

> *Behold, children are a heritage of the* LORD. *The fruit of the womb is [a] reward. As arrows in the hand of a mighty man, so are the children of youth. <u>Happy is the man who has his quiver full of them</u>. They will not be disappointed when they speak with their enemies in the gate.* (Psalm 127:3–5)

> *Your wife will be as <u>a fruitful vine</u>, in the innermost parts of your house; your children <u>like olive plants, around your table</u>. Behold, thus is the man blessed who fears the* LORD. (Psalm 128:3–4)

---

[5] The opposite of this, however, is not necessarily true. Parents who are unable to conceive any, or many children, or parents who have seen many of their children die at very young ages, are not, therefore, lacking the blessing of God. Actually, the Bible describes many righteous parents who desperately desire an abundance of children, but who are unable to have them, as being amongst some of the most blessed people in all of human history. Those who fear God, but nevertheless face barrenness or bereavement, are given this unique (albeit extremely pain-soaked) trial as a sign of their special relation to God. For particular examples of this, see: Genesis 18:10; 25:21; 29:31; Exodus 1:21; 2:9; Judges 13:2; Ruth 4:16-17; 1 Samuel 1:10 (and following); 2 Samuel 12:24-25; 1 Kings 17:23; 2 Kings 2:21; 4:16-17; Esther 2:7; Job 1:18-19; Psalm 113:9; Isaiah 7:14; 49:20-21; 54:1; Jeremiah 31:15-17; Hosea 1:8-10; Luke 1:5-7; 7:12-14; Hebrews 11:11.

This is true of God's blessing upon Israel, and, specifically, upon those who fear Him, before the exile of the Jews in Babylon. But it is also true of the remnant who will return to Jerusalem after the exile:

> *I will gather the remnant of My flock out of all the countries where I have driven them, and will bring them again to their folds; and <u>they shall be fruitful and multiply</u>.* (Jeremiah 23:3)

Moreover, lest all of these biblical evidences concerning God's command for us to be fruitful and multiply through procreation be brushed aside as being "Old Covenant" in nature, and thus no longer binding in the New Covenant age, the words of the Apostle Paul must give us pause. Paul, the great missionary to the Gentiles, *does not* permit the use of "birth control," not even in the name of adapting the Gospel to the host cultures of the Gentiles (who, in his day, regularly practiced various forms of contraception).[6] To the contrary, Paul simply reaffirms the Genesis 1:28 command to procreate in marriage:

> *Let no one be enrolled as a widow under sixty years old, having been the wife of one man, being approved by good works, <u>if she has brought up children</u>, if she has been hospitable to strangers, if she has washed the saints' feet, if she has relieved the afflicted, and if she has diligently followed every good work.* (1 Timothy 5:9–10)

---

[6] Paul's mention of the sin of *"sorcery"* (Greek *pharmakeía*) in Galatians 5:20, following the sins of *"adultery, sexual immorality, uncleanness, lustfulness, idolatry…"* may well be a reference to the common use of certain potions and drugs, the likes of which certainly included both contraceptive drugs and abortifacients. This possibility is strengthened by the fact that the *Didache* (see *Didache 2.2*, in *The Apostolic Fathers: Greek Texts and English Translations* [ed. and rev. Michael W. Holmes; Grand Rapids: Baker Books, 1999], 253), one of our oldest extra-biblical Christian documents, says, "…you shall not abort a child or commit infanticide," *immediately after* it commands, "…you shall not engage in sorcery [*pharmakeúo*]." Also, Minucius Felix (2nd Century AD), in his *Octavius* 30 (*ANF* 4.192), describes "some women who, *by drinking medical preparations*, extinguish the source of the future man in their very bowels, and thus commit a parricide before they bring forth" (emphasis added).

Also,

> *I desire therefore that the younger widows <u>marry</u>, <u>bear children</u>, [manage] the household, and give no occasion to the adversary for insulting.*
> (1 Timothy 5:14)

The image of God in us summons our hearts to respond obediently to God's command to be fruitful and multiply. Every father and mother ought to desire as many children as God will allow them to have.[7] That is, the image of God in us compels us towards abundant multiplication. We are to trust that God will provide all of our needs in Christ Jesus as we continue to ask Him to give us more and more children. In this way, we are to *"fill the earth"* with more and more image bearers (Genesis 1:28).

But what happens when men and women decide to sever the image of God in them from the command to procreate in marriage? What happens when Christians, especially, use contraception to prevent procreation, seeking to limit the number of children that they bring into the world? What happens when believers divorce intimacy in marriage (their one-flesh-ness) from God's desire for believing children?

> *Did He not make you one, although He had the [remnant] of the Spirit? Why one? He [<u>seeks</u>] <u>godly offspring</u>.... (Malachi 2:15)*

Contraception opens wide the door for abortion. Mother Teresa, in her famous speech at the 1994 National Prayer Breakfast in Washington D.C., spoke of a "living love" that husbands and wives ought to have for each other. She then said, "Once that living love is

---

[7] The Bible does explain a very limited numbers of cases in which abstinence is required in marriage, at least for a time. Uriah the Hittite, for example, was righteous in his decision not to be intimate with his wife (and thus to abstain) while his spiritual/military duty beckoned him to stay focused on *"the ark, Israel, and Judah"* who were at that time *"staying in tents"* on the battlefield (2 Samuel 11:11). There are times, then, for abstinence in marriage. When a spouse is sick, wounded, grieving, or frail, or when both spouses agree to a limited season of deprivation and prayer (1 Corinthians 7:5), abstinence in marriage is required. But abstinence in marriage should never be used as a form of birth control. And intimacy in marriage should never be severed from *the desire to beget children.*

destroyed by contraception, abortion follows very easily."[8] Mother Teresa was thus very wise in her ability to see the connection between contraception and abortion.

The truth is that when human beings willfully violate the command to *"be fruitful and multiply"* and to *"fill the earth"* (Genesis 1:28), they give rise to their sin nature's (that is the nature that they inherited from Adam's sin) inclination to destroy children. Instead of always viewing children as a blessing, humanity has been taught, by Satan, to view an overabundance of children as a burden. On large societal levels, people speak of there being too many children to feed, and thus a social responsibility towards population control. On smaller, family-unit levels, parents think that good parenting involves spoiling their children with an excess of material belongings, expensive athletic and extra-curricular programs, exotic vacations, constant entertainments, and costly college educations. They, therefore, conclude that large families are impractical. And, on individual, husband-and-wife levels, our culture has taught married couples that having more than two or three children (or, perhaps, six as a maximum for a wealthy family) would rudely intrude upon their self-centered concepts of recreational sex (that is, marital intimacy without procreative responsibility), social freedom, financial security, vocational ambition, and personal hobbies and enterprises.

Contraception points in a direction opposite that of the Bible. The arrow of fruitfulness and multiplication, whose sharp tip is forged by God in Genesis 1:28, points consistently throughout the Bible towards Christian homes that are "filled" with large numbers of children. It points towards churches "filled" with children, and towards nations "filled" with children. But contraception is a poisonous arrow that points in the very opposite direction. It points towards households, churches, and societies that are no longer "filled" full and overflowing with children.

Here, then, is the frightening connection between contraception and abortion. History tells us, very plainly, that whenever societies

---

[8] In saying this, however, Mother Teresa was, as a loyal member of the Roman Catholic Church, advocating Natural Family Planning as an alternative to contraception. But Natural Family Planning is simply another form of contraception (albeit a less sinful form of contraception, since it at least leaves room for God to override the planned prevention) because it intentionally prevents the fruitfulness of the womb. It, too, is a sinful violation of the image of God in us.

untether sexual intimacy from the desire to procreate within the holy confines of marriage, which is exactly what contraception does, there always follow *unwanted children*. And where there are unwanted children, there are bound to be *abortions*.[9] This was true in ancient Greece and ancient Rome. It is true today in such unthinkable quantities of occurrences that we must cover our eyes, in dismay, on account of it.

A nation whose husbands and wives do not desire to "fill" their homes towards overflowing with children will inevitably "fill" its land with the blood of children. Once the image of God in us is severed, by sin, from our created duty and privilege of bountiful procreation, humans begin to "fill" God's earth not with children, but with the blood of the preborn, and the blood of infants:

> *Because they have forsaken Me, and have estranged this place, and have burned incense in it to other gods, that they did not know, they and their fathers and the kings of Judah; and <u>have filled this place with the blood of innocents</u>, and have built the high places of Baal, <u>to burn their sons in the fire for burnt offerings to Baal</u>; which I did not command, nor spoke it, neither came it into my mind: therefore, behold, the days [of judgment] come....* (Jeremiah 19:4–6a)

---

[9] The argument here is not of logical necessity. The use of non-abortifacient contraception does not logically necessitate the practice of abortion. There are, for example, many advocates of contraception who are vehemently opposed to abortion. The argument here, however, concerns the attitudinal shift that contraception brings about. If God has created intimacy in marriage in such a way that it should *never* be severed from the desire to procreate (and here we note that the Puritan pastor Richard Baxter points out for us that married couples who are intimate beyond the age of childbearing do not violate the underlying God-ordained conjugal desire to procreate), which is the historic Christian position, then *any* severing of intimacy in marriage from the desire to procreate produces a spiritual mindset that is counter to Genesis 1:28, and this spiritual mindset *necessarily undervalues children*. (For example, the question must be asked, "What 'greater good' can result from the use of contraception, a 'greater good' which, itself, outweighs the bringing of a brand new child into the world?"). The spiritual mindset produced by the practice of contraception creates a category of "unwanted children." It is this category of "unwanted children," in turn, that opens wide the door for abortion. (Or, to put the argument another way, Christians violate Genesis 1:28 whenever they decide that they, themselves, have the right to determine the "blessedness" [either in relation to themselves or in relation to the broader world] of their particular family size, instead of trusting God's Word and providence for His own blessed determination of the fruitfulness of the womb).

Contraception Condemned throughout Church History

This explains why all of the giant men of faith of church history (prior to the great Protestant compromise beginning in the 1930's)[10] have associated the sin of abortion very closely with the sin of contraception. The anti-child mindset of both practices is an anti-life mindset. In the end, both practices are anti-God ones.

The quotes from church history about contraception are numerous, unified, and shocking to the contemporary ear. Hippolytus (c. AD 170-236), who was one of the greatest early pastors in Rome,[11] says of contraceptive drugs: "Whence [unmarried] women, reputed believers, began to *resort to drugs for producing sterility*, and to gird themselves round, so to expel what was being conceived...Behold, into how great impiety that lawless one [the heretic Callistus] has proceeded, by inculcating adultery and murder at the same time!"[12] Hippolytus here equates both abortion *and contraception* with "murder," which is a unified line of thought throughout church history. The intentional prevention of conception is seen as "murder" in the sense that it seeks to prohibit a particular human being, an image bearer, from coming into existence.

---

[10] For the very disturbing story of how Margaret Sanger, the founder of Planned Parenthood, used a combination of anti-Roman Catholic fear tactics and the propagation of "soft eugenics" to win mainline Protestant pastors over to her cause, see Allan Carlson, "Margaret Sanger Divides the Christians" in *Godly Seed: American Evangelicals Confront Birth Control, 1873-1973* (New Brunswick: Transaction Publishers, 2012), 79-112.

[11] The spiritual lineage of Hippolytus is significant. A. Cleveland Coxe, "Introductory Notice to Hippolytus," in *ANF* 5.7, says, "Hippolytus was a disciple of St. Irenaeus, St. Irenaeus of St. Polycarp, St. Polycarp of [the Apostle] John."

[12] Hippolytus, *The Refutation of All Heresies* 9.7 (*ANF* 5.131), emphasis added.

The severe warnings from our spiritual fathers continue.[13] In line with Hippolytus, John Chrysostom also equates contraception with murder: "Why sow where the ground makes it its care to destroy the fruit? Where there are many *efforts at sterility*? Where there is *murder before the birth*? ...For I have no name to give it, since it does not take off the thing born, but *prevent[s] its being born*."[14]

During the Protestant Reformation, contraception was universally condemned. Martin Luther (1483-1546), the Father of the

---

[13] Augustine of Hippo (354-430), does, disappointingly, make himself unique in church history by wavering on the actual personhood of a newly conceived baby in the womb. While still remaining opposed to all forms of abortion from conception onwards, he is nevertheless too heavily influenced by the Aristotelian tradition of Greek philosophy in his theory of developmental ensoulment; the rest of the early Church Fathers see the baby, from conception onwards, as fully alive and possessing a soul. (See the *Appendix* for quotations from the early Church Fathers on all forms of abortion as murder). Nonetheless, Augustine, in his *On Marriage and Concupiscence* 1.17 (NPNF¹ 5.270-71), has very serious things to say against the use of contraception in marriage: "They who resort to these [i.e. wrong desires and contraception], although called by the name of spouses, are really not such; they retain no vestige of true matrimony, but pretend the honorable designation as a cloak for criminal conduct....Sometimes, indeed, this lustful cruelty, or, if you please, cruel lust, resorts to such extravagant methods as to use poisonous drugs to secure barrenness [i.e. contraception]; or else, if unsuccessful in this, to destroy the conceived seed by some means previous to birth [i.e. abortion]....Well, if both parties alike are so flagitious [grossly wicked], they are not husband and wife; and if such were their character from the beginning, they have not come together by wedlock but by debauchery. But if the two are not alike in such sin, I boldly declare either that the woman is, so to say, the husband's harlot; or the man, the wife's adulterer."

[14] John Chrysostom, *Homilies on the Epistle to the Romans* 24 (NPNF¹ 11.520). Curiously, the translators of Chrysostom's Romans homilies in the *Nicene and Post-Nicene Fathers* series decided to substitute "abortion" for "sterility" in their English text. However, the Greek text reads, *entha polla ta atokia*, where *atokia* clearly means contraceptive "sterility." For definitions of *atokios* as "a drugged beverage to produce barrenness" and "contraceptive...causing barrenness...medicine for causing it," see, respectively: James Donnegan, *A New Greek and English Lexicon* (Boston: Hilliard, Gray, and Co., 1840), 270; and Henry George Liddell, Robert Scott, and Henry Stuart Jones, *A Greek-English Lexicon* (rev. and new ed.; Oxford: Clarendon Press, 1940), 1:271. Note also the following quote in Chrysostom, *Homilies on the Gospel of St. Matthew* 28 (NPNF¹ 10.194): "...that which is sweet, and universally desirable, the having of children, they esteem grievous and unwelcome: many at least with this view have even paid money to be childless, and have maimed their nature, not only by slaying their children after birth, but by not suffering them even to be born at all."

Reformation, speaks of contraception with exceptional vehemence. He says that there are "many people" in his day "who do not want to have children," a situation which he describes as "worse than barbarous."[15] He further says that, in his day, "most married people do not desire offspring," which makes them "more wicked than even the heathen themselves."[16] They sin against the truth that "the purpose of marriage is not to have pleasure and to be idle but to procreate and bring up children. This, of course, is a huge burden full of great cares and toils. But you have been created by God to be a husband or a wife and that you may learn to bear these troubles."[17] He continues, "Those who have no love for children are swine, stocks, and logs unworthy of being called men or women; for they despise the blessing of God, the Creator and Author of marriage."[18] In sum, speaking of God's command to have a multitude of children in the home, Luther says that "it is inhuman and godless to have a loathing for offspring."[19]

John Calvin (1509-1564), another Reformation giant, is no less grave about the sin of contraception. Describing the sin of Onan in Genesis 38 as, at least in part, a sin of contraception, Calvin says:

> The voluntary spilling of semen outside of intercourse between man and woman is a monstrous thing. Deliberately to withdraw from coitus in order that semen may fall on the ground is doubly monstrous. For this is to extinguish the hope of the race and to kill before he is born the hoped-for offspring. This impiety is especially condemned, now by the Spirit through Moses' mouth, that Onan, as it were, by a violent abortion, no less cruelly than filthily cast upon the ground the offspring of his brother, torn from the maternal womb. Besides, in this way he tried, as far as he was able, to wipe out a part of the human race. If any woman ejects a [preborn baby] from her womb by drugs, it is reckoned a crime incapable of expiation and deservedly Onan incurred upon himself the same kind of punishment, infecting the earth by his

---

[15] Martin Luther, Commentary on Genesis 2:18, *Luther's Works* (St. Louis: Concordia Publishing House, 1958), 1:118.
[16] Martin Luther, qtd. in Charles D. Provan, *The Bible and Birth Control* (Monongahela, PA: Zimmer Printing, 1989), 34.
[17] Ibid., 34.
[18] Ibid., 34.
[19] Ibid., 28.

semen, in order that Tamar might not conceive a future human being as an inhabitant of the earth.[20]

Calvin thus draws the same condemnation upon contraception as he does upon abortion. The two are inextricably linked in his mind.

The list could go on and on.[21] Up until the 1930's, all God-fearing and biblical Christians condemned the practice of contraception. Richard Baxter, one of Protestantism's finest pastors, says, "Another duty of husbands and wives is cohabitation and (where age prohibiteth not) a sober and modest conjunction *for procreation*."[22] John Owen (1616-1683), one of the greatest of the Puritans, speaks of "conjugal duties" in marriage needing to be "subservient unto the due ends of marriage," which include "…the procreation of children."[23] And much later on, Arthur W. Pink (1886-1952), the posthumously renowned expositor, asserts that marriage "results in virgins becoming mothers," that "the propagation of children is the 'normal' end of marriage," and that "…we do not believe in what is termed 'birth control.'"[24]

If church history is a courtroom, then there is a great cloud of witnesses testifying in this courtroom to the inseparable link between abortion and contraception, and also to the mandate of fruitfulness within Christian marriage. The concept of severing intimacy in marriage from the desire to fill our homes, overflowing, with children is unthinkable to the great men and women of church history. And, the very idea that a Christian may be pro-contraception (which means, literally, "positively-for-being-against-conception"), on the

---

[20] John Calvin, qtd. in ibid., 15. Note that Calvin's anti-contraception exposition of Genesis 38:10 is *curiously omitted* in all of the modern editions of his commentary on Genesis.

[21] For an impressive list of the giants of church history who are strongly opposed to contraception, see Bryan C. Hodge, *The Christian Case Against Contraception: Making the Case from Historical, Biblical, Systematic, and Practical Theology & Ethics* (Eugene, OR: Wipf & Stock, 2010), 35-38.

[22] Richard Baxter, *The Practical Works of the Rev. Richard Baxter: with a Life of the Author, and a Critical Examination of His Writings* (ed. Rev. William Orme; London: James Duncan, 1830), 7:119, emphasis added.

[23] John Owen, *The Works of John Owen, D.D.* (ed. Rev. William H. Gould; Edinburgh: T & T Clark, 1862), 24:405.

[24] Arthur W. Pink, *An Exposition of Hebrews*, on Hebrews 13:4 (chapter 108), n.p. [cited: 25 March 2013]. Online: http://www.pbministries.org/books/pink/Hebrews/hebrews_108.htm.

one hand, and "pro-life," on the other, is more than just an oxymoron to them. It is a moral outrage.

The Image of God is *Pro* Procreation

The Bible commands us: *"Be fruitful and multiply"* (Genesis 1:28). It depicts families with more than a dozen children as having a great and abundant blessing from God. The Bible describes the birth of a child as one of the greatest joys in life. Jesus even compares childbirth to the joy of His own resurrection from the dead (John 16:21-22)! It is no wonder, then, that Martin Luther calls procreation "the greatest work of God."[25]

Our modern world is obsessed with money. We think that our perceived need for financial security prevents us from having houses that are overflowing with children.[26] This is an anti-Bible attitude. It cuts against the grain of Matthew 6:31-33:

Therefore do not be anxious, saying, "What will we eat?", "What will we drink?" or, "With what will we be clothed?" For the Gentiles seek after all these things; for your heavenly Father knows that you need all these things. But seek first God's Kingdom, and His righteousness; and all these things will be given to you as well.

The Bible delights in large families. When the book of 1 Chronicles says that *"God gave to Heman fourteen sons and three*

---

[25] Luther, Commentary on Genesis 2:18, *Works*, 1:118.
[26] Luther, in his Commentary on Genesis 30:2, *Works*, 5:332, confronts the sin of using contraception in order to avoid financial hardships in the home: "Although it is very easy to marry a wife, it is very difficult to support her along with the children and the household. Accordingly, no one notices this faith of Jacob. Indeed, many hate fertility in a wife for the sole reason that the offspring must be supported and brought up. For this is what they commonly say: 'Why should I marry a wife when I am a pauper and a beggar? I would rather bear the burden of poverty alone and not load myself with misery and want.' But this blame is unjustly fastened on marriage and fruitfulness. Indeed, you are indicting your unbelief by distrusting God's goodness, and you are bringing greater misery upon yourself by disparaging God's blessing. For if you had trust in God's grace and promises, you would undoubtedly be supported. But because you do not hope in the Lord, you will never prosper."

daughters" (25:5),[27] God announces this to us, through Scripture, with holy glee. The Bible describes the man Heman, with seventeen children, as a man richly blessed by his Creator. Also, righteous Job, whose previous blessings, once lost, are eventually restored to him in abundance, fathers a total of *twenty children*. This large number of children is portrayed in the book of Job as a great blessing from God (1:2; 42:13). In fact, as has been shown already, all throughout the Bible a multitude of children is seen to be a great blessing from God.

This means that even married church pastors and married Christian missionaries, who oftentimes speak of needing to limit their family sizes for the "greater good" of doing "the Lord's work," need to be sharply rebuked by the Jesus of Scripture:

Allow <u>the little children</u> to come to Me, and do not hinder them, for <u>God's Kingdom belongs to such as these</u>. (Luke 18:16)

There is no "greater good" for Christian married couples than the procreation of Christian offspring. Susanna Wesley knew this. She was, herself, the twenty-fifth of twenty-five children in her family. Therefore, giving birth to nineteen children was simply natural and biblical for her. Though she lost nine of them as infants—the sufferings of Christ were not foreign to her—she kept on obeying God's command to procreate. Her *fifteenth* child was John, and her *eighteenth* child was Charles (who was born prematurely and barely survived infancy). John and Charles Wesley would grow up and help spark one of the most important revivals in all of British history, and their preaching would have a great impact on the First Great Awakening in America. However, had Susanna Wesley chosen financial security (the family faced hard financial circumstances at times) over obedience to Genesis 1:28, John and Charles Wesley would never even have been conceived.

God delights in a multitude of children. The greatest joy of Christian marriage is the bringing of godly offspring into the world. In the fruitfulness of the womb, there is great power. We, as Christians, will not change the world by getting fancier graduate degrees and amassing more and more material possessions. We will, like Moses' parents, change the world for the sake of righteousness

---

[27] The present author is indebted to the ministry of Matt Trewhella, founder of Missionaries to the Preborn, for this insight.

only by seeing the eternal worth of procreation for what it really is. God chooses not to save the world through "wise" and "powerful" adults. Rather, He chooses to save the world through little children.

<u>The Image Marred, the Image Restored</u>

All babies, from conception onwards, bear the image of God. Therefore all human beings, in whatever capacities of rulership with which they have been endowed by God, are to work for the protection and nurture of all preborn children in the womb. Moreover, since the image of God includes the mandate of human fruitfulness, there should never be a separation within marriage between the desire for physical intimacy and the desire for more and more children. All pregnancies should be welcomed with mirthful wonder and awe. The idea of a married couple having an "unwanted" child, or choosing to limit the number of children that they bring into the world, should be anathema.

Yes, but now we see just how badly we have marred the image of God in us. It is not that we have accidentally bumped into the portrait of Christ, the image of God, which is hanging in the gallery of our hearts, thus scuffing it up a bit. No, as humans we have forcefully attacked the portrait. We have spit upon it, thrown refuse at it, and driven nails into it. Abortionists have taken needles to the wombs of pregnant mothers, and knives to the foreheads of preborn babies. Rulers have crafted laws that do not protect these weakest of the weak, but rather enable the mass slaughtering of them. And even parents have joined in this anti-life mentality by denying the blessing of houses filled to the point of overflowing with children, and trading that blessing for the lie of "achieving the greater good" through the use of contraception. In all of these things, we are now a people who are greatly bereaved of children.

Where, then, is hope? Have we marred the image of God in us beyond the point of restoration? Are we so addicted to the anti-child drugs and practices of this world that we may never return to the blessing of God-exalting families and churches, filled with children, again?

There is hope, but only the kind of hope that comes at an infinite price. The virgin Mary conceived a child. He kicked inside of Mary's womb. He was *the* Image of God in Mary's womb. After He was born, He grew up into adulthood. He was *the* Image of God in the world. When people looked upon His face, they saw God.

Yet sinful humanity hated this Image of His Father. They hated His exposure of their sins. They despised His life of perfect holiness and perfect justice. Instead of worshipping Him, as God in the flesh, they attacked Him and beat Him:

> *Just as multitudes were appalled at Him, so <u>His appearance</u> was <u>marred <u>beyond that of a man</u>, and His form beyond that of the sons of men.* (Isaiah 52:14)[28]

The horror of human sin is that it attacks Jesus, who is *the* Image of God. He is not merely a portrait of His Father in Heaven. Rather, His flesh is the actual, living Image of His Father. And yet we, sinful humans, attacked that Image. The Jews plotted against Him and betrayed Him with lies. The Romans flogged Him and beat His face until it was so bloodied and abused as to be unrecognizable. Together, they spit upon and mocked the very Son of God.

This is the only hope of "image restoration" within us, and it comes at infinite cost. Jesus has been crucified for our sins. His blood, alone, can cover over all of the sins of abortion in our world. His sacrificial death, in our stead, is the only thing powerful enough to grant forgiveness to those who have had abortions—who have murdered their own offspring—and who are willing to repent of their crimes, and to believe in His name. At the Cross, Mary wept for her Son, whom she carried in the womb. Therefore, at the Cross, weeping mothers, who have been so cruelly betrayed by the lies of the abortionists, can find forgiveness for their sins.

Yet there is more. The hope of the Gospel is brighter still. Not only can the sins of abortion and the anti-child practice of contraception be forgiven at the Cross of Christ, but we must also believe and know that He has been raised from the dead! The body of Christ, the very Image of God, has been raised to life!

Therefore, since Christ is raised from the dead, we know that we, too, shall be raised from the grave: *"But each one in his own order: Christ the firstfruits, afterwards those who are Christ's at His Coming"* (1 Corinthians 15:23). Yet *"those who are Christ's at His Coming"* also includes the precious, preborn children of the Abortion Holocaust.

---

[28] The present author's translation.

They shall be raised from the grave! Their bodies shall be rescued from the grave, and they shall live, everlastingly, with new and resurrected bodies in Heaven! The babies of the Abortion Holocaust shall be raised to everlasting life!

This also means that the image of God in us, which our sin has so horribly marred, can be restored to spiritual perfection in Heaven. The resurrected Christ is *the* Image of God, once crucified, now restored to eternal perfection. Therefore, we, too, can have the image of God within us revived and restored. We, who are born of the Holy Spirit and thus know Christ, are *"predestined to be conformed to the image of His Son, that He might be the Firstborn among many brothers"* (Romans 8:29). Since we have *"borne the image of [the man of dust],"* we also will *"bear the image of [the Man of Heaven]"* (1 Corinthians 15:49). We have taken off the old man, with its cravings for sins, and we *"have put on the new man, who is being renewed in knowledge after the image of his Creator"* (Colossians 3:10). God works in us, through the Gospel of His Son Jesus Christ, to restore His image in us. And He who began a good work of image restoration in us, will see it all the way to completion on the Day of Christ Jesus.

To be human, then, is to be created in the image of God. It is to see all preborn children as created in God's image. It is, also, to desire the overflowing fruitfulness of the womb, for the glory of God. Yet most importantly, to be truly human is to worship Jesus Christ. He, alone, was fully human and fully God. He was the God-man in Mary's womb. He was, therefore, fully human and fully divine upon the Cross. And He was proved to be fully human and fully God through His bodily resurrection from the dead. *The* Image of God, Jesus our Lord, ascended into Heaven. *The* Image of God, the Lord Christ, shall return on the clouds in great glory. Thus to be truly human, created in the image of God, is to see the glory of God revealed in the face of Jesus Christ, to reflect that glory into the world, and thus to worship Him forever:

> *But we all, with unveiled face, reflecting as a mirror*[29] *the glory of the Lord, are [being] transformed into the same image from glory to glory, even as from the Lord the Spirit.* (2 Corinthians 3:18)

---

[29] This is Chrysostom's understanding of *katoptrizō* in his *Homilies on 2 Corinthians* 7 (*NPNF¹* 12), 313.

3

EVE'S CHILDREN:
The Doctrine of Sin and Preborn Children

(Genesis 3:1-8, Part 1)

THE Lord God created Eve to be both beautiful and radiant. Alongside of her husband, Eve walked in the Garden of Eden with a majestic glow and a royal fragrance about her. She joined Adam at his royal side. She carried herself with elegance and grace. Prior to her sin, Eve always opened her mouth with wisdom, and constantly on her tongue was the law of God's covenantal love. She beamed with the propriety of feminine holiness. She was, in her state of innocence, ready to nurse little newborns with gentle gracefulness and uninterrupted joy.

But alas, Eve sinned. Her sin brought pain to her labor, and death to her children. Cain murdered Abel. The sons of God took as wives from the daughters of men *"whomever they chose,"* (Genesis 6:2, NASB),[1] their children were wicked, and God brought a global flood to destroy them. Sarah, the wife of Abraham, was barren. So, too, was Rebekah, the wife of Isaac. Leah was unwanted by her husband, Jacob. Rachel, who was Jacob's favored wife, died during the hard labor of childbirth.

Still, in all of the suffering of the godly women of Scripture, in relation to marriage, labor pains, and the rearing of children, none of

---

[1] Modern academic readings of the Bible (following ancient Rabbinic ones) have greatly distorted the Genesis 6:1-4 history by arguing that it refers to "the angels who abandoned their heavenly position for the sake of illicit relations with mortal women" (Richard J. Bauckham, *Jude, 2 Peter* [WBC 50; Waco, TX: Word Books, 1983], 63). This semi-Gnostic interpretation of Genesis 6:1-4 is sharply rebuked by John Chrysostom. In his *Homilies on Genesis* 22 (vol. 82 of *The Fathers of the Church*; trans. Robert C. Hill; Washington, D.C.: The Catholic University of America Press, 1990), 73, Chrysostom asks, "...who could be so utterly deranged as to admit this blasphemous remark and the folly it betokens, that this incorporeal and intellectual creature could tolerate intercourse with bodily things?" He goes on to define the "sons of God" as the descendants of righteous Seth, while the "daughters of men" he defines as those who were descended from Cain (Ibid., 74).

them could possibly foresee the great bondage and suffering that has engulfed women in our modern age. They did, to be sure, know of the horror of child sacrifice amongst the pagan women of Canaan (Deuteronomy 12:31). They also were acquainted with fellow Israelite women who had decided to practice such Canaanite atrocities (Jeremiah 7:31). They might even have been familiar with the societal concept of radical feminism, but only as a judgment from God (2 Kings 11:1-3; Isaiah 3:12). Nevertheless, living so long ago, they were, in their piety, unable to imagine the kinds of horrific distortions of womanhood that awaited the women of the modern industrialized and scientific age.

Think of a Christian woman, living today, travelling backwards in time in order to inform Sarah, the wife of Abraham, who *"obeyed Abraham, calling him lord"* (1 Peter 3:6), that in the distant future there would be Christian women who would refuse to be submissive to their husbands (thus stridently violating Ephesians 5:22-24 and 1 Peter 3:1-6). Sarah, the mother of faith, would receive with great sadness and bewilderment the news that, in the last days, a significant minority of the very women who profess Christ as their God would be deceived into trading the protective coverings and safety zones of female submission in society and in the Church for the threatening combat zones of political careers,[2] military missions,[3] business leadership networks (contra the *"be sober-minded, chaste, workers at home..."* command of Titus 2:5), and pastoral/elder offices in the Church (in blatant violation of 1 Timothy 2:12). She would be

---

[2] See note 3 in Chapter 5, "Baby Moses in the Nile."
[3] The objection, raised by Evangelical Feminists, that Deborah both held an office of political power and was the leader of the Israelite military, is a naïve one. At a time of extreme spiritual anarchy, when *"everyone did that which was right in his own eyes"* (Judges 21:25), it was the dual sins of male cowardice and male passivity that forced Deborah into leadership. She, herself, knew that it was not God's ultimate design and will for her to lead Israel (Judges 4:6-9). She sang her "Song of Deborah" in order to glorify God for His military victory on behalf of Israel, but also in order to call Israel's *male leaders*, represented by Barak, to *"Arise..."* (Judges 5:12).

appalled to hear of some women "co-pastoring"[4] churches with their husbands, and of other women occupying the pulpit on particular Sunday mornings.[5] In short, Sarah would be mournfully perplexed over the question of why so many modern women in the Church seek to usurp the God-ordained, *masculine positions* of authority in society and in the Church, while simultaneously rejecting their God-ordained, *feminine positions* of submission, homemaking, and physical/spiritual motherhood (and *the incalculable blessings that go with them!*).

Righteous Elizabeth, the wife of Zacharias, too, would be appalled at the modern Church's definition of womanhood. To be sure, she knew, in her own day, of both contraception and abortion. The Romans of the first century AD were steeped in both practices. For contraception, various potions, such as those made with the leaves of barrenwort, were among the most popular forms of "temporary sterilizers."[6] For abortion, the Roman women of Elizabeth's day "took oral drugs"[7] as abortifacients. Also, for surgical abortions, the abortionists in Rome employed cruel and deadly instruments (one with a copper spike and another with a

---

[4] Tertullian, in *On Prescription against Heretics* 41 (*ANF* 3.263), is aghast at the thought of women exercising eldership/pastoral functions in the Church. In his mind, only the heretics allow for this: "The very women of these heretics, how wanton they are! For they are bold enough to teach, to dispute, to enact exorcisms, to undertake cures—it may be even to baptize." Also, in *On the Veiling of Virgins* 9 (*ANF* 4.33), he says, "It is not permitted to a *woman* to speak in the church; but neither (is it permitted her) to teach, nor to baptize, nor to offer, nor to claim to herself a lot in any manly function, not to say (in any) sacerdotal [i.e. pastoral] office." Also, Chrysostom, in *On the Priesthood* 3.9 (*NPNF*[1] 9.49), concurs: "The divine law indeed has excluded women from the ministry, but they endeavor to thrust themselves into it."

[5] For the details of the overwhelming consensus in church history against women teaching from the pulpit, a consensus that is built upon the historic interpretation of 1 Timothy 2:11-14, see Daniel Doriani, "Appendix 1: A History of the Interpretation of 1 Timothy 2" in *Women in the Church: A Fresh Analysis of 1 Timothy 2:9-15* (ed. Andreas J. Köstenberger, Thomas R. Schreiner, and H. Scott Baldwin; Grand Rapids: Baker Books, 1995), 213-67.

[6] John T. Noonan, Jr., *Contraception: A History of Its Treatment by the Catholic Theologians and Canonists* (enlarged ed.; Cambridge, Mass.: Harvard University Press, 1986), 14.

[7] Michael J. Gorman, *Abortion & the Early Church: Christian, Jewish & Pagan Attitudes in the Greco-Roman World* (Eugene, OR: Wipf and Stock, 1982), 16.

frame/annular blade/covered hook composite design) in order to commit their murderous acts.[8]

Yet for Elizabeth to learn that, in the modern age, *Christian* women would both use contraceptives in their own marriages and rally behind pro-abortion political candidates, would be more than disconcerting for her. She would be deeply troubled by this news. For, would not once-barren Elizabeth, who had yearned for the divine gift of children in her womb, and who had, upon the miracle of conception in her womb, treasured little Baby John the Baptist more than most mothers ever think to treasure their babies, be aghast at the thought of Christian women who, in the distant future, would shun procreation and turn a blind eye to the Abortion Holocaust?

How did things become so twisted in the realm of womanhood? How did we arrive at such a horrible place in history? What caused woman to rebel against her very nature? Who deceived the daughters of Eve into hating their highest calling, which is bountiful motherhood, and into exchanging it for the bondage of selfish recreation and lucrative ambition? Who taught women that it was both legal and moral (and, as the lie goes, "sometimes imperative") to kill their own babies in the womb? In order to understand these things, we must return to the Garden of Eden. We must see, afresh, what, exactly, happened when the Serpent deceived Eve with a most cunning and murderous deception.

<u>Obedience, Disobedience, and Abortion</u>

Now the serpent was more subtle than any animal of the field which the LORD *God had made. He said to the woman, "Has God really said, 'You shall not eat of any tree of the garden?'"*

The woman said to the serpent, "We may eat fruit from the trees of the garden, but not the fruit of the tree which is in the middle of the garden. God has said, 'You shall not eat of it. You shall not touch it, lest you die.'"

The serpent said to the woman, "You will not surely die, for God knows that in the day you eat it, your eyes will be opened, and you will be like God, knowing good and evil." (Genesis 3:1–5)

---

[8] Ibid., 17.

The Serpent is cunning; the Serpent is Satan. We know this because Revelation 12:9 equates *"the Devil and Satan"* with *"the old serpent."* Having already fallen from grace and become an evil angel, the Serpent is jealous of God's image bearers and is out to destroy them.

Satan gains influence first over Eve, and then over Adam. In the future, he will gain power over nations. He will rule Egypt. This is why Moses' staff becomes a *"serpent"* (Exodus 4:3); the staff-turned-serpent represents both Pharaoh and Satan. However, the fact that Moses is able to seize it by the tail and thus gain power over it, so that it becomes a hardened staff again, indicates that God has power over both Pharaoh, King of Egypt, who is a slithery foe, and Satan himself. Therefore, the Serpent will rule nations, but God will always rule the Serpent.

Still, in the Garden, it is the craftiness of the Serpent that causes Eve to stumble. He is not a brutish beast. He comes with a kind of dual Ph.D. in philosophy and sociology. He is a studied scientist, with an unmatched mastery of the "scholarly literature" on all things concerning the politics and culture of the Garden. He acts with a dark form of prudence; he uses knowledge to trap his prey.

You Shall *Surely* Die!

A murderer from the beginning, this Serpent brings death into the world through deceit. He is a liar, and the Father of Lies. He spins deceit like a black widow, weaving his own sticky web. He puts false words in God's mouth: *'Has God really said, 'You shall not eat of any tree of the garden?'"* (Genesis 3:1). He builds deception into his question.

The woman responds by quoting Scripture to the Serpent. However, already being partially charmed by the Serpent, she quotes Scripture wrongly:

> *The woman said to the serpent, "We may eat fruit from the trees of the garden, but not the fruit of the tree which is in the middle of the garden. God has said, 'You shall not eat of it. You shall not touch it, lest you die.'"* (Genesis 3:2–3)

Some have supposed, erroneously, that Eve is being legalistic in her response by adding words to the Word of God. They point out that we read nothing in Genesis 2:17 about Adam and Eve not being allowed to "touch" the Tree of the Knowledge of Good and Evil: *"...but you shall not eat of the tree of the knowledge of good and evil; for in the day that you eat of it, you will surely die."* God only says that they must not *eat* from the Tree; He does not say, "...do not touch it." Thus these erring people have concluded that Eve is a legalist. In their view, she has added laws to God's Law, and her legalism has set her up for a great and tragic fall.

This is an unjust reading of the Scripture. For, even though God has not issued a "Do not touch..." command concerning the Tree of the Knowledge of Good and Evil, the utterance that proceeds from Eve's lips, *"You shall not touch it"* (v. 3), is, in fact, a righteous application of the original command. For, elsewhere in Scripture God forbids both the partaking of evil and the *touching* of it:

> *Depart, depart, go out from there; <u>touch no unclean thing</u>! Go out from among her! Cleanse yourselves, you who carry the* LORD's *vessels.* (Isaiah 52:11)

The real problem with the way in which Eve quotes Scripture to the Serpent is not an over-scrupulous application of the principle of moral purity. The real problem is her omission of the word *"surely."* In Genesis 2:17, God says that if they eat from the Tree, they shall *"surely die."* God's Word is emphatic. Death shall *"surely"* follow sin. Yet in Eve's version, it is simply, *"God has said, '...lest you die.'"* Eve, being partially charmed by the Serpent already, has downplayed the gravity of the commandment. She has omitted the word *"surely"* from God's warning to her. In doing so, she has downplayed the gravity of sin, itself.

Sin is everlastingly grave. The wages of sin is *"surely"* death in the presence of a holy, holy, holy God. The Lord is clear about this:

> *You shall set bounds to the people all around, saying, "Be careful that you do not go up onto the mountain, <u>or touch</u> its border. Whoever <u>touches</u> the mountain shall be <u>surely</u> put to <u>death</u>."* (Exodus 19:12)

Sin *"surely"* leads to death. It is very, very grave. To sin against God, even once, is to evoke His everlasting wrath against oneself.

The holiness of God cannot tolerate the presence of sin. In the presence of a holy God, sin must be destroyed. Outside of redemption, the sinner will *"surely"* (Genesis 2:17) face eternal, conscious punishment in Hell:

> *If your eye causes you to stumble, cast it out. It is better for you to enter into God's Kingdom with one eye, rather than having two eyes to be cast into the Gehenna of fire, "where their worm does not die, and the fire is not quenched."* (Mark 9:47–48)

Thus Jesus is emphatic about the wages of sin. He warns not once, but twice in the same sentence that those who reject Him will certainly *"die"* in their sins:

> *I said therefore to you that you will die in your sins; for unless you believe that I am He, you will die in your sins.* (John 8:24)

Sin begets death. There is no way around this reality:

> *Therefore as sin entered into the world through one man, and death through sin; and so death passed to all men, because all sinned.* (Romans 5:12)

There is *"a sin leading to death"* (1 John 5:16), which cannot be remedied. God is gracious and compassionate, forgiving sins. But for those who refuse to repent of their sins, the coming Day of Judgment is worse than death itself:

> *In those days people will seek death, and will in no way find it. They will desire to die, and death will flee from them.* (Revelation 9:6)

Rebellious, unrepentant sinners, who defy Christ and thus continually spit in the face of God, shall face more than the death of their bodies. When God warns, *"You shall surely die,"* He means more than physical death. To be sure, physical death is horrible. But God also means that the wages of sin merit a *"second death,"* which is an everlasting punishment. It means that there will be, for the unrepentant reprobate, conscious torment and suffering, forever, without end, in a lake of fire and brimstone:

> *Then He will say also to those on the left hand, "Depart from Me, you cursed, <u>into the eternal fire which is prepared for the Devil and his angels</u>."* (Matthew 25:41)

This is a sober truth that is reaffirmed by the Apostle Paul in his encouragement to persecuted believers in Thessalonica concerning the future state of their persecutors:

> *…who will pay the penalty: <u>eternal destruction from the face of the Lord</u> and from the glory of His might.* (2 Thessalonians 1:9)

The wicked will *"surely die"* (Genesis 2:17) a *"second death"*:

> *But for the cowardly, unbelieving, sinners, abominable, murderers, sexually immoral, sorcerers, idolaters, and all liars, their part is <u>in the lake that burns with fire and sulfur</u>, which is <u>the second death</u>.* (Revelation 21:8)

The contemporary Church has all but lost the doctrine of Hell. In the name of being "seeker friendly," many contemporary churches have excised, completely, the doctrine of Hell from their statements of faith. Also, under a false pretense of love for unbelievers, Christian preachers have ceased to preach the full force of the doctrine of Hell from their pulpits. In general, Church leaders have made "positivity" their pet deity—for it certainly brings numerical growth to the Church, and who would dare argue with a deity that produces such reliable results?—and the doctrine of Hell certainly does not play nicely with this household god.

The Serpent asks the contemporary Church, feigning an innocent, innocuous goodness of motive, "Has God indeed said, 'Unbelievers, especially the kind-hearted and innocent ones, shall suffer the unjust and cruel punishment of an everlasting Hell'?" His deception is built into his question. Yet the contemporary Church has been charmed by him. Far too many pastors have downplayed the gravity of sin.[9] Far too many have been beguiled, willfully, by the Serpent into trading the authentic Gospel, which includes the full wrath of God against the wickedness of sin, for a cheaper, lesser gospel.

Desire Gives Birth to Sin

Why, then, does Eve sin? She downplays the gravity of sin. Yes, but she has an inner motive for doing so. That is, deception does not come to us by accident. We are never innocently deceived. We deny the truth whenever we want to believe a lie. And we want to believe a lie whenever we crave something that we ought not to crave:

When the woman saw that the tree was good for food, and that it was a delight to the eyes, and that the tree was <u>to be desired</u> to make one wise, she took some of its fruit, and ate; and she gave some to her husband with her, and he ate it, too. (Genesis 3:6)

Sin is conceived in the womb of wicked desire. Eve *wants* to be deceived, for she desires the forbidden fruit so eagerly that she is willing to give up the truth in order to obtain it. She exchanges the truth of God for a lie, so that she may gain what she has coveted.

The strange thing in all of this, though, is how Eve can desire the sinful fruit while God, her loving Creator, has already given to her a plethora of fruit that is both desirable and holy. It is not that Eve lacks *"desirable"* fruit, of the holy kind. To the contrary:

---

[9] Contrast this with Richard Baxter's very pastoral statement about the gravity of sin and the reality of Hell in his *The Saints' Everlasting Rest* (ed. Benjamin Fawcett; Philadelphia: J.B. Lippincott & Co., 1859), 88, "It is one of the hardest things in the world, to bring a wicked man to know that he is wicked or to make him see himself in a state of wrath and condemnation. Though they may easily find, by their strangeness to the new-birth, and their enmity to holiness, that they never were partakers of them; yet they as verily expect to see God, and be saved, as if they were the most sanctified persons in the world....But when they suddenly find themselves in the land of darkness, feel themselves in scorching flames, and see they are shut out of the presence of God for ever; then the application of God's anger to themselves will be the easiest matter in the world."

> *Out of the ground the* LORD *God made every tree to grow that is <u>[desirable]</u> <u>to the sight</u>, and <u>good for food</u>, including the tree of life in the middle of the garden and the tree of the knowledge of good and evil.* (Genesis 2:9)

Every good and perfect gift is from our Father of lights. He gives us holy gifts, which are lovely and desirable. He grants healthy foods to us—holy foods that He invites us to desire.

Still, the great mystery and absurdity of human sin is that we, wanting to be our own gods, have rejected the holy, desirable gifts of God in favor of the wicked desires of our sinful flesh. This is a mystery, an evil mystery. Why we would desire the fruit of the Tree of Death over the fruit of the Tree of Life, or the approval of man over the approval of God, or, ultimately, the deification of self over the worship of God, is a vast mystery. God's glory is infinitely good and desirable. Why, then, do we desire idols? Are we not foolish in our thoughts? Are we not wicked in our hearts?

The Law of God prohibits covetous desires:

> *You <u>shall not [desire] your neighbor's house</u>. You <u>shall not [desire] your neighbor's wife</u>, nor his male servant, nor his female servant, nor his ox, nor his donkey, nor anything that is your neighbor's.* (Exodus 20:17)

This is especially true of the adulteress. Men are not to desire the adulteress:

> *<u>Do not [desire] her beauty in your heart</u>, neither let her captivate you with her eyelids.* (Proverbs 6:25)

But men do desire the adulteress. And women do desire their neighbor's house. Humans are an idolatrous people. Our wicked desires plunge us into self-deception, and self-deception plunges us into a multitude of sins against God.

This explains the folly of idolatry. Why do the Israelites, who have seen the glory of the LORD at Mount Sinai, fall for worthless idols? According to the prophet Isaiah, they desire the kinds of sins that the idols offer to them, and so they enslave themselves to the idols. For example, Asherah, the goddess of fertility, who is worshipped under the terebinth trees, is a prostitute goddess who sells cultic fornication in exchange for gifts and sacrifices. The Israelites go to her because they desire her fornications:

> *For they shall be ashamed of the oaks <u>which you have desired</u>, and you shall be confounded for the gardens that you have chosen.* (Isaiah 1:29)

By contrast, Christ Jesus, when we see Him, has "*no [handsome appearance] <u>that we should desire Him</u>*" (Isaiah 53:2). He does not promise us that we shall become like gods. He never strokes our egos. He has no forbidden fruit to offer us. He tempts us not, and flatters us not, so we desire Him not.

Why, then, do people believe the lies of the Serpent? They only believe his lies because they *desire* his sinful menu items. They reject God's Word in favor of Satan's word so that they can pursue sinful desires, rather than holy ones:

> *…and the cares of this world, the deceitfulness of riches, and <u>the desires for other things</u> entering in <u>choke the Word</u>, and it becomes unfruitful.* (Mark 4:19, NKJV)

In the end, these sinful desires make people slaves to Satan—even children of Satan. The Devil's children desire exactly what their father desires:

> *You are of your father, the Devil, and you want to do <u>the desires of your father</u>.* (John 8:44)

The Word of God is preached, even today, but people whose hearts are set on sinful desires will not listen to it. They will hate sound doctrine, calling it offensive and evil, and, instead, will search for preachers who will affirm them in their own sinful desires:

> *For the time will come when they will not listen to the sound doctrine, but, having itching ears, will heap up for themselves teachers <u>after their own [desires]</u>….* (2 Timothy 4:3)

Why does Eve believe Satan's lie? She believes the Serpent because she desires the forbidden fruit that he is offering to her. God does not tempt Eve. He gives her the freedom to reject Him (which is what love does), but He does not tempt her. She tempts herself:

> *Let no man say when he is tempted, "I am tempted by God," for God cannot be tempted by evil, and He Himself tempts no one. But each one is tempted when he is <u>drawn away by his own [desire]</u>, and enticed. Then <u>the [desire], when it has conceived, bears sin; and the sin, when it is full grown, produces death</u>.* (James 1:13–15)

Eve desires the forbidden fruit. She looks at it and desires it in her flesh (she desires to taste it), with her eyes (she desires to envision its power), and according to her pride (she desires to become her own god). This is the deceptive work of sin. It appeals to our flesh, our eyes, and our pride:

> *For all that is in the world, the <u>lust of the flesh</u>, the <u>lust of the eyes</u>, and the <u>pride of life</u>, is not the Father's, but is the world's.* (1 John 2:16)

A woman's womb is made to desire children. For women, children are *"the desires of the womb"* (Hosea 9:16, the present author's translation). How, then, can Satan deceive women into desiring either contraception or abortion, or both? He can only do this by getting them to desire unnatural things. That is, whereas it is natural to desire a multitude of offspring, it is unnatural to desire a marriage with an *intentionally* limited number of offspring (in exchange for things such as financial security and fleshly diversions). Yet if Satan can get a married woman to desire things such as financial security and the diversions of the flesh more than her natural desire for a multitude of children, then he can easily deceive her into using contraceptives in her marriage.

In the same way, whereas it is natural for a pregnant mother to sing with joy over the baby in her womb—from conception, through the "the soft, butterfly kicking" stage, all the way to birth—it is most unnatural for her to take a drug or to pay a physician in order to murder her own child. However, if Satan can tempt this pregnant mother to desire her deceptively perceived feminine "freedoms" more than she desires the baby in her womb, he may be able to coax her into murdering her own baby.

Or, in the case of a woman who, apart from relational influences, would, in fact, desire to give birth to the baby in her womb, Satan uses other tactics. For example, if he can employ the pregnant mother's husband, boyfriend, father, or mother (or a combination of such family members) for the purpose of threatening and browbeating her, so that she may embrace *their* desire for an abortion, he may succeed in deceiving her into the thought that she is trapped, and that abortion is her only escape from the abuse. And if he can get her to desire escape from the abuse (through the lie that she lacks options other than abortion—which is, indeed, a lie) more than her natural desire to protect her own offspring, he may be able to coerce her into abortion, even as she simultaneously hates it.

The horrendous sin of abortion, then, is conceived in the womb of sinful desire (either a pregnant woman's sinful desire, or her family member's sinful desire, or both). This is a truth that does two important things for Christian Abortion Abolitionists.[10] First, it encourages us not to be overly hard on ourselves. Anyone who has done a lot of work in Abortion Abolitionism knows that discouragement is a guest who visits often, and who is slow to depart. We pour out our sweat, blood, and tears for the preborn. We pray and fast that we may be able to see a sweeping repentance fall over our land with regard to this vast Holocaust. Yet we find many hardened hearts along the way. People are slow to listen to our pleas. They are quick to make us look like the bad guys.

In this discouragement, we begin to question ourselves. For those of us who are pastors, we ask ourselves, "Was my Abolitionist sermon that I preached this past Sunday morning off the mark? Is that why nobody seemed to care much about it?" Or, for those of us who are witnesses for the preborn in our families and social spheres, we ask ourselves, "Am I too uneducated for this task? Did I sound unintelligent? Was that why they stared at me, with such blank expressions on their faces, while I told them about babies in the

---

[10] This is to speak here of distinctly "Christian" Abortion Abolitionism, as opposed to Mormon Abortion Abolitionism, atheistic Abortion Abolitionism, Muslim Abortion Abolitionism, etc., because without the Jesus Christ of the Bible, all Abortion Abolitionism fails to glorify God. The babies in the womb who have been murdered via abortion are an army of martyrs, whose lives belong to Christ Jesus, and they themselves are only honored when their defenders give glory to the One whose blood alone has saved them, and, who alone has made it possible for them to spend eternity in Heaven with God.

womb bearing the very image of God?" And then we sigh, in defeat, and say, "Perhaps I am not cut out for this. There must be better people than me to do this great work."

The Christian work of Abortion Abolitionism is a heavy cross, and a holy work. We must examine ourselves in the midst of it. To be sure, our slothfulness, our indifference, our uncleanness, and, worst of all, our pride can impede our efforts. When we fight for babies in the womb with impure lives or impure motives, we can certainly damage the cause. Our hearts must be pure before God. Our speech must remain full of grace, seasoned with salt.

Yet there are countless times when a lack of "conversions" to a Christian Abolitionist worldview is not our fault. Christian Abolitionist sermons, dialogues, poems, pamphlets, DVD's, bumper stickers, and organized outreaches oftentimes fall on deaf ears. Many people are ever hearing, but never understanding. They are ever seeing, but never perceiving. Their hearts are hardened. They want to believe the lies that they believe precisely because they desire the very sins that led them into those lies in the first place. Therefore, when our God-centered, Abolitionist message is rejected, though it be a holy message, we can be comforted by knowing that we are sharing in the painful rejections of our Savior, the Lord Jesus.

Secondly, the truth that the sin of abortion is conceived in the womb of sinful desire gives Christian women a very important *method* of Christian Abolitionism. This method is one of example. Namely, if the Serpent, today, is tempting women to desire things that are unnatural for women, such as political offices, corporate business titles, and "sexual freedom," and if these unnatural desires move women's hearts away from their innate desire to have children and to be godly homemakers, and thus become strong links to abortion, then Christian women have a vital demonstration to make before the eyes of a watching world. This is the demonstration of Christian chastity and Christian motherhood.

All Christian women (both single and married) have a wonderful *method* of Abortion Abolitionism built into their very lifestyles. That is, by practicing chastity, and thus keeping themselves sexually pure, they are teaching other women how to cut down the murderous tree of abortion at its very roots. Without the sins of immodesty and sexual immorality, abortion might still exist, but its beast-like size would be felled to the ground. Therefore, the biblical imperative for the women of the Church to live chaste and pure lives is one of their greatest weapons against abortion. If the licentious women of the world can observe the women of the Church delighting in chastity with the kind of Heavenly delight that far outweighs the sinful thrills and evil empowerments of feminine seduction and immorality, then they may find themselves drawn to such delightful chastity—through the Gospel.

Also, if Christian women will reject the unnatural desires of radical feminism (and repent of the ways in which they have shared in those desires), and champion the natural desires of Christian motherhood,[11] they will, no doubt, win converts. Their strong desires for godly motherhood and for their own children will, in many cases, awaken those same desires in other women. For, it is one thing for a woman considering an abortion to be surrounded by childless women of the "successful businesswoman" ilk. It is quite another thing for her to keep running into nursing mothers who are so in love with Christian motherhood—even as they are quite honest about its sacrifices and hardships—that their unfading feelings of joy and thanksgiving for their babies are unobtrusively appealing.

The more that Christian women treasure motherhood (and Christian single women can certainly find ways to demonstrate the eternal value of motherhood, as well), the more unbelieving women will smell the aroma of the Gospel in its relation to childbearing. For some unbelieving women, this will come to them as the aroma of death; they will, in their sinful desires, reject the truth, exchange it for a lie, and choose both contraception and abortion. But for other unbelieving women, the sweet aroma of Christian motherhood will come to them as the life-giving aroma of the Gospel. Not only will they find themselves embracing biblical motherhood, but they will also find themselves embracing the Messiah, Himself.

---

[11] This championing of Christian motherhood in no way seeks to belittle the value of single, barren, or bereaved women in the Church. As *spiritual mothers*, such women in the Church have a vital role to play in this public demonstration of femininity. Single Christian women, in particular, are radiant lights of chastity, shining amidst a world of pitch-black sexual immorality, who have received the special calling from God of *uninhibited spiritual motherhood* (1 Corinthians 7:34).

"KNOWING GOOD AND EVIL" IN ABORTION

In regard to sin, in general, and to abortion, in specific, Satan tempts us to "know good and evil." He dangles the knowledge of good and evil before our eyes as a forbidden fruit. God says that abortion is murder; it leads to death. Yet Satan asks us, "Did God really say?" and then tells us that God is withholding the "privilege" of abortion from us because He is hiding good things from us. If we come to know the good and evil of abortion, says Satan, we can become like God.

The Experiential Knowledge of Sin

The serpent said to the woman, "You will not surely[12] die, for God knows that in the day you eat it, your eyes will be opened, and you will be like God, knowing good and evil." (Genesis 3:4–5)

Why is the bad tree, the forbidden one, called the Tree of the Knowledge of Good and Evil? Prior to this, have Adam and Eve been completely ignorant about the existence of evil? Is this a lack of conceptual knowledge about evil?

No, Adam and Eve cannot be said to lack the conceptual knowledge of the difference between good and evil, for the Lord God has already warned Adam about both the existence of evil and the fatal consequences of it:

…but <u>you shall not eat</u> of the tree of the knowledge of good and evil; for in the day that you eat of it, <u>you will surely die</u>. (Genesis 2:17)

---

[12] It is interesting to note that Satan quotes God correctly here, acknowledging that God has warned Adam and Eve that they will *"<u>surely</u> die"* if they eat from the forbidden tree, and thus Satan actually gets the *"surely"* emphasis right, whereas Eve willfully missed it. However, this may be due to the fact that Satan is not, himself, aiming to downplay the gravity of sin (as is Eve). Rather, Satan's aim is different, altogether. He wants to call the very concept of sin into question (making God out to be the guilty party, and making the sinner out to be the victim of God's maltreatment of him), and he does so via an outright denial of the veracity of God's Word. That is, when Satan says to Eve, *"You will <u>not</u> surely die,"* he is, in essence, saying, "God, by His very Word, has lied to you."

Therefore, this is not a matter of cognitive awareness, or lack thereof, concerning good and evil. It is, rather, a matter of experience.[13] Adam and Eve, prior to Genesis 3, have not yet experienced the evilness of evil. They have not yet tasted the sinfulness of sin. It is only after they have eaten from the Tree of the Knowledge of Good and Evil that they come to have *the experience* of what evil really is:

> *Their eyes were opened, and they both <u>knew</u> that they were naked. They sewed fig leaves together, and made coverings for themselves.* (Genesis 3:7)

This experiential knowledge of sin is not what Adam and Eve thought it would be; it is certainly not what the Serpent promised them that it would be. Instead of bringing lasting pleasure, it brings only lasting pain. Rather than enlightening the eyes, it darkens them. Instead of immortality, it ensures their own mortality. They will now surely die:

> *The LORD God said, "Behold, the man has become like one of Us, <u>knowing good and evil</u>. Now, lest he reach out his hand, and also take of the tree of life, and eat, and live forever...." Therefore the LORD God sent him out from the garden of Eden, to till the ground from which he was taken.* (Genesis 3:22-23)

God, of course, does not "know good and evil" in the sense of committing acts of evil, Himself. May it never be! The Lord is holy, holy, holy. He cannot tolerate evil in His holy presence:

> *You who have <u>purer eyes than to see evil</u>, and who cannot look on perversity....* (Habakkuk 1:13)

Still, God "knows good and evil" in the sense that He understands the experiential pain and destruction that evil brings into

---

[13] Again, Chrysostom, in *Homilies on Genesis* 16 (vol. 74 of *The Fathers of the Church*; trans. Robert C. Hill; Washington, D.C.: The Catholic University of America Press, 1986), 219, proves a helpful guide: "...it wasn't because [the Tree of the Knowledge of Good and Evil] supplied knowledge that it is called that, but because the transgression of the command happened to concern the [Tree], and *from that event* knowledge of sin then entered the scene, and shame as well—that was why the name was given" (emphasis added).

His formerly "very good" creation. He knows evil from afar, in that He watches, firstly, Satan fall from grace, and then, secondly, Adam and Eve eat of the Tree, without ever, Himself, becoming entangled in sin. He also knows evil up close, quite personally, since He is *"grieved in His heart"* (Genesis 6:6) over human wickedness, and foresees the day when His only-begotten Son shall have to *"be sin on our behalf"* on the Cross, so that *"in Him we might become the righteousness of God"* (2 Corinthians 5:21).

The knowledge of good and evil, then, is an experiential knowledge.[14] The commission of sin, in blatant defiance to the Law of God, brings about an experiential knowledge of sin. This is why, for example, little children are exempt from the eternally-condemning charge of "knowing good and evil."[15] They are not old enough to be accountable to God's Law, at least in the way in which adults are held accountable to God's Law:

> *Moreover your little ones, whom you said should be captured or killed, and your children, <u>who today have no knowledge of good or evil</u>, they shall go in there, and I will give it to them, and they shall possess it.* (Deuteronomy 1:39)

Childhood does bring with it a certain innocence with regard to the knowledge of good and evil:

> *He shall eat [curds] and honey when he <u>knows to refuse the evil, and choose the good</u>. For <u>before the child knows to refuse the evil, and choose the good</u>, the land whose two kings you abhor shall be forsaken.* (Isaiah 7:15–16)

---

[14] Notice in Genesis 22:12 that God comes to *"know"* that Abraham fears Him only *after* Abraham's faithful act of putting Isaac, his beloved son, on the sacrificial altar. Contrary to the "open theism" heresy, which claims that God does not have exhaustive foreknowledge of all future events, Genesis 22:12 does not mean that God is unable to "know" the future. It simply means that God's "knowledge" of Abraham's piety is now, in Genesis 22:12, an experiential one.

[15] Psalm 51:5 makes it abundantly clear that all children are born with a sin nature, inherited from Adam, and that they are, therefore, naturally alienated from God, and, in their sin nature, children of wrath (see Ephesians 2:3). However, as will be argued in a later chapter, children who die at early ages go directly to Heaven. They are thus not held accountable to the demands of the Gospel in the same way that adults are, and this is due to their inability to "know good and evil" in an adult, experiential way.

Yet if children are not held accountable for "knowing good and evil," grownups certainly are. It is the arrogance of modern man that thinks that we can experience good and evil, and even redefine "good" and "evil," without ever facing the judgment of God. This is not so:

> *You have wearied the* LORD *with your words. Yet you say, "How have we wearied Him?" In that you say, "<u>Everyone who does evil is good</u> in the* LORD's *sight, and He delights in them;" or "Where is the God of justice?"* (Malachi 2:17)

This is not the Christian way. For the Christian, we are to have an experiential knowledge of good, but we are to be ignorant, experientially speaking, of all things evil. We are not to dwell on evil, gossip about evil, or delight in evil. When it comes to the evil acts of unregenerate man, there are some things that the Christian should not even mention by name. Wise as serpents, innocent as doves, the Christian faith demands an experiential innocence regarding evil:

> *For your obedience has become known to all. I rejoice therefore over you. But I desire to have you <u>wise in that which is good</u>, but <u>innocent in that which is evil</u>.* (Romans 16:19)

The Christian may not live, habitually, in experiential evil:

> *Beloved, do not imitate that which is <u>evil</u>, but that which is <u>good</u>. He who <u>does good</u> is of God. He who <u>does evil</u> has not seen God.* (3 John 11)

Millions and millions of people in our world today have tasted of the forbidden fruit of abortion, and found it to be more than bitter.[16] The experiential knowledge of abortion is not what the Serpent promised that it would be.[17] Instead of women's liberation, it has brought about the bondage of lifelong guilt and sorrow. Rather than sexual freedom, it has produced a culture in which women are treated as mere objects of pleasure, and thus has severed the security of the marital bond from the intimacy of what should be a strictly-marital act. Instead of elevating women to a more dignified status, abortion has attacked the very nature of womanhood in society, and has pierced the hearts of countless numbers of women—who have been lied to by both their political leaders and their doctors—to the very core.

Gleams of Hope and a Solemn Calling

There is much hope, however. The hope in all of this is that many people who have participated in abortion, in one way or another, are beginning to speak out against it. Women, in particular, have begun to speak out against the practice of abortion. Thousands of women who have had abortions are courageously standing up,

---

[16] No doubt, some who are reading this book have partaken of the forbidden fruit of abortion. If this is you, dear Reader, then please know that this book is not written with a desire to herald your condemnation. It is, rather, a plea for you to repent of the horrible sin of abortion, to seek the Lord of the Cross who died for the sum total of your sins, and to experience the mysterious power of the Gospel of Christ in its ability to make you *fully* forgiven and *completely* clean. It is the conviction of this author that the forth-telling of the heinous evils of abortion is, for those who have participated in one or more abortions, the very path to the healing waters of the Gospel of God's grace and forgiveness. In the Bible, prophetic exposures of evil necessarily precede the pastoral comforts of grace. Or, to put it another way, the good physician does his surgery with a vision towards the healing, not the demise, of the patient. God is such a Good Physician.

[17] The following is not, in any way at all, to be taken as an attempt to allegorize the Tree of the Knowledge of Good and Evil into a specific parable about abortion. The Tree was a literal tree. The forbidden fruit was literal fruit. And sins against God include *all things that defy His glory and violate His Law*. We could easily apply the "experiential knowledge of good and evil" to other sins, such as idolatry, profaning God's name, neglecting corporate worship on the Lord's Day, dishonoring parents, sexual immorality, theft, perjury, and coveting. However, since our subject at hand is abortion, we apply this principle of the experiential knowledge of sin to the seismic effects of abortion on human lives, and, in particular, on women.

publicly, confessing their sins, and warning other women about the lies that are told to them regarding abortion. They, who were formerly the champions of the abortion movement, are now becoming the courageous advocates of babies in the womb. Having tasted the extreme bitterness of the fruit of abortion, and having gained experiential knowledge of it, these heroines of the Abortion Abolitionist movement are exhorting other women, especially younger women, to guard their own innocence and naivety concerning the sins of contraception, fornication, adultery, and, ultimately, the monstrous practice that our society calls "abortion."[18]

Therefore, in this present generation there is a solemn calling upon the lives of all of the Daughters of Eve (that is, those who are truly Spirit-reborn Daughters of Christ) who are reading this book. It is the calling to live radiant lives of such Christ-like meekness and quietness that they rebuke, even without a word, the wickedness of those who are fighting the pro-abortion war on women and children. Simultaneously, the Daughters of Christ are called to speak with holy courage, and uncompromising fidelity to the Word of God, in defense of the preborn.

On the moral front, since it is a culture of sexual seduction, power mongering, promiscuity, drunkenness, frivolity, and adultery that feeds the abortion industry, Christian women ought to live in such modesty, submission, fidelity to their spouses, sobriety, piety, chastity, and reverent joy that they proclaim, with their lives, by the power of the indwelling Spirit of Christ, a way out of the horror of sexual immorality to those women who are enslaved by it.

On the prophetic front, Christian women are to take up the mantle of the "prophetess" (e.g. Isaiah 8:3) by using the high calling of Christian womanhood, along with the rich spiritual gifts that God

---

[18] Two noteworthy examples of such heroic women are Norma McCorvey and Iman Essiet. McCorvey was the infamous plaintiff known as "Jane Roe" in the 1973 *Roe v. Wade* lawsuit. In 1995, she became a Christian (through the loving witness of a Christian pastor, Flip Benham, and a seven year-old Christian girl named Emily), admitted to fabricating certain portions of her story that contributed to the *Roe v. Wade* case (such as the lie that her pregnancy was the result of gang rape), and has since become an outspoken advocate for the Abortion Abolitionist cause. Essiet is an African-American woman who grew up in Brooklyn, New York, and, after having five abortions, became a born-again Christian. She has subsequently chosen a bold ministry of speaking up, publicly, for the preborn in New York, and beyond.

has bestowed upon them, to speak in defense of preborn life. It is the voice of women, after all, that will, second only to God's Voice, carry the most weight in society when it comes to the subject of life in the womb. And even as Queen Esther had her moment of decision—whether or not to risk her life for the sake of the children of the Most High God—so too do the Daughters of Christ now face their own critical moment of decision. God's irrevocable calling upon Christian women, which is the calling to be tireless advocates for the preborn, is *"for such a time as this"* (Esther 4:14).

4

ADAM'S GUILT:
Male Responsibility and Preborn Children

(Genesis 3:1-8, Part 2)

ADAM is not innocent when he eats from the Tree of the Knowledge of Good and Evil. Far from being blameless, he incurs the greater guilt. Eve has desired sin, but Adam has authorized it. Since his is the spiritual leadership, his is also the bulk of the spiritual responsibility. Thus the blessed Apostle Paul does not say, "For as in Eve all die," but rather, *"For as in Adam all die"* (1 Corinthians 15:22). Thus even the masculine term *"man,"* which is representative both of Adam, as an individual, and, through Adam, of all men and women,[1] shows the greater responsibility of Adam for original sin:

> *Therefore as sin entered into the world through <u>one man</u>, and death through sin; and so death passed to all men, because all sinned....For as through <u>the one man's</u> disobedience many were made sinners....* (Romans 5:12, 19a)

Applied to abortion, the spiritual headship of Adam over Eve means that men are, by no means, off the hook concerning this silent Holocaust. On the contrary, they incur the greater guilt. Seeking to hide behind the cliché that abortion is "a woman's concern," men have, by and large, shirked their God-ordained responsibility to protect all life in the womb. In doing so, they have proven themselves to be twice-guilty. On the one hand, they have not protected women from the Serpent's enticements towards abortion (but rather have selfishly coerced women into it!), and, on the other hand, they have reneged on their duties as God's guardians of life in the womb.

---

[1] There is, therefore, a deeply *theological* reason why "pronoun-neutral, gender-inclusive" Bible translations should be rejected by the Christian.

The Guilt of Men in "Knowing Good and Evil"

Where, then, are the men? Why is so much of the blame for abortion cast upon women, when it has been *men*, primarily, who have promoted the legalization of pornography, the degradation of the nuclear family, the proliferation of fornication, the practice of cohabitation, the widespread acceptance of contraception, and the training of physicians to perform abortions?

Adam is no innocent bystander in the Genesis 3 historical account:

> *When the woman saw that the tree was good for food, and that it was a delight to the eyes, and that the tree was to be desired to make one wise, she took some of its fruit, and ate; and she gave some to her husband <u>with her</u>, and <u>he ate it, too</u>.* (Genesis 3:6)

Where is Adam the whole time that the Serpent is seducing his wife? The horrible answer to this question is that he is there, *"with her,"* standing right beside her. Having been given, by God, leadership and headship over his wife—yes, but for the sole purposes of *serving* her and *protecting* her—Adam is passively allowing the Serpent to destroy his wife. Rather than risking his own neck to defend her, and rather than telling the Serpent to take a hike (which Adam ought to do, especially since he is the one to whom God directly entrusted the Genesis 2:17 commandment), Adam passively allows the whole horror to unfold. He does this because he *wants* the whole thing to unfold. He, too, desires to eat the fruit of the Tree of the Knowledge of Good and Evil.

Men are extremely guilty in this global Abortion Holocaust. God calls men to be the protectors and providers for their families. They are called to lead society, as a whole, and the nuclear family, as a unit, only as under God's own Law. Men are true leaders only when they *fear God* and lead *according to His commandments*. They are to lay down their lives for their wives. They are to be the washers of dirty feet, and the cleaners of dirty toilet bowls in their homes. They are to guard their homes from evil, in order to ensure the holiness of their family members unto God, and they are, without equivocation, to protect human life:

Open your mouth for the mute, <u>in the cause of all who are [appointed to die]</u>. Open your mouth, judge righteously, and serve justice to the poor and needy. (Proverbs 31:8-9)

And,

Defend the weak, the poor, and the fatherless. Maintain the rights of the poor and oppressed. Rescue the weak and needy. <u>Deliver them out of the hand of the wicked</u>. (Psalm 82:3-4)

When it comes to the Abortion Holocaust, men have not been doing this. On the contrary, it has been prominent men, even men of the Church, who have helped to expedite the degradation of women through the legalization of both contraception and abortion.

Regarding contraception, the prominence of *Christian men* in the push towards both its social acceptance and political legalization is shocking, but true. Margaret Sanger, the unrelenting leader of the contraceptive movement, succeeded, first, in winning over Christian pastors from the liberal Protestant persuasion. She did this using the lies of the pseudo-science of human eugenics, a pseudo-science which was, at that time, both fashionable and unabashedly racist. Sanger was particularly inhumane in her attitudes towards impoverished minority groups and special-needs children.[2]

Yet Sanger employed a different method of seduction for Evangelical Protestants. She and her Planned Parenthood colleagues discovered that they, the Evangelicals, were willing to buy the lie of global-overpopulation. By the 1950's, with all of the advances in medical technology and the prolonged life expectancies that came with it, Sanger, with her socialist retinue, convinced many leading Evangelicals that the use of contraception was a moral good, rather than a moral evil. Sanger's league accomplished this by arguing that contraception had the power to prevent a perceived immanent crisis of global-overpopulation, which would include both mass famines and mass starvations.

Notwithstanding the great logical flaw built into this argument, namely, that it would be better for a hungry child (say, living in impoverished Africa) to be denied the right to exist than for him to have to face hunger or starvation, Sanger won over many

---

[2] See Carlson, *Godly Seed*, 92.

Evangelicals to her side. She was a self-proclaimed adulteress, and a hater of the biblical view of marriage. Yet, curiously, she succeeded in winning over none other than the chief editors of *Christianity Today* (which was the flagship publication of American Evangelicalism at that time) to her birth-control cause.[3]

Men, Christian men, were seduced by Sanger's lies. They were "seduced," and not simply hoodwinked, for, just like Adam, God's commandment against this sin had been made clear to them beforehand. The overwhelming consensus of historic Christianity warned them, continually, against the sin of contraception. Yet by the 1960's, even Billy Graham was responding with strong disagreement to Pope Paul VI's *Humanae Vitae* (a papal encyclical which defended the historic Christian ban on contraception) by using the diction that had been fed to him by the likes of Margaret Sanger, "I believe in *planned parenthood*."[4]

Regarding abortion, it was men, even *leading Evangelical men*, who helped pave the way for the legalization of abortion-on-demand in America.[5] The heart-rending truth is that professing Evangelical men contributed to the pro-abortion rhetoric in the 1960's that helped set the stage for the *Roe v. Wade* decision.

In specific, a notorious symposium of Evangelical theologians, called and hosted by *Christianity Today*, took place in 1968. The symposium focused on three major topics: contraception, sterilization, and abortion. During the symposium, Bruce Waltke, then professor of Old Testament at Dallas Theological Seminary, presented a paper in which he said, *"God does not regard the fetus as a soul*, no matter how far gestation has progressed."[6] Evangelical scholars, representing the higher echelons of male leadership in the movement, were thus using Holy Scripture to argue for pro-abortion politics.

The *Christianity Today* symposium, itself, issued a "Statement of Affirmation." Representing the scholarly consensus of the symposium, it exhorted, "Changes in the state laws on therapeutic

---

[3] See ibid., 127-28.
[4] Qtd. in ibid., 133, emphasis added.
[5] True enough, many of the pro-abortion advocates leading up to *Roe v. Wade* in 1973 were also anti-Christian in their philosophical views. The secularization of America certainly drove much of the demand for legalized abortion in America. Yet our focus here is on the *specifically Evangelical* guilt regarding *Roe v. Wade*.
[6] Qtd. in ibid., 135, emphasis added.

abortion…*should be encouraged*," thus advocating the *Roe v. Wade* decision five years before it happened. The "Statement of Affirmation" went on to say, "The Christian physician will advise induced abortion only to safeguard greater values sanctioned by Scripture. These values include *individual health, family welfare, and social responsibility*….Much human suffering can be alleviated *by preventing the birth of children where there is a predictable high risk of genetic disease or abnormality*. This appears to be *a reasonable Christian objective*."[7] This was, therefore, a very murderous "Christian" symposium.

Abortion, then, is not merely a woman's concern. It is very much a man's concern, too. In fact, when God approaches Adam and Eve after they have eaten from the Tree of the Knowledge of Good and Evil, He summons Adam, first, before summoning Eve (Genesis 3:9). This is to signify that, as the spiritual leader of the marriage, Adam will incur a greater responsibility for the couple's guilt. He will receive the stricter judgment. His is the headship; therefore, his is the greater culpability for the transgression.

This means that men cannot excuse themselves from their God-given responsibility to defend life in the womb—at all costs. They cannot, in their sinful passivity, claim that abortion, being a "woman's choice,"[8] as the politicians so deceitfully put it, is out of their male jurisdiction. Nothing could be farther from the truth.

God made men to guard and to protect their wives. He also made men to be brave and valiant in protecting the weakest of the weak:

> <u>Rescue those who are being led away to death</u>! Indeed, <u>hold back those who are staggering to the slaughter</u>! *If you say, "Behold, we did not know this"; does not He who weighs the hearts consider it? He who keeps your soul, does He not know it? Shall He not render to every man according to his work?* (Proverbs 24:11-12)

---

[7] Qtd. in Paul B. Fowler, *Abortion: Towards an Evangelical Consensus* (Portland: Multnomah Press, 1987), 69-70, emphases added.

[8] But why should a woman's choice override the baby's choice? Why is the baby not allowed to choose? Yet the greatest flaw in the "women's choice" propaganda is the failure to recognize that God's holy Law condemns the "choice" of abortion. The Law of God must prevail over the will of the individual, and also over the whims of the society.

Also, the prophet Isaiah's mandate emboldens men to be valiant men of justice:

Learn to do [good]. <u>Seek justice. Relieve the oppressed. Judge the fatherless. Plead for the widow.</u> (Isaiah 1:17)

Where, then, are the men who are willing to die on the battlefield of the Abolitionist cause? Where are the male physicians, especially amongst the academic physicians, who will gladly lose their jobs, if need be, in order to speak up on behalf of babies in the womb? Where are the leading men in the business world who will risk financial ruin in order to invest themselves, without compromise, in the cause of the preborn child? And where, pray tell, are the pastors who are so captivated by God's love for the little ones in the womb that they are willing to speak, unflinchingly, from the pulpit, in their defense,[9] even if it means offending their congregants and being persecuted by their own church members?

Men are responsible for the existence of abortion in our world. In fact, the weight of responsibility falls more heavily upon men than it does upon women.[10] Men are to be leaders in society. Therefore, they are held more accountable for the directions of society.

Thus the Abortion Holocaust can be linked to a host of male sins. There are pornographic materials in society, which men patronize, to their shame. There are also countless numbers of fornications, engagements with prostitutes, and adulteries that occur every day, on account of the lusts of men. It is usually the man, and not the woman, who pushes physical touch in the pre-marital courtship beyond the bounds of piety and purity. Many times it is the man, and not the woman, who advocates the use of contraception within marriage—wanting to limit the number of children in the marriage, out of selfish, financial concerns. And it is far too often the man, and not the woman, who is the first to describe a child in the womb as an "unwanted child."

---

[9] Here it is advised that a pastor's sheepish allusion to abortion once a year, on Sanctity of Human Life Sunday, does not suffice. What is needed from the pulpit is bold, clear, continual, and unequivocal exposure of abortion as a global Holocaust, coupled with the power of Christ's cross to forgive those who have participated in such a global Holocaust.

[10] Consider Hosea 4:14 in this regard.

We need, then, the true men of God to arise. These are the men who will fight for the modesty of women in the world. They will guard, vigilantly, the moral purity of women. The real men of God will never push sexual misconduct upon women. Instead, they will champion federal and state laws that outlaw pornography, without exceptions, along with all other immoral practices that degrade women.[11] They will defend the chastity and honor of women. Faithful to their wives, protective of their daughters, desiring a multitude of godly offspring, they will lead their homes, unwaveringly, in the worship of the triune God.

Also, such men will defend the preborn children of this world, being willing to lay down their own jobs and lives for their sake. They will speak boldly in their defense, and not shrink back when they are verbally assaulted for doing so. These God-fearing men will do their utmost to save the preborn babies who are being threatened under the unjust laws of our world, and they will spend their strength praying for, and laboring towards the abolition of abortion in our world.

The Only Path Back to Innocence

The guilt of Adam and Eve is exceedingly great. They have eaten from the Tree of the Knowledge of Good and Evil. The guilt of our world regarding abortion is exceedingly great. Modern society has eaten from the Tree of Abortion with unprecedented numbers of orgies and gluttonies with regard to the forbidden fruits of abortion. In both cases, God says, on account of the guilt incurred, *"You will surely die."*

What, then, can be done? Can the guilt of Adam and Eve ever be removed? If a man has, in the past, pushed for an abortion, telling his former girlfriend to "fix the problem," how can he ever live with himself, once he realizes that he has murdered his own son or daughter? Or if a woman has, in the past, taken her father's counsel to abort the Down-syndrome baby in her womb, rather than having to suffer the hardship of raising a Down-syndrome child, how does

---

[11] In this regard, note especially the heroic Christian work of Anthony Comstock (1844-1915) in Charles Gallaudet Trumbull, *Outlawed! How Anthony Comstock Fought & Won the Purity of a Nation* (ed. Scott Matthew Dix; reprinted 2013).

she ever find forgiveness for killing her own sweet, innocent little baby boy or girl?

There is hope for the sinner. But this hope must begin with the sober reality that the wages of sin is death. Without the shedding of blood, there is no forgiveness of sins. Someone has to die. Abortion is bloodshed, and for abortion to be forgiven, blood must be shed. This is why God sheds blood in the Garden of Eden. He gives Adam and Eve the hope of forgiveness through the shedding of innocent blood:

> *The* LORD *God made <u>coats of animal skins</u> for Adam and for his wife, and clothed them.* (Genesis 3:21)

Where did these *"coats of animal skins"* come from? The answer is that God shed the blood of animals in order to obtain them. This is the first instance of animal death in the history of the world.[12] Sin is so wicked that blood must be shed in order to cover over it. Only blood can cover over the guilt of our sins:

> *"Come now, and let us reason together," says the* LORD: *"Though your sins be <u>as scarlet</u>, they shall be as white <u>as snow</u>. Though they be red <u>like crimson</u>, they shall be <u>as wool</u>."* (Isaiah 1:18)

How so? If Lady Macbeth could not remove the blood stains from her hands, how can the stain of our sins ever be removed? How can the scarlet stains of abortion, of child murder, which are red like crimson, be removed so that blood-stained human palms can be made *"as white as snow"*?

A literal lamb (or other animal from the flocks or herds) was slain in the Garden of Eden in order to cover over Adam and Eve's nakedness. But a different kind of Lamb has been slain for the forgiveness of our sins:

---

[12] The fossil record is thus not a record of millions and millions of years of Darwinian or Neo-Darwinian evolution. God did not create a world in which lions devour lambs, and then call it *"very good."* Rather, the fossil record is a record of carnivorism and bloodshed that *followed* Adam and Eve's sin, and was, for the most part, laid down during and shortly after Noah's global deluge.

After these things I looked, and behold, a great multitude, which no man could number, out of every nation and of all tribes, peoples, and languages, standing before the throne and <u>before the Lamb</u>, <u>dressed in white robes</u>, with palm branches in their hands. (Revelation 7:9)

Who is this Lamb? And how can we, naked sinners, become clothed with such white robes? Who are these highly favored people, who dwell in Paradise, clothed in white robes?

[The angel] said to me, "These are those who came out of the great tribulation. <u>They washed their robes, and made them white in the Lamb's blood</u>." (Revelation 7:14)

Jesus is the Lamb, sacrificed for us, for our sins! He alone never succumbed to a single one of the Serpent's temptations. He was sinless. He alone lived His whole life without guilt, being perfectly innocent, before God the Father. He alone is spotless.

Therefore, His blood alone is able to cover over our sins. The idolatry of all other religions of this world, including Buddhism, Hinduism, Islam, non-Messianic Judaism, Mormonism, and even atheism, is evident in this: none of them possesses a means by which our sins can be forgiven, in a real (and not symbolic) sense. Only the *historic* act of Jesus of Nazareth dying on that Roman Cross for our sins has the power to forgive our sins.

Being fully God, Jesus' blood is valuable enough to forgive our sins. Being fully human, His blood is able to substitute for our own blood. It was His death in place of our death. It was God's full wrath poured out upon Him, rather than God's full wrath poured out upon us. As the God-man, Jesus is able to forgive sins. He, alone, can forgive sins.

There is no other path back to innocence. Regardless of what globalization has to teach us about a variety of religious traditions in human history, outside of Christ Jesus, all are idolatrous. Only Christianity reveals the true and living God, for in the Man Christ Jesus, the true and living God took on human flesh. In real history, He revealed God to us. Therefore, to refuse to worship Him, alone, as the living God, is to refuse God the Father, as well. If Jesus of Nazareth is the God of Israel, then He, alone, is Lord, and all other claims about God that deny Jesus' exclusive deity and glory are false claims.[13]

Other religions bring false testimonies about God, but the Christian Scriptures testify to the Word of God, who is Jesus Christ. He alone is able to forgive our sins, since He poured out His own blood for the forgiveness of our sins:

> ...*who His own self <u>bore our sins in His body on the tree</u>, that we, having died to sins, might live to righteousness; <u>by whose stripes you were healed</u>.* (1 Peter 2:24)

This is the only path back to innocence: faith in Jesus Christ. He is not only able to forgive our sins, but *willing to do so!* He runs towards broken, repentant sinners in order to welcome them into His arms (Luke 15:20). Our Lord Christ *"came into the world to save sinners, of whom I am chief"* (1 Timothy 1:15). He gently asks the woman who has been caught in the act of adultery, *"Woman, where are your accusers? Did no one condemn you?"* Then, He forgives her sins, washing them away, and adds, firmly, *"Go your way. From now on, sin no more"* (John 8:10-11).

The Gospel of God is liberty from sinful bondage. It is freedom from guilt and condemnation. It forgives those who have eaten from the Forbidden Tree. In the Gospel, Jesus Christ restores repentant sinners to Himself.

The Gospel is thus able to bring the perpetrators of abortion back into a state of peace with God. Jesus Christ forgives those men and women who repent of their abortions, and cling to Him for their salvation. Then, He changes them into loving parents. They, who are now Christians, learn to look forward to Heaven, where they will spend eternity rejoicing in God alongside of the very children whom they were unable to retrieve, after abortion, in this mortal life.

---

[13] Since Jesus claims exclusive glory for Himself, He is either telling the truth, or lying. If He is telling the truth, then He is also denouncing all other religions as idolatrous. There is no way to worship God apart from worshipping the Jesus of Scripture. See, for example, Mark 2:5-11; John 5:43-44; 8:19, 58; 14:6-9; 17:5; Acts 4:12; Colossians 1:15-20; 1 Timothy 2:5-6.

Together, Christian parent and Christian child will live in Heaven in the peace of Christ, and together, according to Revelation 22:1-2, they will eat from an altogether different kind of Tree:

> *He showed me a river of water of life, clear as crystal, proceeding out of the throne of God and of the Lamb, in the middle of its street. On this side of the river and on that was <u>the tree of life</u>, bearing twelve kinds of fruits, yielding its fruit every month. <u>The leaves of the tree were for the healing of the nations</u>.*

<u>Becoming "Like God" through Abortion</u>

The sin of abortion, then, is rooted in original sin, and is, therefore, only overcome by the power of the Gospel of Christ Jesus. Through their participation in sin, which is of the same essence (though not form) as the sin of Adam,[14] many humans are tempted towards the forbidden fruit of abortion. In light of this, we now understand abortion as a temptation both to covet things that are forbidden by the Word of God, and to "know good and evil" in an experiential way.

Yet there is one more powerful temptation that takes place in the Garden of Eden, just prior to Adam's fall into sin. This is the strongest temptation of them all. It is the Serpent's invitation for Adam and Eve to consider doing something in order to become *"like God."*

Satan Attempts to Become "Like God"

At the heart of the wickedness of Satan is his blasphemous attempt to become "like God." He attempts this, himself, and he also tempts Adam and Eve to attempt it, themselves:

---

[14] Without plunging into a prolix discussion of the doctrine of original sin, including the various theories on Adam's headship over the human race, it is the belief of this author that Adam's sin must be seen as both hereditary (that is, we, each and all, have inherited a sin nature from Adam) and representative (that is, had we been in Adam's "shoes," so to speak, we, each and all, would have fallen into sin in the same manner in which he did).

The serpent said to the woman, "You will not surely die, for God knows that in the day you eat it, your eyes will be opened, and you will be <u>like God</u>, knowing good and evil." (Genesis 3:4–5)

    This is Satan's own native language. Satan is tempting Adam and Eve by using his own native tongue. As the Father of Lies (John 8:44), he deceives himself into thinking that he can become like God. Satan actually thinks, at least at one point in world history, that he can usurp God's throne:

How you have fallen from heaven, morning star, son of the dawn! How you are cut down to the ground, who laid the nations low! You said in your heart, "I will ascend into heaven! I will exalt my throne above the stars of God! I will sit on the mountain of assembly, in the far north! I will ascend above the heights of the clouds! I will make myself <u>like the Most High</u>!" (Isaiah 14:12–14)

    As the father is, so are his children. The offspring of Satan are just like their father. Thus, the kingdom of Babylon, personified as Lady Babylon, thinks that she herself can become like God:

Now therefore hear this, you who are given to pleasures, who sit securely, who say in your heart, "<u>I am, and there is no one else besides me</u>. I shall not sit as a widow, neither shall I know the loss of children." (Isaiah 47:8)

    Another one of Satan's children is the king of Tyre. He, too, is chasing the wind. Thinking that he can be his own deity, he pompously presumes that he is able to become like God:

The LORD*'s Word came again to me, saying, "Son of man, tell the prince of Tyre, 'Thus says the Lord* GOD*: Because your heart is lifted up, and you have said, "<u>I am a god, I sit in the seat of God</u>, in the middle of the seas," yet you are man, and not God, though you set your heart as the heart of God...."'* (Ezekiel 28:1–2)

    This is both Satan's rebellion, and his great downfall. He deceives himself into thinking that he can take on the uniquely-divine attributes of God. He assumes the divine prerogative for himself. Satan commits the ultimate sins of disbelieving God's own statements about His exclusive nature and glory, and of seeking to overthrow God by planning a heavenly coup d'état. His desire is to murder God, so that he, himself, can be a ruling god. And when he gets Jesus nailed to the Cross, he tricks himself into thinking that he has finally accomplished his desired end. Yet the Cross is his undoing, and the once-glorious angel, now turned Prince of Darkness, is pierced by the light of Christ's resurrection from the dead, and his head is crushed by the heel of the Son of God.

Prior to being born again in Christ, we are children of the Devil. Unbelievers are the Devil's very offspring. Therefore, in our sin nature, it is tempting for us to want to become *"like God"* (Genesis 3:5). We, in our sinful flesh, are always wanting to *"throw off [the] fetters"* of the Lord, and of His Anointed One (Psalm 2:2, the present author's translation). Sinful humanity sees God's laws as chains, as burdens, since they limit our imaginations and desires. Wanting to be our own gods, we desire self-determination rather than obedience to God.

Abortion is, in this sense, an attempt to dethrone God. He has said, *"You shall not murder"* (Deuteronomy 5:17). Unbelievers, in turn, have taken this commandment as a burdensome ball and chain. They have decided that God does not know what He is talking about. They have said that since He wrote His Book before the dawn of modern science, His own writing was done in a state of ignorance of microbiology and embryology. They have also pointed out that He wrote that Sixth Commandment prior to the dawn of the Feminist movement. Thus they have concluded that God was not enlightened enough to know that modern woman would have needs that demanded, at times, personal freedom from children, and especially for the sake of her career advancement.

God's Throne says that abortion is always a murderous practice. The Throne of God forbids it. Yet modern man says that this Throne of God needs to be displaced. Modern science and modern sociology teach modern man how to become "like God." That is, the archaic Throne of God may be removed, says the goddess Abortion, and in its place the modern Throne of "Choice" may be set up. Abortion thus tempts man to become "like God" in a most murderous and blasphemous sense. It tears down the Laws of God and erects the laws of man. It overturns the judgments of the Most High God in favor of the judgments of the Supreme Courts of man.

There is, In Reality, No One Else "Like God"

It is hopelessly futile, however, for the nations to band together in war against God's Throne. They may band together against the Lord, but they shall never defeat Him. He laughs at them, even scoffs at them, prior to rebuking them in His anger and terrifying them in His wrath. When the great and dreadful *"Day of the LORD"* comes upon this earth, full of *"wrath"* and *"distress"* and *"darkness"* (Zephaniah 1:14ff.), it shall be clear to all that there is, in reality, only one God and King. No one can successfully challenge the "Godness" of the one, true God:

> *There is no one as holy as the LORD, for there is <u>no one besides You</u>, <u>nor is there any rock like our God</u>.* (1 Samuel 2:2)

He alone is God. He is eternally unique. In His saving power and conquering might, He remains unequalled:

> *Your way, God, is in the sanctuary. <u>What god is great like God</u>?* (Psalm 77:13)

The God of Scripture is not like the false gods of the pagans. Nothing, and no one, can be compared with Him. He alone created the stars, set them in place, knows each one of them by name, and makes sure that not one of them goes missing. Therefore, He has no equals:

> *"To whom then <u>will you liken Me</u>? Who is <u>My equal</u>?" says the Holy One.* (Isaiah 40:25)

There is, in fact, only one Man in the history of the world who could ever rightly claim to be "like God." Only He could make this claim, since He, Himself, *is God.* Jesus Christ did not "seem" to be the God-man, like an apparition that merely looked like physical flesh and blood. Nor was He a mere man who happened to have "Godhood" placed upon Him for a season of time. Nor was He merely the physical shell of a Man, with the divine Mind poured into it. Rather, He was fully human and fully divine, having two inseparable natures, perfectly distinct from one another, and perfectly united in His one Person—the Son of God.[15]

Jesus, then, is "like God," by divine right, since He is fully God and fully Man:

The Jews answered Him, "We do not stone You for a good work, but for blasphemy: because You, being a man, <u>make Yourself God</u>." (John 10:33)

The Jews were right about Jesus' self-understanding. He was a Man, and yet He did also claim to be God. However, they were wrong in charging Him with blasphemy. As the God-man, Jesus was, and is the one, true God. No one else is "like God." Only Jesus is "like God," for only Jesus is God.

We Must Obey God's Voice, Again

Who, then, is qualified to decide the matter of abortion? For thousands of years, the kingdom of this world, which the Bible calls the Kingdom of Babylon (Revelation 18:2-8), has claimed its own power to decide on the rightness or wrongness of abortion. It has set up such things as the whims of emperors, the votes of the majority, the dictates of human reason (which are, most of the time, defined by the almost-deified writings of Plato and Aristotle), the progress of modernization, and the invisible machinery of Marxist movements towards perceived social utopias (at the cost of much bloodshed, especially amongst civilians), on the Seat of Justice. In the Kingdom of Babylon, the fate of babies in the womb rests in the hands of men and women who seek to become their own gods.

What is needed, then, is a return to the Word of God. If God alone is God, then His Word must become our only all-authoritative source for judging between right and wrong. In the Garden of Eden,

---

[15] The Chalcedonian Creed (AD 451) speaks, rightly, of "one and the same Christ, Son, Lord, Only-begotten, to be acknowledged in two natures, inconfusedly, unchangeably, indivisibly, inseparably; the distinction of natures being by no means taken away by the union, but rather the property of each nature being preserved, and concurring in one Person and one Subsistence, not parted or divided into two persons, but one and the same Son, and only begotten, God the Word, the Lord Jesus Christ" (trans. in Philip Schaff, ed., *The Creeds of Christendom: with a History and Critical Notes* [Rev. David S. Schaff; 3 vol., 6th ed.; Grand Rapids: Baker Books, 1931], 2:62).

Adam found God's Word to be in conflict with Satan's word. He chose to listen to Satan's word, over God's Word. In abortion, we find the Word of God to be in conflict with the word of man. And when we choose to listen to man's word over God's Word, babies are slaughtered in cold blood.

The Church, therefore, does not simply need more information on the science of embryology. Also, we are not simply lacking good training in logical reasoning in defense of human life. Such things can be very helpful in giving us means by which to engage people while seeking to convince them of the value of human life in the womb. However, they are insufficient, in themselves.

The crisis over the lack of sound Abolitionist thinking in the Church is a crisis over Scripture. The great problem is that we have not believed in the sufficiency of Scripture to address the global Abortion Holocaust. We have been bedazzled by the arguments of biologists, feminists, psychologists, ethicists, and other "doctors of philosophy," and have become confused over the question of what abortion actually is. By fearing the word of man, we have lost the Word of God, and in the process the Church, at least to a significant degree, has been gagged and silenced on the greatest moral issue of our time.

In the Garden of Eden, the great question at hand is the question of authority. Whose voice has more authority, God's voice or Satan's voice? Will God's Word be trusted, or the Serpent's word? The first Adam responds by doubting the Word of God, and thus loses the battle. He sinfully refuses to heed the voice of God. Thus in his new state of sin, he must hear the "voice" of God's judgment:

> *They heard the* LORD *God's <u>voice</u> walking in the garden in the cool of the day, and the man and his wife hid themselves from the presence of the* LORD *God among the trees of the garden. The* LORD *God <u>called</u> to the man....* (Genesis 3:8-9a)

The second Adam, Jesus Christ, wins the victory over the Serpent by believing in the infinite authority of the Word of God. He listens, with perfect faith, to the voice of His Father. His heart is so fixated on His Father's voice that He is able to allow the Scriptures to drown out the voice of temptation coming from the Devil. *"It is written,"* Jesus says to the Serpent.

Adam's Guilt

Are we ready to believe in the infinite power and authority of God's Word, again? If we desire to see the Church win a great victory on behalf of babies in the womb, we must change our abolitionist strategy. Instead of merely trying to win the logical, philosophical argument for the preborn, we must let the Word of God speak, in and through the Church, on behalf of the preborn. We must let *God's own voice* thunder in defense of babies in the womb:

> *Rise up, you women who are at ease!* <u>*Hear My voice*</u>*! You careless daughters,* <u>*give ear to My speech*</u>*!* (Isaiah 32:9)

If we do not heed God's voice concerning abortion, truth will perish from our land:

> *…but this thing I commanded them, saying, "*<u>*Listen to My voice*</u>*, and I will be your God, and you shall be my people…." You shall speak all these words to them; but* <u>*they will not listen to you*</u>*: you shall also call to them; but they will not answer you. You shall tell them, "This is the nation that* <u>*has not listened to the* LORD *their God's voice*</u>*, nor received instruction. Truth has perished, and is cut off from their mouth."* (Jeremiah 7:23-24a, 27-28)

Christians, then, must be taught to hear the voice of Jesus concerning abortion. It is not enough to teach them a general Christian "pro-life" philosophy, or a good Christian apologetic (rational defense) of life in the womb. For Christians to have great love for preborn children, and for them to learn how to weep for them, and how to fight for them, with compassion, they must be taught how to hear Jesus' voice, speaking ever so affectionately about the little ones in the womb:

> *My sheep* <u>*hear My voice*</u>*, and I know them, and they follow Me.* (John 10:27)

Whose voice governs our thinking about abortion? Which voice owns our actions or inactions concerning abortion? Are we trembling at the voice of man, so that we are neglecting the voice of God? Are we listening to the crafty, lying word of the Serpent on abortion, such that we are deaf to the Word of God on abortion?

What is needed is repentance. We need to confess our sins of disbelieving God's Word on abortion, and of not wanting to heed God's Word in summoning us to action on behalf of the preborn. Out of selfishness, we have found it convenient to ignore the voice of God. In our complacency, not wanting to suffer for the truth, we have convinced ourselves that the Bible has no timeless commands to issue concerning Abortion Abolitionism. Thus we have silently ignored the plight of the preborn. Our church services have gone without constant, public prayers for them. Our church preachers have spoken benign words of political correctness about abortion, rather than allowing God's voice for the little ones to boom from their pulpits.

Therefore, we need to repent of these sins, and, in doing so, to return to the only all-authoritative Voice for the preborn:

As many as I love, I reprove and chasten. Be zealous therefore, and repent. Behold, I stand at the door and knock. If anyone <u>hears My voice</u> and opens the door, then I will come in to him, and will dine with him, and he with Me. (Revelation 3:19–20)

Oh, Church of Christ, enough of your headstrong academics and liberalized missions! Away with your psychological anecdotes and your seeker-sensitive outreach theories! No more trembling at the words of man, or clouding the truth with the Serpent's subtle suggestions!

Children, little children, are dying in our world. They are being sacrificed to pagan gods in our world. In this global Holocaust, there are no ends that justify the means. Global poverty does not outweigh global abortion. The alleviation of sickness does not justify human embryonic stem cell research. In vitro fertilization, and especially the kind that involves the freezing of embryos, is not societal advancement, but barbaric to a degree that surpasses the Nazis.

It is time for Christians to return to the Word of God on abortion. This is the only Word that has the authority to end abortion. It transcends governments, and popular opinion. It speaks from above, not from below. Infallible, inerrant, sufficient, and unalterable, the Bible, the voice of God, declaring justice for the preborn, shall be heard. The Lord shall establish His Word. He shall cause His voice, His judgments, on behalf of the little ones, whom He so prizes, to be heard.

Therefore, since time is of the essence for life in the womb, with thousands upon thousands of children being slain in our world every single day, we must return to the proclamation of Scripture, as it speaks in defense of the preborn, without delay. The time is short. It is time for Christians around the globe to rally together under the words of the Prophet:

> *Turn <u>to the law</u> and <u>to the testimony</u>! If they do not speak <u>according to this Word</u>, surely there is no [dawn] for them.* (Isaiah 8:20)

Divine Heartbeat

Part Two:

The Old Testament Heartbeat

Divine Heartbeat

5

BABY MOSES IN THE NILE:
Motherhood and Preborn Children

(Exodus 2:1-10)

A man of the house of Levi went and took a daughter of Levi as his wife. The woman conceived, and bore a son. When she saw that he was a fine child, she hid him three months. When she could no longer hide him, she took a papyrus basket for him, and coated it with tar and with pitch. She put the child in it, and laid it in the reeds by the river's bank. His sister stood far off, to see what would be done to him. Pharaoh's daughter came down to bathe at the river. Her maidens walked along by the riverside. She saw the basket among the reeds, and sent her servant to get it. She opened it, and saw the child, and behold, the baby cried. She had compassion on him, and said, "This is one of the Hebrews' children."

Then his sister said to Pharaoh's daughter, "Should I go and call a nurse for you from the Hebrew women, that she may nurse the child for you?"

Pharaoh's daughter said to her, "Go."

The maiden went and called the child's mother. Pharaoh's daughter said to her, "Take this child away, and nurse him for me, and I will give you your wages."

The woman took the child, and nursed it. The child grew, and she brought him to Pharaoh's daughter, and he became her son. She named him Moses, and said, "Because I drew him out of the water." (Exodus 2:1–10)

Moses is a very special baby, who also has a very special mother. When Moses' mother gives birth to her baby boy, there is a royal decree hanging over her head. Pharaoh, King of Egypt, has decreed that every male baby born amongst the Hebrews must be murdered. The baby boys must be thrown, alive, into the Nile River:

> *Pharaoh commanded all his people, saying, "You shall <u>cast every son who is born into the river</u>, and every daughter you shall save alive." (Exodus 1:22)*

This is the mass murder of children. It happened in ancient times. It is happening in our world today. Just as the screams of the Hebrew baby boys were silenced by the river waters that filled up their lungs, so too are the screams of the preborn babies that are murdered through abortion unable to be heard. The Nile River was a convenient form of mass slaughter. It made murder a quiet, almost sterile affair. So too is abortion a Silent Holocaust. It, too, silences the screams of its victims and attempts to sterilize the messiness of murder. Yet God, the Almighty Judge, heard the screams of the Hebrew babies as they drowned in the Nile, and He hears, today, the silent screams of the preborn children who are being killed in their mothers' wombs.

In Exodus 2, at the time of Moses' birth, amidst the horror of this pogrom launched against the little Hebrew baby boys, God begins opening the eyes of women to the value of their precious little babies. There is, then, a revival of *motherhood* taking place in Exodus 2. While many mothers, under the threats of Pharaoh, are surrendering their babies to the death waters of the Nile River, God is at work, opening the eyes of an elect group of women to see the eternal worth of motherhood. He is showing them that the precious little hiccups and burps of their infants are worth far more than the political favor of Egypt, or the personal security that comes from obedience to the murderous decree.

This is how God saves Israel, *through motherhood*. It is also how God can save our dying world, today. There is no hope for the world, in its current tyrannical and murderous state, apart from a divinely sparked revival of Christian motherhood. The very calling that is so ruthlessly under attack by modern feminism and homosexuality is the one calling that can save modern society from its imminent demise. Biblical motherhood, and not independent woman, is what God chooses to use to bring His most special servants into the world.

The Bible says that God opens the eyes of women to "see" the eternal treasures of motherhood. In this way, the mother of Moses is able to "see" how special Baby Moses really is:

The woman conceived, and bore a son. When she <u>saw</u> [God opens her eyes to see this] that he was a fine child, she hid him three months. (2:2)

It is God who opens her eyes to see how special her son really is. Also, it is God who opens the eyes of Pharaoh's daughter to see how special the baby in the ark really is:

Pharaoh's daughter came down to bathe at the river. Her maidens walked along by the riverside. She <u>saw</u> [God opens her eyes to see this] the basket among the reeds, and sent her servant to get it. She opened it, and <u>saw the child</u>, and behold, the baby cried. She had compassion on him, and said, "This is one of the Hebrews' children." (2:5-6)

What we need today, so pressingly, are women whose eyes are opened to the eternal value of little babies. We need a revival of biblical motherhood in the Church. We are desperate for the ministry of motherhood in the Church. We long for an Exodus out of the radical and anti-biblical forms of feminism that have captured the modern world. The Church is desiring a return to Christian womanhood and Christian motherhood amongst Christian women. We need to see how God uses women through motherhood, and daughter-hood—and not through career—to save His people out of Egypt.

THE WAR AGAINST MOTHERHOOD

A man of the house of Levi went and took a daughter of Levi as his wife. The woman <u>conceived</u>, and <u>bore a son</u>. (Exodus 2:1-2)

There is a war against motherhood raging in the modern world. It is full of *contraception*. That is, our modern culture is, in so many ways, *fundamentally against conception*. The "one-child policy" in China is one of the most wicked examples of this anti-conception culture of the modern age. Through it, Chinese women have been subjected to the barbaric brutality of forced abortions and forced sterilizations. Yet the anti-conception culture of modernity is also quite militant in the "Free World" nations, including the United States. Statistics from 2006-2010 indicate that "nearly all (99.1%) [non-celibate] women in the United States have used contraception at some time in their lives," and that 62% of women of child-bearing ages in the United

States are actively using contraception.[1] Such anti-conception militancy has existed, to be sure, since ancient times, but it has reached unprecedented levels of violence against motherhood in our current age.

Motherhood is under siege in modern culture. Sure, it might be modish for a woman today to have a biological baby in a designer stroller, here, or an adopted baby in a designer front-pack, there, so long as her total number of children does not exceed two or three. But large families are frowned upon in so much of the "civilized" world. The modern woman is trained, by our society, to be a career woman, not a homemaker. She is told that her worth is only to be found in the currencies of academic, political, humanitarian, economic, and athletic achievement. The biblical currencies of infant nursing, child raising, homeschooling, hospitality, and mother-to-mother discipleship are seen to be quite devalued, if not utterly worthless, in her eyes.

Yet God saves Israel out of Egypt through _conception_. Moses' mother _conceives_ and, nine months later, gives birth to a handsome baby boy. The Lord sets up the downfall of Pharaoh not by calling Hebrew women into the workplace (so that the Hebrews can make more bricks?), nor by summoning them into the military, but by creating a new little baby in the womb of a brave and faithful Hebrew mother.

This is how God works. He brings down kingdoms not with great armies, but with little babies. For example, when the Israelites need deliverance out of the hand of the Philistines, God saves them through a miraculous conception and birth:

> *The LORD's angel appeared to the woman, and said to her, "See now, you are barren and childless; but you shall conceive, and bear a son."* (Judges 13:3)

In Elisha's day, God uses a miraculous conception to bring forth a son for a barren woman. Yet this son, having grown into a boy, suddenly dies, and this happens because God, through Elisha, has

---

[1] Jo Jones, William Mosher, and Kimberly Daniels, "Current Contraceptive Use in the United States, 2006-2010, and Changes in Patterns of Use Since 1995," *National Health Statistics Reports, no. 60* (October 18, 2012), 2, 5. Cited 17 July 2013. Online: http://www.cdc.gov/nchs/data/nhsr/nhsr060.pdf.

determined to raise him, instantaneously, from the dead. Thus the power of resurrection from the dead is preceded by a miraculous conception:

The woman <u>conceived</u>, and <u>bore a son</u> at that season, when the time came around, as Elisha had said to her. (2 Kings 4:17)

The prophet Isaiah issues a heavenly prophecy about how God shall save the world through motherhood. The Lord God will place a "sign" in history, which is the sign of His salvation. This sign is that of a miraculous conception:

Therefore the Lord himself will give you <u>a sign</u>. Behold, the virgin will <u>conceive</u>, and <u>bear a son</u>, and shall call his name Immanuel. (Isaiah 7:14)

Isaiah's wife, the prophetess, serving as a type of the coming virgin Mary, conceives and gives birth to a son, and he, too, is a great sign to Israel. This baby boy, Maher Shalal Hash Baz, heralds to the world that Judah's enemies, Syria and Ephraim, shall be judged and destroyed, under the gracious and protective providence of God:

I went to the prophetess, and she <u>conceived</u>, and <u>bore a son</u>. Then the LORD said to me, "Call his name 'Maher Shalal Hash Baz.'" (Isaiah 8:3)

Yet the glory of motherhood does not climax in world history until the coming of the New Testament age. Living in the days of Caesar Augustus, two Jewish women conceive and give birth to two sons, who, together, change the course of world history in a most supernatural way. The first mother is an elderly woman named Elizabeth. Though far too old to have a child by any natural reckoning, she conceives, according to God's promise to her, and becomes a mother:

After these days Elizabeth, his wife, <u>conceived</u>, and she hid herself five months.... (Luke 1:24)

Elizabeth's pregnancy, in turn, becomes the forerunner of the greatest pregnancy of all. Mary is a virgin. She has never known a man. Yet the Holy Spirit comes upon her and the power of the Most High overshadows her. Thus she conceives and brings forth a Son:

> *Behold, you will <u>conceive</u> in your womb, and <u>give birth to a Son</u>, and will call his name "Jesus."* (Luke 1:31)

Do you "see" it? Does God, right at this moment, open your eyes to "see," as Moses' mother saw, the eternal worth of motherhood? The Lord God has called women to be neither combat soldiers,[2] nor members of the Congress or Senate.[3] He has not summoned them to be the heads of state.[4] He does not permit them to be in the pulpit.[5] Rather, He has summoned them to be distinctly feminine, and to receive a glorious calling in their womanhood. He has called women to one of the greatest vocations throughout the history of the world. He has exclusively and benevolently ordained for them the great world-changing work of motherhood:

> *Let a woman learn in quietness with all subjection. But I do not permit a woman to teach, nor to exercise authority over a man, but to be in quietness. For Adam was first formed, then Eve. Adam was not deceived, but the woman, being deceived, has fallen into disobedience; but she will be saved <u>through her childbearing</u>, if they continue in faith, love, and sanctification with sobriety.* (1 Timothy 2:11–15)

---

[2] Rather than challenging it, the *full content* of Judges 4:9 (the verse in which Deborah agrees to lead Israel into battle) shows that this verse actually supports a male-only fighting military by demonstrating *the shame of Barak, who was too afraid to lead his people into battle*. Thus Deborah says in Judges 4:9, *"…nevertheless there will be no glory for you in the journey you are taking, for the L*ORD *will sell Sisera into the hand of a woman."*

[3] The elders (i.e. political officers) of Deuteronomy 1:15 are exclusively male, since God designed men, and not women, to fulfill these verbally combative and socially wearisome offices. Accordingly, God despises the violation of this gender-based law of His created order. As the great Scottish Reformer, John Knox (1514-1572), in his *The First Blast of the Trumpet against the Monstrous Regiment of Women* (Southgate, London, N.: Edward Arber, 1878), 11 [with spelling modernized by the present author], so boldly puts it, "To promote a woman to bear rule, superiority, dominion or empire above any realm, nation, or city, is repugnant to nature, contumely to God, a thing most contrary to His revealed will and approved ordinance, and finally it is the subversion of good order, of all equity and justice."

[4] Athaliah (2 Kings 11:1-21) is the quintessential example of a nation that, under God's judgment, is handed over to a female head of state. See also Isaiah 3:12.

[5] See note 5 in Chapter 3, "Eve's Children."

The preacher announces salvation to the world by preaching. He is a man. The mother announces salvation to the world through childbearing. She is a woman.[6] Both are evangelists, and both have the power to bring down nations.

America's current President gnashes his teeth at the thought of highly educated women giving up their careers in order to become homemakers. He shoves birth control pills down their throats[7] because he despises the biblical blessings of motherhood. But the New Testament defends motherhood. The New Testament knows that mothers who stay at home to nurture and to educate their children have the power to change the world:

> *I desire therefore that the younger widows marry, <u>bear children</u>, [<u>manage</u>] <u>the household</u>, and give no occasion to the adversary for insulting. For already some have turned aside after Satan.* (1 Timothy 5:14–15)

And,

> *...[the older women must] train the young women to love their husbands, to love their <u>children</u>, to be sober minded, chaste, <u>workers at home</u>, kind, being in subjection to their own husbands, that God's Word may not be blasphemed.* (Titus 2:4–5)

God loves motherhood. He calls women into the ministry *of the home*. Yet in today's Church, pastors can get fired from their churches for saying this. The American Church has become so enticed by radical feminism that Paul's words to women in the First Timothy and Titus passages quoted above are no longer permitted to be spoken in the Church, unaltered. If, for example, a pastor simply were to quote them from memory, verbatim, but without letting on to his listeners that they are actually in the Bible, he would, in many of today's compromised churches, be labeled a legalist, a Pharisee,

---

[6] This is not to say that men have no roles to play in child rearing (far from it!), nor that women have no roles to play in public evangelism (may it never be!). It is, however, to point out that a woman's greatest evangelistic power lies in her gift of childbearing.

[7] It hardly needs to be said that we here refer to the notorious HHS Mandate of the Obama Administration.

and a divisive person. Biblical motherhood is now despised in the very household of God.

It is not so with the Gospel. The Gospel, itself, is not ashamed of the traditional, biblical roles of women in motherhood. Rather, it elevates motherhood back to its proper status of great importance. In the Gospel, God brings the Messiah into the world *through motherhood*:

> *A great sign was seen in heaven: a woman clothed with the sun, and the moon under her feet, and on her head a crown of twelve stars. She was <u>with child</u>. She cried out in pain, laboring to <u>give birth</u>. Another sign was seen in heaven. Behold, a great red dragon, having seven heads and ten horns, and on his heads seven crowns. His tail drew one third of the stars of the sky, and threw them to the earth. The dragon stood before the woman who was about to give birth, so that when she gave birth he might devour her Child. She <u>gave birth to a Son</u>, a male Child, who is to rule all the nations with a rod of iron. Her <u>Child</u> was caught up to God, and to His throne.* (Revelation 12:1–5)

God saves Israel out of Egypt through the motherhood of Moses' mother. As a mother, she has the courage to conceive, to give birth to, and to protect her baby boy. She risks her life in order to save her son.[8] She does not *"cast"* her son into the Nile River, allowing him to drown, as Pharaoh's government has ordered her to do (Exodus 1:22). Rather, she gently places him into the Nile River, in an ark, a little baby's ark, in order to save him. In doing so, she prepares the way for the salvation of Israel.

In the same way, God saves humanity through the motherhood of Mary. The virgin Mary believes the angel, and receives the gift of the Lord in her womb. She then risks her life in order to flee to Egypt, so that she can protect her baby Boy. She does not surrender Jesus to Herod. She guards little Jesus with her own life.

---

[8] What, then, of the argument that we ought to allow for abortions when the life of the mother is in danger? Would not every loving mother want to risk her own life for the sake of her child?

Mothers change the world through their motherhood.[9] There was a woman in the fourth century AD, living in the city of Antioch, named Anthusa. By age twenty, she was already married and had a daughter and a son. But at age twenty, her husband died. Alone, and facing many trials, she took the raising of her children exclusively upon herself. She homeschooled them, as a single mother, and she taught them to fear God and to love the Scriptures. Her God-fearing motherhood shaped her children into God-fearing Christians.

Anthusa's son was named John. When he learned how to preach, some began to call him "Golden Mouth" or, in Greek, Chrysostom. John Chrysostom became one of the greatest preachers that Christianity has ever known. He changed the world through his preaching. His mother changed the world through her motherhood.

There are, then, two great lies from the Devil that women in today's upside-down world have to face. First, there is the lie of career. Women are taught in our society—this is spoken to them with great force and repetition during the high school and college years—that a successful career will prove to be the fulfillment of their potentials. The lie is that without a career, women are wasting their educations and wasting their talents.

The second lie concerns submission. The Bible calls for wives to submit to their husbands. But Satan tells women today that submission is for the spiritually weak. Submission, according to Satan's lie, is degrading and belittling. It is like slavery. It is, according to Satan, a menace to society.

Thus we see a great war at hand. In Moses' time, Pharaoh declared war on the Hebrew baby boys. He had them all murdered in the Nile River. In our time, there is a war against motherhood, itself. Women think that motherhood, homemaking, and submission in marriage are the very chains of slavery. So they shun them, spitefully,

---

[9] The present author owes his own life to his mother. If it had not been for the prayers and biblical counsel of his mother, he most likely would have committed suicide when he was nineteen years old. She talked him out of the idea of suicide, using Scripture to guide him. Also, if it had not been for a very precious letter, full of Scripture and summoning him to Jesus, that his mother mailed to him when he was in that suicidal state, he may not have become a Christian. In fact, this act of quoting Scripture to him was habitual. His mother quoted the Bible to him from childhood onwards. She was a *"homemaker"* (Titus 2:4, NKJV), and she gave up career and social status so that she could stay home with her children and instruct them in the things of God.

and in doing so, ironically, they find themselves enslaved to the workplace, in bondage to the day care center, and shackled by the reality of passive, pushover husbands.

This is the war that is raging against the family. Babies are being murdered in this war, by the millions. And motherhood, itself, is being murdered in this war. The nations are raging against childbearing, whereas Jesus, being born of a woman, shows, by His birth, the everlasting value of childbearing. Also, the nations are raging against the concept of submission (and especially the concept of wives submitting to their husbands), whereas Jesus, who submits Himself, unreservedly, to His Father in Heaven, demonstrates that submission is for the spiritually strong, and not the spiritually weak. Jesus, born of Mary, calls women to the exalted mission of Christian marriage, and of Christian motherhood. But the world continually wars against it.

Where, then, are the brave Christian women of this generation? Who are the Christian women who will be known in Heaven as the ones who shone most radiantly for Christ amidst one of the darkest eras in world history? The Bible says that a large number of them shall be found in the humble, yet glorious service of Christian motherhood.[10]

God's best women die to the world, and live for Christ, through motherhood (either physical motherhood or spiritual motherhood). These women are the ones who are laboring to restore the glory of motherhood to its proper place in the Church. They are the ones who voluntarily walk away from their tenured faculty positions at prestigious universities and medical schools, solely for the purpose of pursuing Christian motherhood. They give up lucrative careers and large houses in order to homeschool their children, and thus raise them in the Christian faith. Trading the upper-middle-class amenities of a career track for the hardships of the discipleship of children in the home, they carry their crosses of motherhood with gentleness and grace. The world looks down upon them in wonder, baffled by their willingness to sacrifice so much for their children. It also looks

---

[10] Surely many wonderful Christian women are called to the gift of singleness, and shall serve as God's missionaries in their singleness. Amy Carmichael never married, but she is one of the Lord's best and brightest stars in church history. Yet she still, in her singleness, demonstrated the eternal value of motherhood. Her adopted orphans called her "Amma," or "Mother."

down upon them in scorn, hating their Christ-like humility and their silent, exemplary rebuke of modernized womanhood. Still, these daughters of God press on, unintimidated by the threats of the world, up the Narrow Road of Christian motherhood. They do it for their children, whom they love. But most of all they do it as unto the Lord, whom they worship.

THE NEED FOR INTERCESSORS

Preborn children need their mothers. They weep in the womb for their mothers. They feel, in their own bodies, the anguish of their mothers when their mothers are contemplating abortion. They hear their mothers' weeping and sobbing on the way to the abortion clinics. They weep for their mothers' love, even as the doctors prepare the instruments, or prescribe the drugs for their abortions.

The baby in Exodus 2 is crying. The baby needs help. The baby in the ark is weeping for his mother:

Pharaoh's daughter came down to bathe at the river. Her maidens walked along by the riverside. She saw the basket among the reeds, and sent her servant to get it. She opened it, and saw the child, and behold, <u>the baby [was weeping]</u>. She had compassion on him, and said, "This is one of the Hebrews' children." (Exodus 2:5-6)

Baby Moses is weeping. He is weeping for his mother. He is also weeping on behalf of all of his fellow Hebrew baby boys who have died in the very river on which his little ark is floating. He weeps in solidarity with the babies of Israel.

Abortion brings weeping. Baby Moses, weeping in the basket in the Nile River, teaches us to weep for the millions upon millions of babies who have been killed by the hands of the gods of abortion. We weep, then, for these babies, just as the exiles, in Babylon, wept for their babies who had been murdered by the hands of the Babylonians:

By the rivers of Babylon, there we sat down. Yes, we <u>wept</u>, when we remembered Zion. (Psalm 137:1; see also v. 9)

We weep for the preborn just as Rachel wept for her children who had been taken from her:

The LORD says: A voice is heard in Ramah, lamentation, and bitter <u>weeping</u>, Rachel <u>weeping for her children</u>; she refuses to be comforted for her children, because they are no more. (Jeremiah 31:15)

But why are there today a number of professing Christians who know not how to weep for babies in the womb? There ought to be more pastors who know how to lead their churches in weeping for the preborn. If we believe them to be persons, full human beings, then we ought to weep for them. Every true Christian (that is, those who truly love God and do not merely profess Christ with their lips) ought to spend time weeping for the preborn. If we love them, we shall weep for them.

The baby is weeping. Baby Moses needs help. The Princess of Egypt has seen him, and has had compassion on him. But the baby is weeping for *his mother*. He wants *his mother*. So he needs an advocate. He needs someone to come forth, courageously, as his intercessor:

She opened it, and saw the child, and behold, the baby cried. She had compassion on him, and said, "This is one of the Hebrews' children."

<u>*Then his sister said to Pharaoh's daughter,*</u> *"Should I go and call a nurse for you from the Hebrew women, that she may nurse the child for you?"*

Pharaoh's daughter said to her, "Go."

The maiden went and called the child's mother. Pharaoh's daughter said to her, "Take this child away, and nurse him for me, and I will give you your wages."

The woman took the child, and nursed it. (Exodus 2:6–9)

Miriam, Moses' sister, courageously steps in as his intercessor. She risks being exposed as an accomplice to her mother's act of civil disobedience, and through her courageous intercession, Baby Moses is restored to his mother. Miriam, Moses' intercessor, risks her life on behalf of her baby brother. His weeping moves her to intercession.

The result is fantastic. Moses' own mother, Jochebed, becomes his private wet nurse! Thus Pharaoh's imperial money unwittingly pays Jochebed a salary to nurse her own baby, and Pharaoh's very daughter becomes a secret accomplice to the downfall of his own kingdom. This is irony in real, historical cloth; it is also the providential power of God.

When babies are weeping, in danger at the hands of others, they need an intercessor. God uses intercessors to save His people. For instance, only a chapter earlier in Exodus, Shiphrah and Puah become courageous intercessors for the little Hebrew baby boys who are being slaughtered under Pharaoh's murderous edict. In order to protect the baby boys from the blood-filled waters of the Nile River, they risk their own lives. They are thus heroines of the faith on account of their intercessory work:

The king of Egypt spoke to the Hebrew midwives, of whom the name of the one was Shiphrah, and the name of the other Puah, and he said, "When you perform the duty of a midwife to the Hebrew women, and see them on the birth stool; if it is a son, then you shall kill him; but if it is a daughter, then she shall live." But the midwives <u>feared God</u>, and <u>did not do what the king of Egypt commanded them, but saved the baby boys alive</u>. (Exodus 1:15-17)

Queen Esther is another courageous intercessor in the Bible. She risks her own life in order to save the lives of the Jews:

Then Esther asked them to answer Mordecai, "Go, gather together all the Jews who are present in Shushan, and fast for me, and neither eat nor drink three days, night or day. I and my maidens will also fast the same way. <u>Then I will go in to the king, which is against the law; and if I perish, I perish</u>." (Esther 4:15–16)

Consider also the Ethiopian friend of the Prophet Jeremiah, who risks his life in order to save Jeremiah:

Now when Ebedmelech the Ethiopian, a eunuch, who was in the king's house, heard that they had put Jeremiah in the dungeon (the king then sitting in the gate of Benjamin), <u>Ebedmelech went out of the king's house, and spoke to the king, saying</u>, "My lord the king, these men have done evil in all that they have done to Jeremiah the prophet, whom they have cast into the dungeon;

and he is likely to die in the place where he is, because of the famine; for there is no more bread in the city." (Jeremiah 38:7–9)

Still again, note the courage of the Apostle Paul's nephew, boldly interceding for Paul after he overhears the Jews plotting to ambush and murder Paul. He risks his own safety in order to report the matter to the Roman commander, who, in turn, saves Paul's life:

So the commanding officer let the young man go, charging him, "<u>Tell no one that you have revealed these things to me</u>." (Acts 23:22)

Sadly, though, at the end of Paul's life, no Christians have the courage to intercede for him. All abandon him. The courageous intercessors are no more. But Jesus Christ never abandons His children. He stays with Paul. Jesus is Paul's intercessor:

At my first defense, <u>no one came to help me</u>, but all left me. May it not be held against them. <u>But the Lord stood by me</u>, and strengthened me, that through me the message might be fully proclaimed, and that all the Gentiles might hear; and I was delivered out of the mouth of the lion. And the Lord will deliver me from every evil work, and will preserve me for his heavenly Kingdom; to whom be the glory forever and ever. Amen.
(2 Timothy 4:16–18)

If preborn children are weeping in our world, weeping in the hands of the abortion doctors who are about to murder them, then we must intercede for them. No true Christian can stay silent about abortion. No true follower of Jesus can passively sit by and watch this Holocaust march on into the future, leaving the corpses of God's little image bearers in its wake. We must become outspoken intercessors for the preborn.

Mary Wagner is a Canadian Christian who has spent years in prison for working alongside of her mentor and co-worker, Linda Gibbons. Both women are strong in their Christian faith. So what do these women do? Why are they in prison so often? They are in prison for being intercessors for the preborn children of Canada. They practice civil disobedience by going into abortion clinics, giving the women inside flowers, and handing them literature that asks them to rethink the imminent killing of their babies.

The police arrest Mary Wagner and her mentor on a very consistent basis. They throw them into prison, for months at a time. When they let them out of prison, they scold them and warn them not to go back into the abortion clinics. But Mary and her mentor go right back to their work of intercession.

One day, in prison, an inmate approached Mary Wagner. She asked Mary, "Do you remember me?" Mary did not. So the inmate reminded Mary that they had first met two years earlier on the way into an abortion clinic. The woman was entering the clinic to have an abortion—to ask a physician to murder her baby. Mary followed her into the abortion clinic, gently pleading with her to reconsider, but the woman would not change her mind.

However, once inside the clinic, the police came to arrest Mary. They were very rough in pushing her up against the wall and handcuffing her. The woman with the baby saw Mary's willingness to suffer for the preborn. She reconsidered, right on the spot. She kept her baby. The inmate, having recognized Mary, said that she wanted to thank her for *saving her little son* from abortion.[11]

How many babies are weeping, crying out for intercessors, around the globe today? The international numbers on abortion are more than the human mind can grasp.[12] As many as 18,000 abortions occur every day in India.[13] Forty percent of all babies in the womb in New York City find themselves weeping in their mothers' wombs in

---

[11] Peter Baklinski, "Inmate Tells Arrested Pro-lifer: 'Your Arrest in the Abortion Clinic Saved My Baby,'" *Life Site News* (October 16, 2012), n.p. [cited 12 July 2013]. Online: http://www.lifesitenews.com/news/inmate-tells-arrested-pro-lifer-your-arrest-in-the-abortion-clinic-saved-my.

[12] The statistics on global abortion rates are very slippery and hard to be precise about, especially since so many abortions go unreported or uncounted (e.g. consider the countless abortions that take place via the birth control pill, IVF, and other medical drugs/procedures that are not normally considered to be abortions). The following estimates are as current as the author could find, and, considering that they reflect, for the most part, only reported and/or estimated abortions, they are certainly lower than the actual numbers, themselves.

[13] Malathy Iyer and Pratibha Masand, "Mumbai Saw 44% More Abortions Last Year," *The Times of India* (May 20, 2013), n.p. [cited 12 July 2013]. Online: http://articles.timesofindia.indiatimes.com/2013-05-20/mumbai/39392038_1_abortions-dr-nikhil-datar-dr-nozer-sheriar.

abortion clinics.[14] For every ten live births in Russia, there are thirteen babies in Russia who weep over their mothers' decision to have them killed in the womb.[15]

Where, then, are the intercessors for these weeping babies? Where are the seminary professors? Why are Christian seminary professors so silent about the Abortion Holocaust? And where are the Christian doctors? Why are the Christians physicians, with a few very notable exceptions, so muted concerning the mass slaughter of abortion? Where are those who will be the courageous advocates for the children in the womb?

Part of the problem seems to be that many Christians today have decided to view abortion as "just another social issue." Following Western political polemics, the gravity of abortion is oftentimes downplayed in the Church by reducing its degree of urgency and importance. "What about taking care of the poor? What about those orphans who are not aborted, but still need care?" one Christian will object in response to the cry for obligatory Abortion Abolitionism.[16] Yet abortion cannot be brushed aside as simply one important political issue among many others. In Nazi Germany, there were plenty of social and economic issues to think about. Yet the *one issue* of the concentration camps captured the attention of those Christians who feared God and knew that, as His people, they were obligated to intercede for the Jews, and for others (including those with disabilities) who were being so brutally slaughtered in their land.

Why, especially amongst Protestants, is there a dearth of courageous intercessors for the preborn? Another part of the problem concerns a particular approach to the Gospel known as "Dispensationalism" that was popularized amongst conservative Protestants in the eighteenth and nineteenth centuries. In its classical expressions, Dispensationalism tends to teach a strong bifurcation

---

[14] Paul Vitello, "Religious Leaders Call for New Efforts to Lower the City's 'Chilling' Abortion Rate," *The New York Times* (January 6, 2011), n.p. [cited 12 July 2013]. Online: http://www.nytimes.com/2011/01/07/nyregion/07abortion.html?_r=0.

[15] Robert Greenall, "Russia Turns Spotlight on Abortion," *BBC News Online*, (September 16, 2003), n.p. [cited 12 July 2013]. Online: http://news.bbc.co.uk/2/hi/europe/3093152.stm.

[16] Ironically, most of these critics of obligatory Abolitionist activism do not, themselves, practice sacrificial care for the widow and the orphan (James 1:27). Few of them, for example, have actually taken orphans into their own homes.

between Law and Gospel, between Old Testament and New. It narrows the definition of the Gospel away from passages such as Isaiah 40:9, where the Gospel is as big as God, Himself,[17] and creates an unbiblical boundary around the Gospel that restricts it to "how one gets saved." One of the bad fruits of this over-narrowing of the term "Gospel" is a practical bifurcation between the Gospel and politics. Thus a Dispensationalist might say, "Abortion is an important issue, but we do not want to spend too much of our time preaching against it, lest we neglect the preaching of the Gospel." This is in stark contrast with the thinking of William Wilberforce, who saw his Abolitionist efforts as *a means by which* he could receive open doors to preach, boldly, about God's wrath against idolatry, about repentance from sins and faith in Jesus Christ, and about the judgment to come.

Still, the greatest reason why so few Christians are willing to make sacrificial intercession for babies in the womb is their own selfishness. Just like the priest and the Levite in the Parable of the Good Samaritan (Luke 10:30-37), many Christians today are so full of selfish interests that they simply *"pass by"* their preborn neighbor (vv. 31-32). It is not that they deny, intellectually, the tragedy of abortion. They simply are too caught up in planning vacation cruises, in monitoring their investments in stocks and bonds, in watching football on television, and in building bigger, fancier church buildings to really care much about the preborn. *The issue is one of love.* They have learned to love their own selfish desires so much that it has blinded them to a proper, biblical love for babies in the womb. If they loved, as God does, the babies in the womb who are being slaughtered in abortion clinics just down the highway from them, they would weep for them. And then, inevitably, their love for them would propel them into courageous intercession on their behalf.

---

[17] John Piper, in *God is the Gospel: Meditations on God's Love as the Gift of Himself* (Wheaton: Crossway Books, 2005), 129, makes the point that faith, by itself, without the exaltation of Christ *as its object*, is not the center of the Gospel: "Faith is not saving faith if it tries to trust Christ for the wrong things. So this makes clear that trust per se, without reference to what we trust [Him] for, is not the essence of a saving relationship to Christ. Something else must be present in faith if it is to be saving faith that honors Christ rather than just using [Him]. Saving faith must have a quality to it that tastes what is Christ-exalting and embraces it."

BABY MOSES AND SALVATION

Baby Moses heralds the gift of a baby to the world. A baby is a gift given to mothers. Mothers, through their motherhood, have the power to dethrone kings and to bring down evil kingdoms. But babies need intercessors. They need courageous voices to speak up on their behalf. As biblical Christians, then, we champion motherhood, for God's glory. We also intercede for the preborn, as God would have us to do.

Ultimately, however, Baby Moses' plight, floating in a basket down the Nile River, gives us a glimpse of salvation. The rescue of Baby Moses out of the Nile River is a miraculous event, a free gift from God, and it is thus a portrait of salvation, itself:

The child grew, and she brought him to Pharaoh's daughter, and he became her son. She named him Moses [which, in Hebrew, means "the one who draws out"], and said, "Because I drew him out of the water." (Exodus 2:10)

Salvation happens when God *draws us out* of the death waters of the Nile River. In Exodus, He draws Baby Moses out of the waters of the Nile River. Also in Exodus, He draws Israel out of the death waters of the Red Sea. In the Gospel of Matthew, He draws Baby Jesus out of the death waters of King Herod's slaughter of baby boys in Bethlehem. And, in salvation, He draws us out of the death waters of our own sins:

He sent from on high and he took me. He drew me out of many waters. (2 Samuel 22:17)

Also,

When you pass through the waters, I will be with you; and through the rivers, they will not overflow you. (Isaiah 43:2)

Baptism signifies this salvation. Regeneration precedes physical baptism (Acts 10:47), but physical baptism is an act of obedience to Christ that proclaims our salvation. Just as Moses was lowered into the waters of death, but raised up out of those waters, so too are

Christians lowered into the death of Christ, so that we are also raised with Him. We are immersed in the water, only in order to be raised up, out of the water:

We were buried therefore with Him <u>through baptism</u> to death, that just as Christ was raised from the dead through the glory of the Father, so we also might walk in newness of life. (Romans 6:4)

God rescued Baby Moses out of the death waters of the Nile. He kept the waters from overtaking him, and causing him to drown. The same is true for the Church. Satan wants to drown the Church in the floodwaters of his cruel hate. Yet God will not allow the Church to drown:

The serpent spewed water out of his mouth after the woman like a river, that he might cause her to be carried away by the stream. The earth helped the woman, and the earth opened its mouth and <u>swallowed up the river</u> which the dragon spewed out of his mouth. (Revelation 12:15–16)

Baby Moses was lowered into the death waters of the Nile River, so that God could draw him out of the Nile River, into salvation. Israel was lowered into the death waters of the Red Sea, so that God could draw Israel out of the Red Sea, into salvation. Are we, the Church, willing to follow Moses and Israel into this dangerous cycle of first being lowered into death, and subsequently being raised into life? Will we allow God to place *us* in the little ark, floating down the Nile River? Will we allow Him to draw *us* out of the waters of death? If we will allow Him to do this, if we will trust Him to care for us, then we shall see His saving power in the world, once again. For, when He draws us out of danger, He will also draw many others out, with us. Moses' salvation becomes Israel's salvation. In the same way, our own rescue out of the waters of death becomes a witness to many others, so that they, too, may believe and be saved.

There must, then, be a revival of Christian willingness to suffer on behalf of the preborn. We must be willing to lower ourselves into the "little ark" on the Nile River, for the sake of children in the womb. This, for example, is Pastor Randy Alcorn in the early 1990's, facing arrest, imprisonment, and a horrific lawsuit from an abortion clinic following his peaceful intercession[18] for the preborn.[19] It is Mary Wagner and Linda Gibbons sitting in prison[20] in Canada for the sake of the preborn. It is a high-profile political candidate losing his candidacy because his intercession for babies in the womb is viewed as "too extreme" by his own party. It is a Christian woman who works as a nurse being fired from her hospital for her outspoken advocacy for the preborn. And, on a less visible, yet still very painful level, it is a Christian man facing the loss of friendships, or the wrath of family members, simply because he will not stop reminding his friends and family members—using speech that is full of grace, seasoned with salt—about how the Lord of Hosts views the plight of the preborn.

God loves to rescue babies out of the death waters of abortion. He has, thousands upon thousands of times, used the little "arks" of crisis pregnancy centers around the world to rescue His precious little ones. He has also used, in countless ways, the courageous Christian side-walk counselors who have stood outside of abortion clinics, rain or shine, to encourage women to rethink abortion. The Lord has appointed and ordained Christian missionaries to go to public places, such as the universities campuses of the world, in order to speak, from the Scriptures, His message of justice and life for the preborn. He has rescued babies through all of these heroic efforts.

Yet there is much more work to be done. The persecution, sorrow, social ostracism (even coming from misguided wings of the Church) and loneliness of God's great intercessors for the preborn may intensify greatly before things start to get better. There is, therefore, an increasing need for Christians to possess a willingness to carry their crosses on behalf of the little ones in the womb. We must feel called by God to labor, to sweat, and, if necessary, to lay down our lives, gladly, on their behalf. And when we do so, God shall do the supernatural work, the mighty work of salvation on their behalf. He will draw them, one by one, out of the rivers of death.

---

[18] This author does not condone the use of violence in the defense of the preborn. It is one thing to advocate the sword of government with respect to justice for the preborn (see chapter 6), and quite another thing for Christians to take the sword into their own hands (Matthew 26:52).

[19] For Pastor Alcorn's story, see Randy Alcorn, *The Treasure Principle: Unlocking the Secret of Joyful Giving* (Sisters, OR: Multnomah, 2001), 21-24.

[20] At the time of this writing, Linda Gibbons is currently out of prison, but Mary Wagner is still in prison, awaiting trial.

And when He does so, He will demonstrate to the world the saving power of His eternal Gospel.

Remember Christ Jesus, the only-begotten of His Father. God lowered His own Son not into the safety of a baby-ark, floating in the Nile River, but into the waters of death itself. Jesus went down into the dark waters of death for us. God lowered Him into death itself. For Jesus, there was no way out of death. He humbled Himself all the way to death. He died. He drowned in the suffocating waters of the Cross. He took death for us.

Yet on the first day of the week, in real, literal history, God drew Him out of death. He drew His Son out of the grave. Christ is risen! God has drawn Him out of the dark waters of the tomb, into the bright light of the morning. Sin is defeated! Life in Christ has been drawn out of the waters of death. Christ is alive! Thus salvation, through the remission of sins, which is by grace alone, through faith alone, is found in Christ alone.

Divine Heartbeat

6

THE DEATHBLOW OF ABORTION:
Political Law and Preborn Children

(Exodus 21:12-27)

One who strikes a man so that he dies shall surely be put to death, but not if it is unintentional, but God allows it to happen: then I will appoint you a place where he shall flee. If a man schemes and comes presumptuously on his neighbor to kill him, you shall take him from My altar, that he may die.

Anyone who attacks his father or his mother shall be surely put to death.

Anyone who kidnaps someone and sells him, or if he is found in his hand, he shall surely be put to death.

Anyone who curses his father or his mother shall surely be put to death.

If men quarrel and one strikes the other with a stone, or with his fist, and he does not die, but is confined to bed; if he rises again and walks around with his staff, then he who struck him shall be cleared: only he shall pay for the loss of his time, and shall provide for his healing until he is thoroughly healed.
(Exodus 21:12–19)

In August of 1979, cruel violence struck and killed a baby girl who was only eight months old. She was the daughter of an Amish couple, Mr. and Mrs. Levi Schwartz, living near Berne, Indiana. Her name was Adeline. Her parents loved her very much.[1]

A group of reckless, bigoted young men killed her. They hated the Amish who lived in their community, calling them "Clapes" (presumably short for "Clay apes"), and they made it a sport to drive their pick-up trucks at night, cloaked in darkness, in order to hunt for

---

[1] The historicity of this event is documented by Bryan D. Byers, "Amish Victimization and Offending: A Rural Subculture's Experiences and Responses to Crime and Justice," *Southern Rural Sociology* 23:2 (2008), 235-37.

Amish buggies. When they found the buggies, they would throw rocks and clay tiles into them.

One night, while speeding down the road in a pick-up truck, the young men hurled debris at an Amish buggy, and the debris struck little eight-month-old Adeline, penetrating her head via her ear. Her mother was holding her at the time, but since it was dark outside, she did not know that Adeline had been hit. Only after the buggy arrived at their home did the young couple bring Adeline into the light, and realize that she was dead.

What followed was a monumental lack of justice. The Amish, of course, are known for not pressing charges against their persecutors. As a result of the Schwartzes' refusal to press charges, combined with a law of the land that was very lax on the young men, Adeline's murder went virtually unpunished. The young men hid behind the lie that the whole thing had been an accident—that they had never intended to inflict harm on the Amish—even though there had been local reports about them, at an earlier time, bragging about having made another Amish person bleed from the face. These violent young men walked away from their crime, unpunished. They never spent time in prison; they never faced criminal justice, at all, at least in this life.

These kinds of historical injustices prompt many questions. They summon the compassionate hearer of them to the types of hard questions that involve biblical justice. For example, how big of a blow was that event to Adeline's parents? How did they ever recover from the deathblow that was dealt to their daughter? And what would God say about the proper course of justice in this case? What would real, biblical justice look like for Adeline?

Such stories haunt those who believe in a God of justice. The striking lack of justice in this world haunts us. Yet, as believers, we gain some comfort in learning that the Bible does, indeed, speak to these kinds of awful things. It describes, through its own divine law codes, the blow of battery, the blow of manslaughter, and the blow of murder, and it portions out justice according to the degree of the blow. If the crime is a smaller blow, the justice is less severe. But if the crime is a bigger blow, the justice is much more severe.

As Christians, we define abortion as a deathblow. It is the killing of an innocent person, a baby. We thus want to understand biblical justice for the baby in the womb. We want to ask the questions,

"How big, exactly, is the deathblow of abortion?" and "How should political law be employed to protect babies in the womb?" But before we can answer these questions, we must first explore the twenty-first chapter of Exodus as it relates to the deathblow of murder, in general.

LESSER BLOWS AND NON-CAPITAL OFFENSES

Exodus 21 is full of heavy crimes, involving heavy blows. But some blows are lesser ones. They are not capital offenses:

If men quarrel and one strikes the other with a stone, or with his fist, and he does not die, but is confined to bed; if he rises again and walks around with his staff, then he who struck him shall be [acquitted]: only he shall pay for the loss of his time, and shall provide for his healing until he is thoroughly healed. (Exodus 21:18–19)

Moses, Israel's prophet and judge, is describing injurious blows on a case-by-case basis. Here, he describes that a man will be *"acquitted"* if his victim does not die. But this only means that he will be acquitted *of murder*. He is still guilty *of battery*. He still must make restitution for his crime:

…only he shall <u>pay for the loss of his time</u>, and shall <u>provide for his healing until he is thoroughly healed</u>. (v. 19)

More literally translated, *"He shall give [to him] his 'rest,' that he will surely heal,"* [2] this verse describes a kind of "disability" restitution. The perpetrator has injured a man, and so he must pay for the victim's working wages while the victim rests and heals. The victim must be compensated for his wounds, and for the duration of time during which he is unable to work.

This, in turn, introduces one of the major categories of legal punishments within the Mosaic Law: the sentence of restitution. Some crimes are not capital crimes. They do not demand the death of the perpetrator. Yet they do call for restitution. The thief must pay back double, or even five-fold for the livestock that he stole (22:1, 4). The arsonist must make restitution for the crops that he destroyed

---

[2] The present author's translation.

(22:6). And in the case of battery, the violent offender must give monetary restitution to his victim, and commensurate with the victim's injuries and time away from work.

THE DEATHBLOW OF MURDER IS A CAPITAL OFFENSE

Yes, but in Exodus 21 there are more severe blows, and they call for capital punishment. These more severe blows introduce a second major category of legal punishments within the Mosaic Law: the death sentence. Capital crimes call for capital punishment:

Anyone who kidnaps someone and sells him, or if he is found in his hand, he shall surely be put to death. (Exodus 21:16)

This first type of capital offense in Exodus 21 is surprising. Most people know that kidnapping and slave trafficking are bad things, but God says that they are *capital crimes*. The Bible is *not* pro-slavery in the sense of pre-Civil War slave owners in the American South thinking that kidnapped Africans could be treated as their own property. Rather, the Bible says that anyone who kidnaps people from their native lands and sells them as slaves in foreign lands ought to be put to death![3]

Another surprising type of capital offense is the blow against a father or mother:

Anyone who attacks his father or his mother shall be surely put to death. (Exodus 21:15)

---

[3] Thus when the American South's leading theologian, James Henley Thornwell (1812-1862), used the Bible to advocate his pro-slavery views, boasting confidently, "That the relation betwixt the slave and his master is not inconsistent with the [Word] of God, we have long since settled…" (qtd. in Mark A. Noll, *America's God: From Jonathan Edwards to Abraham Lincoln* [Oxford: Oxford University Press, 2002], 393), he was not applying the Bible to the African slave trade and American slavery the way that he should have. Rather than using texts such as Ephesians 6:5-9 to defend American slavery, he should have used Exodus 21:16 to advocate the abolition of American slavery.

Also,

Anyone who curses his father or his mother <u>shall surely be put to death</u>. (Exodus 21:17)

These verses show the intensity of the sinful blow of a child blatantly violating the Fifth Commandment. A child does not have to murder his father or mother in order to be guilty of a capital crime. He simply has to attack his parent, or curse his parent, and God counts this as a capital crime. But our current culture has reached such an advanced stage of rebellion against this kind of reverence for parents that many hearts have become hardened to it. In our current, debased culture, people have come to believe that children have the *right* to curse their parents. By way of stark, holy contrast, God says that children ought to be put to death for such crimes.[4]

Finally, there is the deathblow of murder, itself:

One who strikes a man <u>so that he dies</u> shall surely be put to death, but not if it is unintentional, but God allows it to happen: then I will appoint you a place where he shall flee. If a man schemes and comes presumptuously on his neighbor to kill him, you shall take him from My altar, that he may die. (Exodus 21:12–14)

Murder is the greatest blow; it calls for capital punishment:

One who strikes a man so that he dies <u>shall surely be put to death</u>. (Exodus 21:12)

The murderer willfully caused death, and so he must die. He willfully shed blood, and so his blood must be shed. He must *"surely die,"* which phrase points us back to the severity of sin, in general:

---

[4] The present author surmises, reasoning from God's patience and longsuffering, and especially His compassion towards little children (see, for example, Deuteronomy 1:39) that these laws of capital punishment for violent, rebellious children do not apply to the sinful acts of children that are common to almost all children, such as a toddler hitting his mother during a temper tantrum. Rather, the laws are designed to address an idolatrous, blasphemous older child (see Leviticus 24:10-23) who habitually defies his parents' authority, even to the point of Satanically cursing them, or seeking to injure them, severely, by attacking them.

The LORD God commanded the man, saying, "You may freely eat of every tree of the garden; but you shall not eat of the tree of the knowledge of good and evil; for in the day that you eat of it, <u>you will surely die</u>."
(Genesis 2:16–17)

    The wages of all sin is death, but murder is a much greater sin than most. It calls for capital punishment, for the immediate death of the murderer, since he shed the blood of another man:

One who strikes a man so that he dies <u>shall surely be put to death</u>.
(Exodus 21:12)

    How, then, does the Bible speak to the case of young adults who cruelly murder (even if violent harm, but not murder, was their intent) an eight-month-old baby girl by throwing rocks and clay tile at her parents' horse-drawn buggy? It does speak to this case. It calls for justice. It demands capital punishment:

But if he struck him with an instrument of iron, so that he died, he is a murderer. The murderer shall surely be put to death. <u>If he struck him with a stone in the hand, by which a man may die, and he died, he is a murderer. The murderer shall surely be put to death</u>. (Numbers 35:16–17)

    When it comes to protecting human life, God is deadly serious. If acts of intentional violence, even when committed with non-murderous intent, lead to death, capital punishment follows. It is "life for life." How much more, then, do intentional, premeditated murders demand capital punishment. That is, if God is wrathful towards the kind of reckless, hateful violence that killed Baby Adeline, how much more is He wrathful towards the kind of premeditated murder that happens through abortion. God is holy; therefore, He hates all sin. Yet He hates the sin of murder with a particularly great hatred. The Author of human life *hates* the murderous taking of human life at the hands of a fellow human being.

Murder defiles a land, for blood defiles a land:

> *Moreover you shall take no ransom for the life of a murderer who is guilty of death; but he shall surely be put to death.*
>
> *You shall take no ransom for him who is fled to his city of refuge, that he may come again to dwell in the land, until the death of the priest.*
>
> *So you shall not pollute the land in which you are; for blood pollutes the land. <u>No atonement can be made for the land for the blood that is shed in it, but by the blood of him who shed it</u>.* (Numbers 35:31–33)

In fact, murder is such a great sin that even a man who has run to God's altar of forgiveness and has grabbed hold of the altar, though he may be spared judgment in the final state, should not be spared the sentence of capital punishment:

> *If a man schemes and comes presumptuously on his neighbor to kill him, <u>you shall take him from My altar, that he may die</u>.* (Exodus 21:14)

Joab is such a murderer, and King Solomon calls for Joab's execution, even after Joab has fled from Solomon in order to take hold of the horns of God's altar. After Joab has told Solomon's messenger, Benaiah, that if he would strike him down, he would have to kill him right at the altar of God, Solomon responds to Joab's words, relayed through Benaiah, with words of biblical justice:

> *The king said to [Benaiah], "Do as he has said, and fall on him, and bury him; <u>that you may take away the blood, which Joab shed without cause, from me and from my father's house</u>."* (1 Kings 2:31)

Yet all of this talk about capital punishment is very offensive to modern ears. If, in the medieval ages, the government was too quick to pronounce the death penalty over the heads of even some of its thieves, we, in the contemporary age, have gone to the opposite extreme. We have almost shunned capital punishment, altogether.[5] And we have used Jesus' words to do it. Many have quoted Jesus in order to defy the biblical commandment of the necessity of capital punishment in sinful human society:

> *You have heard that it was said to the ancient ones, "You shall not murder"; and "Whoever murders will be in danger of the judgment." But I tell you, that <u>everyone who is angry with his brother without a cause will be in danger of the judgment</u>.* (Matthew 5:21–22)

Some people greatly misinterpret these verses. They believe that Jesus is equating murder with hatred, as if the sins were equal sins. But He is not doing this. He is, indeed, pointing out the horror of the sins of the heart, like hatred, and how internal sins such as hatred are so grave as to be likened to murder, in that they merit everlasting punishment in Hell. But Jesus is not saying that all sins are equal. He is not downplaying the severity of murder.

Rather, the Bible, in both Old and New Testaments, does uphold capital punishment for murder. This is clear for at least two reasons. First, the origin of capital punishment for the crime of murder comes from God's words to Noah:

> *I will surely require your blood of your lives; at the hand of every animal I will require it. At the hand of man, even at the hand of every man's brother, I will require the life of man. <u>Whoever sheds man's blood, his blood will be shed by man, for God made man in His own image</u>.* (Genesis 9:5–7)

This command from God, given to Noah, comes *before the Law is given to Moses*. This means that it is *designed for all people*, and not just the nation of Israel. Also, the rationale that God gives for capital punishment in cases of murder is that man is created *"in the image of God."* To murder anyone, at any time in world history, is to shed the

---

[5] Interestingly, one of the first major voices in Western civilization against capital punishment was that of atheist Jeremy Bentham (1748-1832). Yet his utilitarian ethics, especially as applied to civil government, also deeply influenced the Western world towards the legalization of homosexuality and same-sex "marriages." See Kevin Swanson, *Apostate: The Men who Destroyed the Christian West* (Parker, Colorado: Generations with Vision, 2013), 86-94.

blood of an image bearer, and, therefore, to forfeit one's own blood. God gave this command as a timeless one.

Secondly, let us keep in mind that capital punishment is also *a New Testament teaching*. The Apostle Paul wrote Romans 13, to be sure, but let us remember that the Holy Spirit, the Spirit of Jesus, is the ultimate Author of Romans 13. Therefore, it is not just Paul speaking in Romans 13; it is, in the end, Jesus who is speaking in Romans 13:

> *...for [the governing authority] is a servant of God to you for good. But if you do that which is evil, be afraid, for he does not <u>bear the sword</u> in vain; for he is a servant of God, <u>an avenger for wrath to him who does evil</u>.* (Romans 13:4)

Jesus wrote these words. He says that the government of a land has the responsibility to use the *"sword"* when it needs to. And He says *"sword"* rather than "prison door" because He means, amongst other things, capital punishment. When a citizen of a nation commits murder, the governing authority of that nation has the obligation to exercise the sword of capital punishment. This is God's law concerning murder.

So how big is the deathblow of murder? It is big enough to require the return deathblow of capital punishment. God is very serious about this.

Former Nazi leaders are convicted of horrific crimes against the Jews during the Holocaust in Germany. Some of these crimes involve torture, and all of them involve murder. Should the Nazi leaders face the death sentence for their crimes? Exodus 21 gives a very clear answer to this question.

Saddam Hussein is captured, after years of slaughtering thousands upon thousands of innocent people in his own country of Iraq. Should Saddam Hussein have been put to death for his murderous crimes? The Bible says, "Yes. The deathblow of murder is that severe."

Of course, some Christians will object to this line of biblical reasoning. They will say that governments should "turn the other cheek" at murder. They will argue that we can magnify the grace of the Gospel by eliminating capital punishment from society, even in the face of murder.

But this is simply not true. The truth is that *when we shirk capital punishment, we actually belittle God's grace, rather than magnify it.* For, in the Bible, capital punishment is a grace. It is a grace in that it serves as a severe warning about the gravity of murder. It publishes a message to society that the deathblow of murder is much, much more evil than we like to think that it is. And it also issues to all people, everywhere, the warning that, lest they think that capital punishment is overly severe, Hell is a million times more severe.

The Deathblows of Servant Murder and Abortion

But what about a servant? Perhaps capital punishment is merited for the murder of a citizen. But what about the murder of a servant? Did not the ancient world view servants as less valuable than freemen? And if so, would the murder of a servant merit a lesser punishment?

> *If a man strikes his servant or his maid with a rod, and he dies under his hand, he shall surely be [avenged]. Notwithstanding, if he gets up after a day or two, he shall not be [avenged], for he is his [silver].* (Exodus 21:20–21)

Correct Bible translation skills are really crucial here. Some modern translations make it sound as if the murdered servant's master only faces punishment for the murder (perhaps a slap on the wrist or a monetary fine?), but not capital punishment. These translations see the servant as property, and not a man or woman with full human rights.⁶ But this is not the right way to translate verses 20-21. Rather, the right way to translate verses 20-21 is to hear that the murdered servant will be *"avenged."* And this changes things dramatically, for the idea of *"vengeance"* on behalf of a murdered servant certainly means *capital punishment for the master*. That is, in the Bible, the one on whom *"vengeance"* falls is inevitably put to death:

> *Set yourselves in array against Babylon all around, all you who bend the bow; shoot at her, spare no arrows: for she has sinned against the LORD. Shout against her all around: she has submitted herself; her bulwarks are fallen, her walls are thrown down; for it is <u>the vengeance</u> of the LORD: <u>take vengeance</u> on her; <u>as she has done, do to her</u>.* (Jeremiah 50:14–15)

Also,

> *Let the saints rejoice in honor. Let them sing for joy on their beds. May the high praises of God be in their mouths, and <u>a two-edged sword</u> in their hand; <u>to execute vengeance</u> on the nations, and punishments on the peoples.* (Psalm 149:5–7)

In the Bible, vengeance puts wicked people to death. Therefore, vengeance for the murdered servant is not a slap on the master's

---

⁶ The NIV translation of Exodus 21:21 (following the KJV) reads, "…*but they are not to be <u>punished</u> if the slave recovers after a day or two, since the slave is their <u>property</u>.*" This makes it sound as if the masters are merely to be "punished" (that is, they do not face capital punishment) when they murder their servants; and, if their servants do not die after they strike and injure them, they are not to be "punished" at all! Yet the Hebrew text should be translated as *"avenged"* (referring to the injured servant) rather than *"punished"* (referring to the guilty master). Also, the Hebrew text literally says *"silver"* rather than *"property."* The ESV gets this right: "*But if the slave survives a day or two, he is not <u>to be avenged</u>, for the slave is his <u>money</u>.*" This is significant because the point of Exodus 21:20-21 is that the murder of a servant by his master requires that the slain servant be *"avenged"* (through capital punishment), while the injury of a servant, though it does not require vengeance (since the servant survives), nevertheless requires that the servant, who is the master's *"silver"* (that is, the master has purchased his work/servitude and thus has heavily invested his own money into him), be set free! His compensation for the crime committed against him is his freedom from servitude. This is in line with Exodus 21:11: *"And if he does not do these three for [his female servant], then she shall <u>go out free, without paying [silver]</u>."* Note also the parallel passages in Exodus 21:26-27: *"If a man strikes the eye of his male or female servant, and destroys it, he shall <u>let him go free for the sake of his eye</u>. And if he knocks out the tooth of his male or female servant, he shall <u>let him go free for the sake of his tooth</u>."*

wrist. The word *"avenged"* is, in many ways, a stronger word than the previous phrase used in Exodus 21 to describe capital punishment, the phrase *"put to death."* This hints at the fact that the murder of one's own servant is *even more severe* than more typical kinds of murder, since the servant is more vulnerable than the freeman. What this means is that *servants require extra protection by God from deathblows, for they are more vulnerable members of society.*

What, then, of the baby in the womb? If servants are protected from murder by God's law, and protected with a vengeance, then what about preborn children?

> *If men fight and hurt <u>a pregnant woman</u> so that she gives birth prematurely, and yet no [calamity]*[7] *follows, he shall be surely fined as much as the woman's husband demands and the judges allow. But if any [calamity] follows, then you must take life for life....* (Exodus 21:22–23)

Just as was the case with the previous verses on the murder of a servant, these verses about the preborn can be translated and interpreted in two opposite directions. The Revised Standard Version (RSV) translation of the Bible takes the liberal position in this debate, translating the *"gives birth prematurely"* clause in verse 22 as a *"miscarriage."* The RSV's (grossly inaccurate!) translation envisions two men fighting, when during their struggle one of the men strikes a pregnant woman. In the RSV's view, the woman *"miscarries"* her child in verse 22, but is, herself, not injured. Therefore, according to liberal theology, there is no murder, here, since the miscarried child is not yet "a full person." This is proved, they say, by the fact that the only punishment commanded for this event is a monetary fine. Had the child been an actual "person," the event would have been a murder, and the punishment for the crime would have been a capital one.

But this, itself, is a murderous interpretation of these verses of Holy Scripture. Consider how Thomas McDaniel, a theologian writing from his current teaching position at a professing Evangelical

---

[7] The usage of the Hebrew term *'āsôn* in Genesis 42:4, 38; 44:29 requires a meaning for the term that is much more severe than *"harm"* (as the WEB and NKJV translate it in Exodus 21:22-23). The Hebrew term implies a horrible loss or death. Therefore, *"calamity"* seems to be a much better translation for it here. Thus Ludwig Koehler and Walter Baumgartner, *The Hebrew and Aramaic Lexicon of the Old Testament* (2 Vol. Study Edition; Leiden: Brill, 2001), 1:73, suggest the translation of *'āsôn*, in all of these biblical occurrences, as *"fatal accident."*

seminary, *uses Exodus 21:22 to craft a pro-abortion doctrine from it.* He says, "…in Mosaic law a woman's fertilized egg or an imperfectly formed fetus was not considered to be a person. Only a fetus that was 'fully formed' was recognized as a person."[8]

This is worse than murderous. It is twisting the very Word of God in order to justify abortion. And it is blatantly wrong. Arrogantly following the RSV translation, McDaniel recklessly fails to disclose to the reader that the Hebrew language has words for "stillborn child" and "miscarriage" that *are utterly absent from Exodus 21:22*, even though the Hebrew word for "miscarriage" appears only two chapters later:

No one will <u>miscarry</u> or be barren in your land. I will fulfill the number of your days. (Exodus 23:26)

Moses, then, obviously knew the Hebrew word for "miscarriage," and the fact that he did not employ it in Exodus 21:22 means that *he was not thinking about miscarriage in this verse.* He was, instead, thinking about the baby *"coming out"* of his mother's womb, *fully alive,* which is why the crime in verse 22 is not a capital crime.

The proper interpretation of Exodus 21:22-23, then, is that the baby does not die in the event of verse 22—the case in which a *"calamity"* does not occur—and it is only in the contrary event, in verse 23—the case in which a *"calamity"* does occur—that the baby dies as a result of the blow. In other words, when verse 22 says that the baby *"comes out"* or is born *"prematurely,"* it has in mind a case in which the baby lives and thrives. However, when verse 23 refers to the occurrence of a *"calamity,"* it describes the case in which the baby is seriously injured, or even dies from the blow. This, in turn, explains both the absence of capital punishment from verse 22 (for, the baby was not seriously injured in this case) and the presence of capital punishment in verse 23 (for, the baby, being seriously injured in this case, sometimes does die, and thus is murdered).

Therefore, the right way to translate verses 22-25 is as follows:

---

[8] Thomas F. McDaniel, "The Septuagint Has the Correct Translation of Exodus 21:22-23," online paper (not published elsewhere), 2012, n.p. [cited 29 July 2013]. Online: http://tmcdaniel.palmerseminary.edu/LXX_EXO_%2021_22-23.pdf. McDaniel is an Emeritus Professor of Old Testament at Palmer Theological Seminary.

> *If men fight and hurt a pregnant woman so that she gives birth prematurely, and yet <u>no calamity</u> [meaning, "<u>no serious injury to, or no death of the baby</u>"] follows, he shall be surely fined as much as the woman's husband demands and the judges allow. But if <u>a calamity</u> [meaning, "<u>serious injury to, or death of the baby</u>"] follows, then you must take <u>life for life</u>, eye for eye, tooth for tooth, hand for hand, foot for foot, burning for burning, wound for wound, and bruise for bruise.* (Exodus 21:22–25)

Here, then, is the broad picture of Exodus 21. Every murder is a deathblow that God hates, and must be answered with the deathblow of capital punishment. Specifically, however, the murder of a servant or the murder of a preborn child is particularly wicked, for the servant and the preborn child *are weaker and more vulnerable than other people*. In other words, God protects all people from the deathblow of murder, but God particularly guards, with a vengeance, the servant and the preborn. He says, in effect, in Exodus 21, "Thou shall not murder, lest thou be put to death." But He also adds special emphasis on protecting the weakest of the weak when He says, in effect, in Exodus 21, "Thou shall not murder the servant or the preborn, lest thou be put to death *with a vengeance.*"

This severe warning from Exodus 21 against murdering the baby in the womb lines up well with the general wrath of God against all child sacrifice in the Bible:

> *Moreover, you shall tell the children of Israel, "Anyone of the children of Israel, or of the strangers who live as foreigners in Israel, who gives any of his offspring to Molech [via child sacrifice]; <u>he shall surely be put to death</u>. The people of the land shall stone him with stones."* (Leviticus 20:2)

And where does the punishment for unrepentant, willful abortion, and unrepentant, willful advocacy of abortion appear in the New Testament? There are passages in the New Testament that may deal more directly with the murder of babies. For example, Luke 1:44 is written in such a way as to protect, deliberately, the "personhood" of babies in the womb.[9] And the Apostolic Decree to the Gentiles in Acts 15 may, in fact, include a direct prohibition against infanticide.[10]

---

[9] See Chapter 10, "The Baby Leaped! Elizabeth, Mary, and Preborn Children."
[10] David Instone-Brewer, "Infanticide and the Apostolic Decree of Acts 15," *Journal of the Evangelical Theological Society* 52:2 (June 2009): 301-21.

But in general in the New Testament, abortion falls under the category of murder:

> *But for the cowardly, unbelieving, sinners, abominable, <u>murderers</u>, sexually immoral, sorcerers, idolaters, and all liars, their part is in the lake that burns with fire and sulfur, which is <u>the second death</u>.* (Revelation 21:8)

In contemporary terms, this means that we must put the 2012 fatal shooting of twenty children (mostly six-year-olds) at Sandy Hook Elementary School in Newtown, Connecticut, side by side with the reality of a licensed physician who is teaching OB/GYN medical residents how to perform abortions. America's current president does not want to put these things side by side, but Exodus 21 demands that we do so. And when we compare the Sandy Hook shooting, which was incomprehensibly horrific (and the horror of it should not be minimized one bit), with a medical resident being taught how to perform abortions, Exodus 21 says that the abortion performed by the teaching physician is just as heinous a crime. Both horrors deserve the death penalty,[11] and both horrors are punishable by God with a vengeance, for both of them involve the murdering of *the weakest of the weak*, in cold blood.

How big is the deathblow of abortion? It is big enough to be a capital offense in the Bible, but more than that, it is one of *the worst* of capital offenses in the Bible. There are degrees of sin. There are degrees of murder. Abortion is of the highest degree, for abortion is the killing of the most vulnerable of human beings.

Roe v. Wade happened in America partly because of a great lie. The lie is that abortion ought to be made legal because, whether legal or not, women will have abortions. And since back-alley abortions are dangerous for the mother, we ought to protect women's lives by providing sterile abortions for them.

The Bible says that such reasoning is clouded by a dark and murderous lie. The lie is that abortion *ought* to be made safe. Much to the contrary, God's Word says that abortion *ought* to be considered a

---

[11] In this regard, let us not forget the political axiom given to us by William Wilberforce, *A Letter on the Abolition of the Slave Trade: Addressed to the Freeholders and Other Inhabitants of Yorkshire* (London: Luke Hansard & Sons, 1807), 73, while reflecting on his fight for the abolition of the Slave Trade: "…*from law* arises security" (emphasis added).

capital offense in every nation (at the very least with regards to the physician or practitioner who performs or prescribes the abortion), and it *ought* to be dangerous for the abortion-seeking parents. Just as murdering two-year-olds ought to be considered a life-threatening action for the murderer, and just as suicide bombing is inherently dangerous for the suicide bomber, so too willful, informed, voluntary abortion ought to be dangerous both for the physician or practitioner and for the abortion-seeking parents. It is an informed physician or practitioner and informed parents willfully and voluntarily murdering a child.[12]

The crime of abortion is a capital crime. God, Himself, says so. Therefore, every OB/GYN physician must tremble before this decree of God, and vow to protect life in the womb. Every abortion-hungry boyfriend of a pregnant girlfriend, or abortion-focused father of a pregnant daughter must immediately repent, and recant, with holy fear. The biblical truth is that those who perform or prescribe medical or chemical abortions are murderers. Those who push women towards abortion (e.g. by lecturing, as a professor on a university campus, in favor of abortion) and those who seek to coax expectant mothers into abortion are guilty of murderous intent. Thus the laws of any nation that claims to be a just nation ought to reflect these truths. The purest statutes regarding abortion are those that *protect women from the abortion "option,"* so that women are guarded, by law, from the lustful and manipulative coercions of perverse and wicked men.

These are heavy, prohibitive truths. Yet the gravity of Exodus 21 also teaches us, positively, how to see babies in the womb as God sees them—as amongst His most prized possessions, whom He guards more fiercely than any other. God protects all people from murder, but especially the preborn. This is because God delights in the vulnerability, dependency, fragility, and beauty of the little ones in the womb. He watches them kick and burp in the womb. He, alone, can see their growth in the womb in vivid, real-life ways. God is the One who prompts mothers to talk to their preborn children, and

---

[12] The present author here *does not* direct this grave statement towards mothers who have been coerced, deceived, or even physically forced into having abortions. He also *does not* direct this statement towards fathers who have sought, with tears, to prevent the abortion of their own preborn offspring, but whose pleadings were cruelly ignored. The grave guilt in such cases lies elsewhere.

God is the One who hears those preborn children coo whenever they hear their own mothers' voices. And when they leap and play in the womb, and only God sees them do it (though, of course, the mothers may feel it), it is God who smiles upon them with joy. Jesus loves the little babies in the womb.

THE **D**EATHBLOW TO **A**BORTION THROUGH THE **G**OSPEL

The deathblow of abortion is severe; it demands capital punishment:

> *But if a calamity [meaning, "serious injury to, or death of the baby"] follows, then you must take <u>life for life</u>, <u>eye for eye</u>, <u>tooth for tooth</u>, hand for hand, foot for foot, burning for burning, wound for wound, and bruise for bruise.* (Exodus 21:23–25)

Yet millions of women have had abortions, legally, in America, since 1973. If over 50,000,000 babies have been legally murdered on American soil, this also means that millions of fathers and mothers have aborted their own babies on American soil.

So where does the Bible leave them? Are they simply to be left as murderers? Does the Bible leave them there, legally condemned, and thus without any hope? It is simply, "an eye for an eye, a tooth for a tooth, and a life for a life?" Is justice so exacting that those who have committed murder, through abortion, are left with only an everlasting death sentence hanging over their heads?

Praise be to God that this is not the case. Praise be to our Lord Jesus that the crime of abortion can be forgiven through the power of the Cross.

> *David's anger burned hot against the man, and he said to Nathan, "As the* L<small>ORD</small> *lives, <u>the man who has done this deserves to die</u>!"* (2 Samuel 12:5)

David demanded the death sentence for the murderer, once Nathan told him the parable about the murderer. But then Nathan sprung the trap of the parable on David, exposing David, himself, as the murderer. David had taken Uriah's wife and had murdered Uriah. Thus he ought to have been put to death. Yet God spared him. Instead of David being put to death, it would be a child, a son, who would *"surely die"* on account of David's murder. And just as this son died, as it were, in David's place, so too the Son of God has died in the place of all murderers who will repent of their sins and believe upon His name:

> *However, because by this deed you have given great occasion to the LORD's enemies to blaspheme, <u>the child</u> also who is born to you <u>will surely die</u>.* (2 Samuel 12:14)

    Fathers and mothers, millions of them, live in America today with the blood of abortion on their hands. Some of them are calloused and unrepentant. They reject God's grace and oppose the Gospel of God. They trample upon the blood of the Son of God. Therefore, their murderous acts will be avenged on the great and dreadful Day of the Lord. At the final Judgment, the blood of the preborn will be on their heads.

    Still, there are those fathers and mothers who hear the truth about abortion and desperately want forgiveness for their crimes against their own offspring. They see the blood on their hands, and they cry out to God for their guilty stains somehow to be removed. They cannot go back in time and undo what they have done, but they plead for mercy and forgiveness, and long to see their preborn children someday, in the future, in Heaven.

    For these parents, there is astounding hope. Yet the hope of the Gospel is not that justice will be cast aside. The Gospel of Christ does not teach that murderers are given a slap on the wrist, and then all is forgiven. Rather, the Gospel of Christ teaches that Someone Else is able to pay the justice penalty for their crimes. Murderers deserve not only capital punishment, but everlasting punishment. And yet Christ, in His amazing love for them, takes that punishment in their place.

    Once this transaction happens, by faith, wherein guilty criminals allow the death of Jesus on the Cross to become the payment for their crimes against God and against their fellow human beings, including the crime of abortion, their sins are washed away. And the permanence of this forgiveness is astounding: their sins are cast into the ocean, never to be brought to the surface again.

    From the opposite vantage point, once their parents become Christians, aborted babies, who are in Heaven, are no longer *witnesses against* their parents. Rather, they now become *advocates for* their parents in Christ. They wait, in Heaven, for the day when they can greet their parents, in love and joy, in the Kingdom of God. Only the Gospel of God can accomplish this kind of glorious forgiveness, and glorious reunion.

In the Bible, God greatly employs former murderers in His Kingdom. God loves former murderers, made clean by the blood of Christ, just as He loved the Apostle Paul:

But Saul, still <u>breathing threats and [murder]</u> against the disciples of the Lord, went to the high priest, and asked for letters from him to the synagogues of Damascus, that if he found any who were of the Way, whether men or women, he might bring them bound to Jerusalem. (Acts 9:1-2)

Saul was murderous. Yet Christ transformed him, by the Gospel, into a great missionary, whom God loved. The Father in Heaven changed Saul's name to Paul, gave him a new life and a grand purpose, and loved him all the way to his martyrdom—his life had become a drink offering, poured out for the glory of God—in Rome.

Justice demands an eye for an eye, a tooth for a tooth, and a life for a life. But the Gospel is that Jesus gave His perfect, sinless life in place of our guilty, sinful lives. Abortion takes life, but Jesus gives life. There shall be, according to biblical justice, an eye for an eye and a tooth for a tooth, but the Gospel is that God gives us the life of His only-begotten Son, in place of the deathblow of abortion.

How big, then, is the deathblow of abortion? It is as big as the Cross. It takes the Cross of Jesus Christ to overcome the sting of abortion. There is no other way to be healed from it. No psychology, and no personal counseling can do this. Nothing in our human society has the power to heal our land from abortion. Only the Cross of Christ is big enough to do it.

Christ is crucified at Calvary. Therefore, abortion can be nailed to the Cross and our land can be cleansed of its bloodshed, if we, as a nation, will repent before the Savior who bled for us on the Cross.

Christ is risen from the dead. The tomb is empty. Therefore, those children who have received the deathblow of abortion in our land will, at the resurrection of the dead, rise again. They shall arise, like a mighty army, and the mortal blow of abortion shall be shown to have power over them no more. Under the triumphal banner of

Christ's resurrection, the preborn saints who have been murdered through abortion shall arise as a great choir, a victorious multitude, and they shall sing of the glory of their Shepherd and of their God, and the sound of their voices will be as the sound of rushing waters, and the voice of mighty waters, singing, "Hallelujah! For the Lord our God, the Almighty, reigns!"

7

DAVID'S LITTLE BOY:
Bereavement and Preborn Children

(2 Samuel 12:15-23)

Nathan departed to his house.

The LORD struck the child that Uriah's wife bore to David, and [the child] was very sick. David therefore begged God for the child; and David fasted, and went in, and lay all night on the ground. The elders of his house arose beside him, to raise him up from the earth: but he would not, and he did not eat bread with them. On the seventh day, the child died. David's servants were afraid to tell him that the child was dead, for they said, "Behold, while the child was yet alive, we spoke to him, and he did not listen to our voice. How will he then harm himself, if we tell him that the child is dead?"

But when David saw that his servants were whispering together, David perceived that the child was dead; and David said to his servants, "Is the child dead?"

They said, "He is dead."

Then David arose from the earth, and washed, and anointed himself, and changed his clothing; and he came into the LORD's house, and [bowed down]. Then he came to his own house; and when he requested, they set bread before him, and he ate. Then his servants said to him, "What is this that you have done? You fasted and wept for the child while he was alive, but when the child was dead, you rose up and ate bread."

He said, "While the child was yet alive, I fasted and wept; for I said, 'Who knows whether the LORD will not be gracious to me, that the child may live?' But now he is dead, why should I fast? Can I bring him back again? I will go to him, but he will not return to me." (2 Samuel 12:15–23)

The parks and hillsides of our towns and cities are not full, but relatively empty. They should be brimming with little children. Sure, there are toddlers stumbling up the stairs of most public playground sets. And yes, there are hives of child-sized soccer jerseys swarming around on most public soccer fields. Nevertheless, for every child that we see playing in the grass, romping up a rugged hill, or picking wildflowers near a stream, there are many unseen children who are missing.

Not a few of these unseen children have been denied the right to exist, altogether, since the modern contraception culture has barred them from conception. Others of these unseen children have died not at the hands of men, but rather through miscarriage, according to God's providence.[1] Yet far too many of these unseen children have been killed, through abortion, while they were still in their mothers' wombs.

The modern world is thus, in many ways, a global war zone that deceives itself into thinking that it is living in an age of relative peace. Children dress up in their winter formal attire in order to sing secularized holiday songs in their chorales, while their parents applaud them, proudly cooing over their well-groomed offspring. Yet the truth, which is never acknowledged in such high-brow social circles, is that the chorale, itself, represents a remnant. The children singing on stage are merely the survivors. Some of their siblings have been slain, legally, and in a sanitized fashion, by their own fathers and mothers.

The same is true of the university campus. At the university, undergraduate students walk to their classes on red-brick pathways, outlined by flowerbeds filled with daisies and mums, and they read their textbooks under green, spreading oak trees. Yet while their professors wax eloquent about issues of globalization and social justice, the students, themselves, are never told by their teachers that they are a remnant, a lonely group of survivors. They plunder the rich resources of the modern world, not having to share them quite like their great-grandparents once did, only because many of their peers

---

[1] This passing reference to miscarriage is not made with indifference. Rather, miscarriage is a wound to a parent's heart that is so severe as to be a permanent one, this side of Heaven. The Church's need to exercise extreme compassion towards those fathers and mothers in this world who have suffered through the bereavement of miscarriage is discussed, in detail, below.

were slaughtered while they were still in the womb. The survival of the fittest—which is Darwin's great lie—has played out on the battlefield of abortion, and the survivors, themselves, have been bereaved of their own sisters and brothers.

Now is not the time for rejoicing. It is the time for grieving. Those who love themselves, firstly, and worship themselves, proudly, are those who rejoice today. They eat, drink, and are merry, saying to themselves, "Let us suck the marrow out of life, today, for tomorrow we die." Yet tomorrow will come for them, closing in upon them like a trap. If they do not repent, then, in the not-too-distant future, they will grieve and gnash their teeth, in Hell.

Yet for those who fear God, it is the time for grieving. We must learn how to grieve the loss of little children in our world. We need to come to view our modern society not as a rich, iconic dream world, full of exotic foods and spices, and the thrills of sterilized, electronic adventures, the very utopian triumph of modern science and engineering. Rather, Christians must become aware of the judgments of God that are falling upon our increasingly Babylonian world. People in the New Babylon have forsaken the fruitfulness of the womb, and so they have been given over to the judgments foretold by the Prophet:

No birth, no one with child, and no conception….Their root has dried up. They will bear no fruit. (Hosea 9:11, 16)[2]

Therefore, the glory of Christians in an age of unprecedented bereavement of babies in the womb is not their ability to "turn lemons into lemonade." The "don't worry, be happy" spirituality of false teachers who name the name of Christ, but who promote a Gospel devoid of intense Christian suffering and intense divine wrath, is nothing less than heretical. Instead, the glory of Christians in this horrific age of globalized abortion is our unique ability to grieve and mourn, in God-centered ways, on behalf of preborn children. We herald God's coming glory in the New Heavens and

---

[2] In context, these judgments include bereavements of children who are born, too. And, yes, they originally spoke to Israel, in her idolatrous rebellion against God. Yet the New Testament pattern is that God's judgments tend to have multiple fulfillments, and they become more and more global the closer that we get to the Second Coming of Christ.

New Earth whenever we shed distinctly Christian tears for the little ones in the womb.

DAVID'S CHASTISEMENT

Nathan departed to his house. The LORD struck the child that Uriah's wife bore to David, and [the child] was very sick....On the seventh day, the child died....Then David arose from the earth, and washed, and anointed himself, and changed his clothing; and he came into the LORD's house, and [bowed down]. (2 Samuel 12:15, 18a, 20a-b)

King David is not like his predecessor, King Saul. David is a brave warrior, a man after God's own heart (1 Samuel 13:14; Acts 13:22), while Saul is a coward and spiritual rebel, who is rejected by God (1 Samuel 15:23). Still, David, much like Saul, has to face God's chastisement. It is God who appoints the kings of Israel. So it is God who also chastens the kings of Israel.

Having been anointed unto kingship, David must face God's chastisement. He has taken the sacred responsibility of kingship and used it for evil. King David has committed adultery with Bathsheba, and has murdered Uriah, her husband, in order to conceal his adultery. Thus, like Saul before him, he must face the chastening hand of the Lord.

There are two similarities between Saul's chastisement and David's own chastisement. The first involves the verb "to strike." David, in his earlier, youthful state, trusted that he need not lift his own sword to strike down Saul, who was persecuting him (in fact, David shielded himself from the sin of striking down God's anointed), since God would, in time, come with a judgment on David's behalf and strike down Saul, Himself:

David said, "As the LORD lives, <u>the LORD will strike him</u>; or his day shall come to die; or he shall go down into battle and perish." (1 Samuel 26:10)

Yet the chastening *"strike"* of the Lord, which eventually did fall upon Saul, also comes David's way, but in a different manner. After David has murdered Uriah, the chastening strike of the Lord falls upon David's own offspring:

David's Little Boy

<u>The LORD struck the child</u> that Uriah's wife bore to David, and [the child] was very sick. (2 Samuel 12:15)

God chastens His kings. He brings them into His own courts of justice. He strikes down Saul for all of his murderous crimes against David and his supporters, and for his idolatrous disobedience towards God's own commandments. Yet He also chastens David. He *"strikes"* David's child, on account of David's dual crimes of adultery and murder, such that the child dies—despite David's fasting and pleading before God for the sparing of the child's life. Both Saul and David fall under the Lord's chastisement.

The second similarity between Saul's chastisement and David's own chastisement is the way in which both men acknowledge God's right to discipline them. When God sends Samuel, unexpectedly, to interrupt the divination of the medium of En Dor (whom Saul has sought out), Saul is both terrified, and ashamed. He yields to Samuel's rebuke. He recognizes God's authority over him (yet without a changed heart) by *"bowing down"* before Him:

He said to [the medium], "What does he look like?"

She said, "An old man comes up. He is covered with a robe." Saul perceived that it was Samuel, and he [stooped] with his face to the ground, and <u>[bowed down]</u>. (1 Samuel 28:14)

In the same way, David perceives that the death of his son is a result of God's severe chastisement upon him. Responding to God's chastisement as Saul did (yet with sincerity, and thus without Saul's hypocrisy), David *"bows down"* before God, yielding to Him in deep, broken-hearted repentance and worship:

On the seventh day, the child died.... Then David arose from the earth, and washed, and anointed himself, and changed his clothing; and he came into the LORD's house, and <u>[bowed down]</u>. (2 Samuel 12:18a, 20a-b)

David, like Saul before him,[3] commits murder. And David, like Saul, *"bows down"* under the chastening hand of God. Yet David, *unlike* Saul, responds to God's discipline with a truly repentant heart

---

[3] For example, Saul murders the priests of the LORD in 1 Samuel 22:11-21.

(Psalm 51:17). Thus his broken-hearted act of *"bowing down"* (in contrast to Saul's empty act of *"bowing down"*) is an example for all who have committed great crimes against God, and yet truly desire to repent of them. Even horrific crimes can be atoned for under the mercy of the Gospel of God.

The crime of abortion brings with it God's chastening hand. Like David, those who are involved in abortion are oftentimes guilty of both sexual immorality (in David's case, adultery; in their case, fornication or adultery) and cover-up murder (in David's case, the cover-up murder of Uriah; in their case, the cover-up murder of the baby). Like David, therefore, those have committed acts involving abortion and who, subsequently, feel God's chastening hand upon them—perhaps physically, but oftentimes more spiritually—ought to submit, broken-heartedly, to His loving chastisement. If they will submit to the angry rebuke of God regarding their abortion-related sins by choosing to repent, humbly, of their deeds (rather than proudly refusing to acknowledge the horrific nature of their crimes), they will find Him to be *such a merciful God* that even their great sins can be forgiven by His grace, through faith in the atoning blood of Christ Jesus.

There are Christians in this world who, very regrettably, have committed sins leading up to, and including abortion. Yet their Christian faith is evident in the fact that they respond to God's chastening hand upon them (on account of their crimes) not like Saul (whose repentance was self-centered and phony), but more like David. They humbly bow down on their faces before God, in true, heart-rending repentance. They acknowledge the kingship of Christ and submit to His divine rebuke. These are the ones who love much, for they know that they have been forgiven much. They understand the vast magnitude of God's mercy that is able to cover over both David's horrific sins, and their own.

JOB'S BEREAVEMENT

Yes, but there is a great need for caution here. Bereavement in the Christian life, and especially the incalculable pain that Christian parents face whenever they lose their own children, *is not to be equated, recklessly, with God's chastisement.* While David's bereavement of a baby boy was due to God's hand of chastisement upon him, Job's bereavement of his own children was certainly not!

In fact, the book of Job exists to refute the simplistic, reckless theology that equates parental bereavement with God's chastisement. Specifically, when Job's "friends" (who really turn out to be envious foes) accost Job with the false teaching that his sufferings must have been caused by his hidden sins, God vindicates Job by demonstrating that his great tribulations have *not* been a result of divine chastisement:

> *There was a man in the land of Uz, whose name was Job. That man was <u>blameless and upright</u>, and one who <u>feared God, and turned away from evil</u>.* (Job 1:1)

What is so exemplary about Job is that although he knows that his bereavements—the worst of which have been the sudden deaths of all ten of his own children—are *not* divine judgments for heinous, hidden sins in his life, he nevertheless accepts them, by faith, as sanctifying sufferings. That is, there is both a contrast and a similarity between David and Job. David, being *guilty* of great crimes against God, *"bows down"* after recognizing God's *judgmental chastisement* upon him; Job, being *innocent* of great crimes[4] against God,[5] still chooses to *"bow down"* after recognizing God's *sanctifying sufferings* ordained for him:

> *Then Job arose, and tore his robe, and shaved his head, and <u>[bowed] down</u> on the ground, and worshiped. He said, "Naked I came out of my mother's womb, and naked shall I return there. The LORD gave, and the LORD has taken away. Blessed be the LORD's name."* (Job 1:20-21)

There are, then, many piercing trials and sufferings in the Christian life that have been ordained by God, and yet have nothing

---

[4] There is, no doubt, a sense in which all sins are "great crimes" against God (James 2:10). However, the phrase "great crimes" is used here to connote degrees of sin, such that particularly heinous and blatant crimes against God oftentimes do, in fact, evoke His direct and immediate judgments.

[5] The Bible does not suggest that Job is sinless. However, it does suggest that his faith in God has propelled him into righteousness (or, in New Testament terms, "sanctification") of a very high order, such that his sufferings *cannot* be said to be the result of God's judgmental chastisement upon him.

to do with God's chastisement. They are, rather, sanctifying sufferings. For strong believers in the Lord, tribulations and sorrows are, more often than not, sanctifying sufferings, ordained by God to make us holy. Our faith is purified by them, much as gold or silver is refined by the fiery furnace.

Bereavement is filled with suffering. As such, it sanctifies us, as believers. It plunges us into the kind of grief and suffering that will, through the compassionate and tender work of His Spirit in us, press us closer to God and remove more of the dross of "autonomy" from our hearts.

It must be said, however, that the sanctifying nature of bereavement is not to be used, callously, in order to seek to comfort the bereaved. Pastorally speaking, Romans 8:28, *"We know that all things work together for good for those who love God,"* is not an appropriate verse to quote to the bereaved.[6] Doing so only trivializes the actual pain of bereavement. It is much like someone saying to Jesus, when He was on the Cross, "Well, do not dwell on the pain of this. God will, in the end, use it for much good." Such recklessness is not only misguided; it is also inhumane and heartless.

It is individual believers, themselves, who must seek God, intimately and personally, in order to work out the agonizing "Why, O Lord, did You allow this to happen?" and "Why do You, O God, allow such dear loved ones to be taken away?" questions of Christian bereavement. Yet these questions are not easy to sort out in the midst of bereavement. When a wife has lost her husband, or when a son has lost his mother, the pain is so great as to preclude much abstract reflection. The head is assaulted by the storms of the heart. Therefore, only after the storms of mourning (which are violent storms) have subsided, can the believer begin to think through the gracious aspects of God's sanctifying sufferings.

This is no easy path. The strongest man of faith will find himself undone by the loss of his dearest relation. To *"bow down"* before God, in submission to Him, even when His providence has ordained the greatest of bereavements, is an act of faith that feels, at the time when the pain is at its peak, virtually impossible to do.

---

[6] This precious verse of Scripture may, indeed, minister, very comfortingly, to the bereaved, but it is one thing for the bereaved to embrace it in his own Bible, and quite another for someone to quote it to him as if it were a quick fix to his pain.

We need, then, vast supplies of grace, from above, in order to make it through the horror of bereavement. In specific, we need the comfort of our Father in Heaven, the One who allowed His only-begotten Son to be *"cut off out of the land of the living"* (Isaiah 53:8), even by way of death on the Cross, for our sins. He, who grieved over the death of His Son, shedding the largest tears of Heaven on that great and dreadful day of the Crucifixion, knows how to comfort us in our bereavement.

We also need the Son of God to help us. He knew no sin. He was completely sinless before His Father. Yet He, who was sinless, nevertheless submitted, willingly, to the sufferings that had been ordained for Him by His Father. He is, therefore, able to help us through our own immense losses and pains:

…though he was a Son, <u>yet learned obedience by the things which He suffered</u>. (Hebrews 5:8)

Are you, beloved Reader, going through bereavement? Has your precious loved one been snatched, by the cruel hands of death, out of your arms? Do you feel that, while the world around you rejoices and celebrates the blessings of life, you have been consigned to an invisible prison of loneliness and grief?

If so, take heart in the knowledge that God is inviting you into the fellowship of His sufferings. Christ Jesus has scars. During His earthly life, He nursed many wounds. On the Cross, He was given new wounds, which the Roman soldiers made deep and terrible. He is a suffering Christ. His Kingship over us has been won through suffering. O precious Christian, O grieving Christian, know that He is sharing His wounds with you, in divine love. For, as William Tyndale (c. 1494-1536) puts it, "Tribulation for righteousness is not a blessing only. But also a gift that God give[s] unto none save [His] special friends."[7]

Also, in specific, if you, dear Reader, have been bereaved of *a child*, then know that God, the Father, invites you into the fellowship

---

[7] William Tyndale, *The Obedience of a Christian Man* (ed. David Daniell; London: Penguin Books, 2000), 9.

of His own sufferings. He, Himself, did not suffer on the Cross,[8] but He did suffer to see His Son on the Cross.[9] He suffered a mysterious, infinite kind of pain over the death of His beloved Son.[10] Thus, if you grieve over your own precious child who has been taken from you, then be assured that the Father understands your grief. He weeps with you. Or, better put, He invites you to weep with Him.

For the true Christian, bereavement is a mark of Christ upon one's life. It shows that we belong to Christ, the suffering Savior, and that we share in His scars and wounds. Your tears are His tears, and your pain is His pain. You have been invited into the sorrows of the Man of Sorrows:

> *...that I may know Him, and the power of His resurrection, and the fellowship of His sufferings, becoming conformed to His death; if by any means I may attain to the resurrection from the dead.* (Philippians 3:10-11)

Has Christ given you a scar? Has your deep wound of bereavement produced a large and permanent scar? If so, take heart, you who are loved by your Father in Heaven, for He has marked you as His own. The dearly loved children of the Father, those who are His most prized possessions, are the very ones whom He marks with such a scar:

---

[8] The Church Fathers, such as Athanasius, are adamant about the doctrine that *God the Father does not suffer on the Cross*. In saying this, they are not implying that God the Father never suffers (with respect to His creation). Rather, they are simply saying that we must distinguish between the Persons of the Godhead when we speak of "Who," exactly, died on the Cross. God the Son, and not God the Father, was the One on the Cross. We must believe this, lest we attribute physicality to God the Father. Thus Athanasius, *Statement of Faith* 2 (*NPNF*² 4:84), says, "Neither do we ascribe *the passible body* which He [the Son] bore for the salvation of the whole world to the Father" (emphasis added).

[9] For the reality that God does, indeed, suffer, note that He is "grieved" in both Genesis 6:6 and Isaiah 63:10.

[10] In this regard, listen to D.A. Carson, *How Long, O Lord? Reflections on Suffering and Evil* (2d ed.; Grand Rapids: Baker Academic, 2006), 165, responding to the "impassibility" doctrine of modern theologians (a doctrine which says that God cannot suffer): "With all respect to the many fine theologians who uphold this line of reasoning, I sharply disagree....The crucial question for this book can be simply put: Does God suffer? And if [He] does not, why does the Bible spend so much time depicting [Him] as if [He] does?"

> Hast thou no scar?
> No hidden scar on foot, or side, or hand?
> I hear thee sung as mighty in the land;
> I hear them hail thy bright, ascendant star.
> Hast thou no scar?
>
> Hast thou no wound?
> Yet I was wounded by the archers, spent,
> Leaned Me against a tree to die; and rent
> By ravening beasts that compassed Me, I swooned.
> Hast *thou* no wound?
>
> No wound? No scar?
> Yet, as the Master shall the servant be,
> And piercèd are the feet that follow Me.
> But thine are whole; can he have followed far
> Who has nor wound nor scar?[11]

Therefore, it is by grace that we humbly submit to God's sanctifying sufferings in bereavement. We trust Him, even as we grieve. Having been bereaved of loved ones, and especially when we have lost children, we, who worship Christ Jesus, wait upon Him to comfort us (2 Corinthians 1:3-5). We mourn, though not as those who are without hope:

> *For if we believe that Jesus died and rose again, even so God will bring with him those who have fallen asleep in Jesus.* (1 Thessalonians 4:14)

DAVID'S BEREAVEMENT AND PARENTAL WEEPING

How, then, do Christian parents weep, in a biblical manner, for their children who have been taken from them through death? What does it mean for Christian mothers who have miscarried children in the womb to weep for their little ones? And how do we, as Christians, teach the world to weep over the slaughter of children in the womb, which takes place through abortion?

---

[11] Amy Carmichael, *Mountain Breezes: The Collected Poems of Amy Carmichael* (ed. Elisabeth Elliot; Fort Washington, PA: Christian Literature Crusade, 1999), 173. "No Scar?" by Amy Carmichael, © 1999 by The Dohnavur Fellowship. Used by permission of CLC Publications. May not be further reproduced. All rights reserved.

King David is, indeed, a man after God's own heart. Part of what makes him such a man is his strong, Spirit-empowered inclination to weep for his dying baby boy:

> He said, "While the child was yet alive, I *fasted and wept*." (2 Samuel 12:22a)

Yet this introduces us to David's strange, unpredictable behavior. His actions are enigmatic. While the child is very sick, but still alive, he fasts and weeps for him. Yet once he learns that the child has died, David gets up off of the ground, washes, spruces himself up, and goes to the House of the Lord to worship. It is as if he celebrates the baby boy's death (at least, that is how his actions appear). One would expect his fasting and weeping to come *after* the boy's death, and not just prior to it. Also, one would *not* expect the King of Israel to wash himself and to perk up, so to speak, right upon receiving the news of the death of his child.

Why such strange behavior? The answer to this enigma eludes us until we finish listening to the historical account, in its entirety. Yet before that is accomplished, we first pause to reflect upon the sober reality that King David is a man who is used to weeping. The fact that he does not weep in the immediate interval after the death of his son is shocking and enigmatic precisely because his normal habit is to weep immensely for the deceased:

> Then David took hold on his clothes, and tore them; and all the men who were with him did likewise. They *mourned, wept, and fasted* until evening, *for Saul, and for Jonathan his son*, and for the people of the LORD, and for the house of Israel; because they had fallen by the sword. (2 Samuel 1:11–12)

It is the habit of righteous persons, who understand the love of God, to weep for the deceased. Lazarus, whom Jesus loves, becomes sick and, shortly thereafter, dies. Jesus weeps (John 11:35). Just like Jesus, David weeps over the death of his son Absalom, whom he loves:

> Joab was told, "Behold, the king *weeps and mourns for Absalom*." (2 Samuel 19:1)

David has learned this kind of weeping by imitating some of the great men and women of Scripture. He, too, reads the Bible. He watches his biblical heroes, especially in the Law of Moses, weep for their deceased loved ones. This is true, for example, with Abraham:

Sarah died in Kiriath Arba (also called Hebron), in the land of Canaan. Abraham came <u>to mourn for Sarah</u>, and <u>to weep for her</u>. (Genesis 23:2)

Jacob, also, is a man who weeps. When he is deceived into thinking that wild beasts have killed his beloved son, Joseph, he weeps for him:

Jacob tore his clothes, and put sackcloth on his waist, and <u>mourned for his son many days</u>. All his sons and all his daughters rose up to comfort him, but he refused to be comforted. He said, "For I will go down to Sheol to my son mourning." His father <u>wept for him</u>. (Genesis 37:34–35)

Righteous Hannah, the wife of Elkanah, weeps not for children whom she has lost, but for the children whom she has not been able to conceive:

As he did so year by year, when she went up to the LORD's house. Her rival provoked her; therefore she <u>wept, and did not eat</u>. Elkanah her husband said to her, "Hannah, <u>why do you weep</u>? Why do you not eat? Why is your heart grieved? Am I not better to you than ten sons?" (1 Samuel 1:7–8)

There is, in life, *"a time to weep"* (Ecclesiastes 3:4). David, following the patriarchs, shows us that this is especially true when our loved ones die. And, later in Scripture, this principle is elevated to its greatest heights when the deceased are children. The loss of children always summons godly people to weep for them:

The LORD says: A voice is heard in Ramah, <u>lamentation, and bitter weeping</u>, Rachel <u>weeping for her children</u>; she refuses to be comforted for her children, because they are no more. (Jeremiah 31:15)

Also,

> *For these things I <u>weep</u>; my eye, my eye <u>runs down with water</u>; because the comforter who should refresh my soul is far from me: <u>my children</u> are desolate, because the enemy has prevailed.* (Lamentations 1:16)

When a teenage son dies of leukemia, his father and mother weep, with uncontrollable weeping. When children die, in the midst of this turbulent and wicked world, their parents mourn and wail for them. The sobs of the daughters of Jerusalem, who wept for Jesus during His passion, are turned towards their own children (Luke 23:27-28). Christian people, whose hearts have been quickened by the Holy Spirit and made alive in the love of Christ Jesus, know how to weep, with passionate weeping, when their children die.

Yet Christians also learn how to weep for all of God's children, when they die. Elijah felt the searing pain of the death of the only son of the Widow of Zarephath, even though the boy was not his own son. He mourned for him, since he was to him a son in the Lord. In like manner, the death of a toddler, who has been born into the Church, or the death of a young girl who has grown up in the fellowship of the Church, causes the whole Church to mourn. The church members weep over the child, as if the child were their very own. This is because all of the Church's children are God's children.

Yet if this is true for children who die in the Church, is it not also true of children who die elsewhere? Are not all children who die prior to adulthood immediately ushered into the Kingdom of Heaven?[12] Are they not, then, children of the Kingdom? And if they are children of the Kingdom, then is it not true that we should weep for them?

What, then, of aborted children? Is there any difference in personhood, essence, or value, between a two-year-old child and a child in the womb? If not, then should we not mourn for aborted children as much as we mourn for those two-year-old children whose pictures we see in the news, having been murdered at the hands of vicious men? Is it not the duty of Christians to honor the personhood and intrinsic value of preborn children by weeping for

---

[12] See the discussion in this chapter, below, for the truth that all children who die in childhood go directly to be with Jesus Christ, in Paradise.

those preborn children who have been so brutally murdered in the contemporary Abortion Holocaust?

There was a Holocaust in Nazi Germany. It was an unthinkable Holocaust. And the sights and smells of this Holocaust caused the strong, ruddy American GI's, who swept into the Nazi concentration camp at Dachau as liberators, to weep:

> Nothing the American infantrymen encountered battling across Europe and into the German heartland steeled them for what they found at Dachau. After storming through the concentration-camp gates, *some of the GIs wept.* Parked at a railway siding were 40 freight cars with 2,000 corpses inside. Thousands more bodies were stacked like cordwood near the crematorium. The SS guards had run out of coal with which to burn them.[13]

Similarly, but even more grievously, there is a contemporary Holocaust taking place around the globe, today. It has taken many, many more human lives. This Holocaust has preyed upon the weakest of the weak. It has invaded lands of "liberty," bringing the bloodstain of the ruthless murder of children in the womb to "free" nations such as England and America. This contemporary Holocaust ought to cause us to weep.

What the American GI's found at Dachau, some employees of the Martin Container Corporation discovered in a wealthy man's backyard in Los Angeles, California, in 1982. The wealthy man's name was Malvin Weisberg, and he operated a home-based business, doing research on the bodies of aborted babies. Needing somewhere to discard the bodies of the babies after he was finished with them, he rented a twenty-foot storage container from Martin Container Corporation, and placed it in his backyard. However, when his rent check for the container bounced, the container was repossessed. Upon coming to repossess the container, the workers of the Martin Container Corporation discovered 16,433 bodies of aborted babies in, or near the container. The discovery, once examined for autopsy and subsequently revealed to the public, was revolting and horrific:

---

[13] Terrence Petty, "At Dachau, The GI's Wept—Allies Liberated Nazi Camps 50 Years Ago This Month," *The Seattle Times* (April 2, 1995, emphasis added), n.p. [cited 5 August 2013]. Online: http://community.seattletimes.nwsource.com/archive/?date=19950402&slug=2113520.

Dr. Eva Hauser, assisted by Dr. Joseph Wood, weighed and measured at least 43 of [the] larger baby bodies. Some had been dead for more than 2 years. Some were at least 30 weeks old. All were severely mutilated through poisoning or dismemberment with surgical knives. The putrid smell, the constant buzz of flies, and the horrifying sight of mangled infant bodies made the autopsy procedure difficult for the doctors.[14]

Christians weep over such horrors. We tear our garments, spiritually speaking, and are aghast that such atrocities take place in our own lands. We grieve, mourn, and wail over such evidences of the contemporary Holocaust that surrounds us, and plagues our nations. We think upon the delicate fingers, the tiny toes, the rhythmic heartbeat, the precious innocence, and the vibrant life of the preborn, and we weep and wail for them. As Christians, the Spirit of Christ in us teaches us to mourn for them, with tears and sobs of love.

Why did David weep only before he knew that his son had died, but not after? Why, upon receiving the news of the death of his son, did he not weep? This is an enigma, upon which we will meditate in the next section, but for now we pause, in order to notice *where David goes* to find comfort after his son has died. He goes, to find comfort, not to the funeral home, but to the House of the Lord:

…*and he came <u>into the LORD's house</u>, and [bowed down]*. (2 Samuel 12:20b)

Comfort for parents who have been bereaved of their preborn children ought to be found in the Lord's house, in the Church. We are not speaking here of the physical church building. Rather, we are speaking of the living, breathing Church of Christ Jesus. Parents who

---

[14] See the historical documentation in, "16,433 Bodies Found Dead in a Shipping Container in Los Angeles," distributed by *The Center for Documentation of the American Holocaust*, 1983, n.p. [cited 5 August 2013]. Online: http://tildensc .org/nav/The%20American%20Holocaust.pdf. See also President Ronald Reagan's comments on the need for memorial services and burial "for these children" in order to "strengthen our resolve to end this national tragedy" in Philip Hager, "Court Clears the Way for Disposal of Fetuses," *The Los Angeles Times* (March 19, 1985), n.p. [cited 5 August 5 2013]. Online: http://articles.latimes.com/1985-03-19/news/mn-31700_1_state-supreme-court.

are weeping for their children, whom they aborted, need to find the Lord's house, the Church, a place wherein they can weep and find the Lord's forgiveness. Also, people who are awakening to the true personhood of the preborn baby, and who are thus only now awakening to the horror of abortion, need a place where they can express their shock and grief, in tears. This place ought to be the Church.

In the Church, we ought to find ourselves weeping, together, for the preborn. Our church services should hold regular, solemn times of prayer on behalf of the preborn.[15] We should teach the world how to weep for the preborn by doing so, ourselves, with sincere hearts. In the Church, people ought to observe God's enormous heart for children in the womb by watching the members of the Church love them, with sacrificial tears.

There is, then, a very practical way that the Church of Christ can teach a watching world the value of life in the womb. We are to weep over abortion, to be sure. But we can also demonstrate the value of human life in utero by the way in which we approach miscarriages amongst our church family members. When we, the Church, join together to weep for babies in the womb who, under God's mysterious providence, have been miscarried, we also inherently affirm the precious value of all life in the womb.

Due to Darwinian lies and pro-abortion rhetoric, many people, including Christians, have been trained to think of miscarriage as something less than true bereavement. It is as if a newly-conceived baby is less "human" than a baby who has been in the womb for six months, and that a baby who has been in the womb for six months is still less "human" than a newborn. For this reason, an early-stage miscarriage is oftentimes, ever so coldly, treated as "less human" than a later-stage miscarriage, which, in turn, is treated as "less human" than a stillbirth.

This kind of reasoning does unthinkable damage to human society. It tells fathers and mothers who experience early-stage

---

[15] The current author's local church sets aside a special time during the worship service, once a month, for silent prayer on behalf of the preborn. The church thus prays, regularly and publicly, with tears for the preborn, and with spiritual petitions on behalf of Christians who serve in various Abortion Abolitionist ministries. The church also extends Christ's forgiveness and healing to those who repent of the sin of abortion, and it encourages its members to learn the acronym **P.R.A.A.**, which stands for "**P**ray **R**everently for the **A**bolition of **A**bortion."

miscarriages that they merely have a "fertility issue." Culturally speaking, it discourages these parents from mourning, even privately by themselves, and certainly shuns any forms of public mourning. This deceptive thought also tells fathers and mothers who experience later-stage miscarriages that they "almost made it" to parenthood, but did not arrive at full parenthood. It issues a steely, cruel "better luck next time" statement to the privately-grieving couple.

This is understandable in pagan thought, which does not recognize full life and personhood in the womb. However, the presence of this type of thinking and speaking in the Church ought to be alarming. It ought to betray the stealthy intrusion of foreign ideas and foreign gods into the Church. Christians ought not to tolerate this kind of thought in the Church.

Rather, the Church should be a place where grieving mothers, who have miscarried their children, find comfort and solace. Our members ought to console the parents of miscarried children with the same measure of compassion and care that they would extend to parents who have lost toddlers, or even older children. Our church buildings ought to be made readily available to parents who desire to hold private memorial services for their miscarried children, and our pastors ought to be trained in how to officiate at such services. In short, churches that seek God's heartbeat for the preborn will become places in which fathers and mothers who have been bereaved of children through miscarriage can find biblical compassion, healing, and hope.

It is only when a watching world sees us, as Christians, weeping over abortion that it will begin to understand the gravity of abortion. It is only when it sees us honoring life in the womb, through bereavement ministries for families that lose children through miscarriage, that it will be forced to face—experientially and relationally, and not just abstractly—the reality of full personhood in the womb (from conception onwards). It is, after all, much easier for a pro-abortionist to dismiss an Abolitionist's philosophical treatise against abortion than it is for him to say to a grieving, weeping mother, "Stop crying. Your six-week-old in the womb was not a real person, anyway."

David's Bereavement and Heavenly Hope

We now return to King David's strange, enigmatic behavior. Why does the King of Israel weep and fast prior to his son's death, but then wash himself and eat immediately after receiving the news that the boy has died? Surely, David knows how to weep over the death of a loved one. He is a compassionate, weeping king. Why, then, does he not weep over the death of his own little boy?

Surprisingly, enigmatic acts are oftentimes performed by God's prophets for the sake of very important spiritual lessons. For example, the prophet Ezekiel is not allowed to weep, publicly, or to show any signs of public mourning over the death of his beloved wife:

> *Also the* LORD's *Word came to me, saying: Son of man, behold, I will take away from you the desire of your eyes with a stroke: yet <u>you shall neither mourn nor weep, neither shall your tears run down</u>. Sigh, but not aloud, make no mourning for the dead; bind your headdress on you, and put your shoes on your feet, and do not cover your lips, and do not eat men's bread. So I spoke to the people in the morning; and at [evening] my wife died; and I did in the morning as I was commanded.* (Ezekiel 24:15-18)

Is Ezekiel, then, a bad husband? Is he cold and calloused towards the death of his own wife? Not at all! To the contrary, she is the *"desire of [his] eyes"* (v. 16) and his most treasured companion. His lack of weeping for his deceased wife is shocking to the people only because of how much his love for her was known to them. This shocking, enigmatic behavior from Ezekiel, then, sets the stage for his powerful prophecy about the destruction of God's sanctuary in Jerusalem, which is the *"desire of [the people's] eyes"* (v. 21). This destruction will come upon them with unexpected suddenness, the speed and devastation of which will inhibit them from mourning.

In similar fashion, David's strange behavior after the death of his son, his own little boy, is prophetic. It is shocking and enigmatic due to the well-known character of David, as a man who both weeps passionately over the deceased and loves his son with a great, fatherly love. Therefore, if he does not weep, with great passion, upon receiving the news that his son has died, something prophetic must be afoot. His lack of weeping is shocking and enigmatic. It has a message to convey to us. Here, then, is that message:

Then his servants said to him, "What is this that you have done? You fasted and wept for the child while he was alive, but when the child was dead, you rose up and ate bread."

He said, "While the child was yet alive, I fasted and wept; for I said, 'Who knows whether the LORD *will not be gracious to me, that the child may live?' But now he is dead, why should I fast? Can I bring him back again? <u>I will go to him, but he will not return to me.</u>"* (2 Samuel 12:21–23)

Ezekiel's shocking behavior, not grieving publicly over the death of his wife, sets the stage for a great prophecy of impending judgment. God's sanctuary in Jerusalem shall be destroyed. Similarly, David's shocking behavior, not weeping upon receiving the news that his little boy has died, sets the stage for a great prophecy, but this time one of heavenly hope. Namely, all little children who die go directly to Heaven!

There is no stated and specific "age of accountability" in the Bible, before which children are not held accountable to the Gospel of Christ in the same way that adults are. However, there is a wonderful statement in the book of Deuteronomy about children lacking "the knowledge of good and evil," and thus not being barred from the Promised Land on account of the sins of their parents:

Moreover <u>your little ones</u>, whom you said should be captured or killed, and <u>your children</u>, who today <u>have no knowledge of good or evil</u>, they shall go in there, and I will give it to, and <u>they shall possess it</u>. (Deuteronomy 1:39)

Children are the ones who are humble, meek, dependent, and filled with faith. They instinctively trust their fathers and mothers to be their rescuers in times of trouble. This is why Jesus says that the Kingdom of Heaven belongs to them:

But Jesus said, "Allow <u>the little children</u>, and do not forbid them to come to me; for <u>the Kingdom of Heaven belongs to ones like these</u>." (Matthew 19:14)

In their faithful, trusting postures, children recognize the praiseworthiness of Jesus Christ without questioning His authority:

But when the chief priests and the scribes saw the wonderful things that he did, and <u>the children</u> who were crying in the temple and saying, "<u>Hosanna to the son of David</u>!" they were indignant.... (Matthew 21:15)

To enter Jesus' Kingdom, where He is unceasingly praised as King of kings and Lord of lords, one must come to God *"like a little child"*:

Most certainly, I tell you, whoever does not receive God's Kingdom <u>like a little child</u>, he will in no way enter into it. (Luke 18:17)

King David, then, recognizes this. He chooses not to weep over the news of the death of his little boy, so that he can announce to the Church, through Holy Scripture, that his boy, along with all little children who die prematurely, is in Heaven with God: *"I will go to him, but he will not return to me"* (2 Samuel 12:23). This means that all miscarried babies go to Heaven. It means that all toddlers who have died in their toddler-hood are in Heaven. And it means that every aborted baby, so unwanted by this world (though not always unwanted by his or her parents, for there are forced abortions in this cruel world), is living, without tears or pain, in Paradise with Jesus Christ.

This changes our picture of the saints in Heaven quite dramatically! Instead of a vast multitude of adult converts to Christ, many of whom have been martyred for the faith throughout the centuries, and yet nothing more, we must picture Heaven as being filled with all children who have died prematurely, and for whom people have grieved, during the six millennia of human history. Thus the number of saints in Heaven is far greater than what we previously imagined it to be. King David's prophecy concerns all children who die premature deaths: every out-of-the-womb child untimely taken away; every stillborn child and every miscarried baby; every embryo (the smallest of human babies) murdered through in vitro fertilization and human embryonic stem cell research; every baby in the womb murdered through the birth control pill and other abortifacients; and every preborn child murdered through abortion. All of these are now with Christ, our Lord, in Heaven. This means that the multitude of saints in Heaven is a vast, seemingly countless one. We can certainly imagine it to be more than the number of sands on the seashore, or the stars in the sky!

And how does Heaven house so many children? How can there possibly be enough room in Heaven for so many children? Jesus does not seem to have a problem with this kind of dilemma:

"<u>In My Father's house are many [abodes]</u>. If it were not so, I would have told you. I am going to prepare a place for you." (John 14:2)

The Church Fathers, as well, did not question the doctrine that those children who die in childhood go directly to Heaven. They simply assumed it to be true, based on both the biblical evidence and the compassionate and just character of God:

And again, who are they that have been saved, and received the inheritance? Those, doubtless, who do believe God, and who have continued in His love; as did Caleb [the son] of Jephunneh and Joshua [the son] of Nun, *and innocent children, who have had no sense of evil.*[16]

Also,

I must compel you to determine (what you mean by Hades), which of its two regions, the region of the good or of the bad. If you mean the bad, (all I can say is, that) even now the souls of the wicked deserve to be consigned to those abodes; if you mean the good, why should you judge to be unworthy of such a resting-place *the souls of infants* and of virgins, and those which, by reason of their condition in life were pure and innocent?[17]

Believers in Christ mourn, with great mourning, for all of the little ones who have died in childhood. Yet we mourn in a way that is distinctly Christian. This is because we know that we will see them, and embrace them, someday, in Heaven. They are not taken from us

---

[16] Irenaeus (c. AD 130-200), *Against Heresies* 4.28.3 (*ANF* 1:502), emphasis added.
[17] Tertullian, *A Treatise on the Soul* 56 (*ANF* 3:233), emphasis added.

forever. They shall not return to us, in this mortal life, but we shall go to them, in Paradise.

A Christian couple miscarries a ten-week-old child in the womb. They both feel led, by the Holy Spirit, to give him a boy's name. They name him Titus, picturing the pastor-teacher that he might have been, had he grown of age. A week after he has been taken from them, they invite their church members to a private memorial service, so that they can grieve for him, and celebrate his life, together. They say, at the memorial service, that they are confident that God, over time, will begin to heal their wounds (though they also know that the wounds will never heal completely, this side of Heaven). They announce at the memorial service that they plan to mark the passing of Titus' due date, calendar year after calendar year, and to remember him, always, with affectionate, parental love.

At the same church where Titus' parents are members, there is another Christian couple who previously had two abortions prior to converting to Christ. Having been born of the Spirit, they have repented of their murderous crimes against their own offspring, and have found a miraculous, spiritual healing in their souls that has come to them through the Gospel. Having faith that the blood of Christ has been applied to their guilt-stained consciences, they have felt within them the warm, piercing love of His mercy and forgiveness. They know and believe that the Lamb of God has paid, in full, the enormous debts that they incurred through their abortions. They have since grown to love, with a deep, parental love, their two aborted children, naming the older one Samuel and the younger one Mary.

It is not, however, until the church memorial service for Baby Titus that the latter couple has a spiritual breakthrough concerning the hope of Heaven. They know, intellectually, that they shall meet their own children, Samuel and Mary, someday in Heaven. Yet as Baby Titus' life is celebrated, with family testimonies, with many tears, and with the singing of heavenly songs, the Holy Spirit descends upon this couple. Grieving, once again, for Samuel and Mary, and longing to hold them in their arms, they are given a spiritual light from Holy Scripture, a supernatural assurance that their children are safe in the Celestial City, and that their own children love them, as their parents, with Jesus' love. Tears of joy burst from their eyes as they hear King David's prophetic words read out loud by the pastor, *"I will go to him, but he will not return to me."*

Thus the life and death of Baby Titus has, so gently and quietly, preached the hope of Heaven to a Christian couple that has been desperate for it. Titus' meek and humble death has opened the door for Christ's hope of Heaven to be preached to his entire church family (and countless others, too). In many ways, then, some of God's best evangelists (through miscarriage) and martyrs (through abortion) are the little ones in the womb.

What, then, was it like for King David, upon his own death, to meet his little boy, again, in the House of God? When their eyes first met in Heaven, did not David recognize his son's eyes as the same ones that he knew on earth? And did not his son immediately recognize David's voice as the voice of his earthly father? What were their first words to each other? And since there are no tears in Heaven, how did they keep from bursting into tears of joy?

Bereaved and grieving Christian parents, there are little faces in God's eternal Kingdom that are waiting to greet you there. Their faces and hair texture resemble yours. Their eyes are just like your eyes, only slightly different and unique. Their hands are clean, and holy. They speak with the wisdom of angels, for they have been reared and educated in the very courts of God. These children, your children, are God's children. They live, and move, and have their joyful existence in Christ. They shall greet you, some great and eternal Day, and invite you to join them in worshipping God, with the countless multitudes, whose perfected hearts are fixed upon Him.

Therefore, bereaved and grieving parents in Christ, remember that our Lord has made an everlasting promise to you:

Blessed are <u>those who mourn</u>, for they <u>shall be comforted</u>. (Matthew 5:4)

8

WOVEN IN THE WOMB:
God's Omniscience and Preborn Children

(Psalm 139:1-24)

O LORD, You have searched me, and You know me. You know my sitting down and my rising up. You perceive my thoughts from afar. You search out my path and my lying down, and are acquainted with all my ways. For there is not a word on my tongue, but, behold, O LORD, You know it altogether. You hem me in behind and before. You laid Your hand on me. This knowledge is beyond me. It is lofty. I cannot attain it. Where could I go from Your Spirit? Or where could I flee from Your presence? If I ascend up into heaven, You are there. If I make my bed in Sheol, behold, You are there! If I take the wings of the dawn, and settle in the uttermost parts of the sea; even there Your hand will lead me, and Your right hand will hold me. If I say, "Surely the darkness will overwhelm me; the light around me will be night"; even the darkness does not hide from You, but the night shines as the day. The darkness is like light to You. (Psalm 139:1–12)

God knows all things. He knows the exact number of sands on every seashore, and the exact number of stars in every galaxy. The Lord of Hosts knows, presently, the precise coordinates of every fish in the sea, every bird in the air, and every creature on the dry ground. He knows every event that has ever happened in all of world history, including those events to which no human being was a witness. He also has exhaustive knowledge of every future event, including the future actions of His enemies, and the exact day on which His Son will return in glory, with the holy angels. There is nothing that escapes His knowledge.

At the same time, God knows us, His children, in a very *personal* way. He watches over us as a father might watch over his own son or daughter, yet with perfect omniscience.[1] He has perfect knowledge of both our outward lives, and our inward thoughts. He *"knows"* when

---

[1] The doctrine of "omniscience" simply states that God has perfect and complete knowledge of all things, and that He is not lacking true knowledge in any way, whatsoever. He is perpetually the Teacher, and never the "student."

we wake up in the morning, and when we go to bed at night (Psalm 139:2). He also *"know[s]...altogether"* the exact words that we will speak before they are ever on our tongues (v. 4). The hidden recesses of our minds are not hidden from Him. The dark places of the human heart are as light to Him. He sees all, and knows all about us.

Psalm 139 is a worshipful tribute to the all-knowing nature of God. It is, in the words of the great American theologian, Jonathan Edwards (1703-58), a "meditation on the omniscience of God."[2] Primarily, then, about the glory of God's knowledge, the Psalm also celebrates how such knowledge translates into God's love for us, as Christians. He loves us, His children, through His intimate knowledge of our comings in and goings out. He listens in on the conversations of our hearts, and He loves us in all of our inner weaknesses, vulnerabilities, and needs.

How, then, shall we describe God's knowledge of little babies in the womb? It is both an omniscient knowledge, and a personal knowledge. Yet before we explore this further, we must first follow the mountainous contours of the opening verses of Psalm 139 in order to better understand what they teach us about the grand heights of God's omniscience, itself.

LEARNING TO FEAR THE OMNISCIENT GOD

The Bible does not condone the pursuit of knowledge when it is done purely in the abstract. According to Holy Scripture, knowledge that is divorced from the fear of God is dangerous. It leads to foolishness. For God is the One who:

...frustrates the signs of the liars, and makes diviners mad; who turns wise men backward, and <u>makes their knowledge foolish</u>. (Isaiah 44:25)

Thus the Apostle Paul rebukes the kind of knowledge that is secular, or this-worldly:

Where is the wise? Where is the scribe? Where is the [debater] of this world? Has not God <u>made foolish the wisdom of this world</u>? (1 Corinthians 1:20)

---

[2] Jonathan Edwards, Sermon XXXI in *The Works of President Edwards* (Worcester 8th ed. in 4 vol.; New York: Leavitt and Allen, 1858), 4:502.

In the Bible, the only path to true knowledge is the fear of God. True knowledge cannot be obtained without a holy trembling before the majesty and grandeur of God. The Lord, *"He is to be feared"* (Psalm 96:4). Since God is the Founder and Architect of all things, we must fear Him in order to understand the world in which we live. As finite creatures, we must learn to tremble before the infinite heights of the infinite God. Thus to know anything, rightly and truly, is to know it in the light of the fear of God:

<u>The fear of the LORD is the beginning of knowledge</u>; but the foolish despise wisdom and instruction. (Proverbs 1:7)

This theme, that true knowledge cannot be divorced from the fear of God, echoes its way throughout the book of Proverbs:

…then you will understand <u>the fear of the LORD</u>, and find <u>the knowledge of God</u>. (Proverbs 2:5)

And,

<u>The fear of the LORD</u> is the beginning of wisdom. <u>The knowledge of the Holy One</u> is understanding. (Proverbs 9:10)

The indestructible bond between true knowledge and the fear of the Lord is, later on in Israel's history, picked up in the oracles of Isaiah, the great Prophet. He, too, sees only one path to true knowledge, which is the path of fearing the Lord:

The LORD's Spirit will rest on him: the Spirit of wisdom and understanding, the Spirit of counsel and might, the Spirit of <u>knowledge</u> and of <u>the fear of the LORD</u>. (Isaiah 11:2)

Also,

There will be stability in your times, abundance of salvation, wisdom, and <u>knowledge</u>. The <u>fear of the LORD</u> is your treasure. (Isaiah 33:6)

But why is this so? What explains the indissoluble bond between true knowledge and the fear of the Lord? To be sure, the holiness of

God is at the heart of the answer to this question. Since all of reality is, in essence, created to be God-centered, and since God is a God whose holiness requires us to fear Him, with a joyful fear, there is no true knowledge apart from the fear of God.[3]

Still, as a subset to the more general knowledge of God's majestic holiness, we can speak of the knowledge of God's omniscience as part of what it means to fear Him. As evidence of this, there is, in Psalm 139, a large amount of joyful trembling before God—which is the fear of the Lord—that takes place whenever we read, with humility, its verses concerning His omniscience.

The fact that God knows our every movement (Psalm 139:2) and has complete foreknowledge of our spoken words (v. 4) humbles us before Him. When we consider that His omniscience wraps us up, like a blanket, and envelopes us, like a cloud (v. 5), we exclaim with David, *"This knowledge is beyond me. It is lofty. I cannot attain it!"* (v. 6). After pondering God's omniscience concerning the formation of our bodies in the womb, we rejoice, with holy fear, and say, *"I will give thanks to You, for I am fearfully and wonderfully made. Your works are wonderful. My soul knows that very well."* (v. 14). God's omniscience means that His thoughts of us are infinite in number (v. 17). We gaze upon the heights of this lofty knowledge of God, like travelers at the bottom of the Grand Canyon, looking up towards its rim, so high above us, and we tremble.

We only come to "know" things, rightly, when we come to believe that God knows all things. The wicked do not believe this. They believe that they can hide their evil works in the dark, and they ask, mockingly, *"'Who sees us?' and 'Who knows us?'"* (Isaiah 29:15). But the righteous believe that God, indeed, knows all things. He is not like the gods of the nations, for, *"Who taught Him knowledge?"* (40:14). In particular, the idols of the world cannot know the future. It is only the God of Israel who is able to declare *"the end from the beginning, and from ancient times things that are not yet done"* (46:10).

When we think correctly upon the omniscience of God, meditating upon it with humble hearts, we necessarily fear Him. This

---

[3] That the fear of God is a very Christian (New Testament) posture of the heart, and not just an Old Testament one, is proved by its importance in the commandments of the New Testament Gospel: Luke 12:5; Acts 9:31; Romans 11:20; 2 Corinthians 7:1; Ephesians 5:21; Philippians 2:12; Colossians 3:22; Hebrews 12:28; 1 Peter 1:17; 2:17; Revelation 11:18; 14:7; and 19:5.

is reasonable and right, since who would not fear and give glory to the One who sees the future just as clearly as He does the present? If God knows all things, if He can simultaneously pinpoint both the speed and the location of electrons (all of them, and without any uncertainty!), and if He can predict the weather, not by probability, but by the complete exactness of His foreknowledge of it (since He, Himself controls the weather), then should we not fear Him? And if God can see, with exhaustive knowledge, into the inner recesses of our hearts, knowing the hidden, sinful desires that we try so hard to conceal from the world, then should we not fall down on our faces before Him, in repentance, and worship Him?

The God of Israel is omniscient. Therefore, so too is Jesus Christ omniscient. Since He is of the same essence as His Father (there is only one God), God the Son has full knowledge of all things.[4] Not quite fully grasping the truth of this, His disciples nevertheless catch a glimpse of it prior to His death and resurrection:

"Now we know that <u>You know all things</u>, and do not need for anyone to question You. By this we believe that You came from God." (John 16:30)

Yet once Jesus has been crucified, laid in the grave, and then raised from the dead on the third day, just as He foretold, the truth of His omniscience is fully and gloriously affirmed. It is Jesus who shall judge the living and the dead, in His perfect omniscience. He is the eternal King, before whose judgment seat all shall stand, and before whose all-seeing and all-knowing eyes nothing shall be hidden:

There is no creature that is hidden from His sight, but <u>all things</u> are naked and laid open before the eyes of Him to whom we must give an account. (Hebrews 4:13)

Knowledge, in the abstract, divorced from the knowledge of God's omniscience, inevitably leads to idolatry. In today's information age, far too many people worship at the altar of

---

[4] Though Jesus Christ, in His earthly sojourn, humbly took on flesh, and humbly surrendered the right to exercise, at will, all of His divine attributes—so that He could share in the frailties and sufferings of our fallen humanity (Philippians 2:6-8)—He nevertheless retained all of the divine attributes, including omniscience.

secularized knowledge. They assume that erudite doctoral dissertations, rigorous (peer-reviewed) scientific research, and well-funded, government-run systems of public education are the keys to a healthy and prosperous world. They go to university campuses not in order to marvel at the God who made the heavens and the earth, but rather to worship science, reason, humanism, and psychology, so that these academic disciplines become the great deities of our age. They thus turn lecturers into priests, and lecture halls into temples.

The sinful arrogance of modern learning is astounding. Someone who has studied to know a plethora of facts in an esoteric realm of botany or biochemistry is conditioned by our culture to believe, ever so presumptuously, that he is, by nature of his lofty educational status, a wise individual. He knows the immune systems of plants, or the three-dimensional structure of proteins, and on account of this knowledge he presumes to be able to speak to matters of great moment. Thus the professor of botany thinks that he is wise enough to comment on the origins of man. And the medical school biochemistry researcher (who also happens to be a neonatal physician), thinks that he has the high-priestly authority to determine whether or not it is ethical to slay a preborn child in his mother's womb.

It is not that learned men have no right to speak to subjects outside of their fields of expertise. It is, rather, that learned men who lack the fear of God have no right to claim to possess true wisdom, at all. True wisdom begins with the fear of the Lord. Lacking it, the philosophical and ethical speculations of men will always be grossly distorted.

The doctrine of God's omniscience, then, is designed to humble all men. We, who claim to know so much in this age of electronic journals and Google Books, actually know very little.[5] With all of our mathematical knowledge, our highest levels of calculus and abstract

---

[5] Most people today have an evolutionary view of knowledge, thinking that our learned men have evolved, epistemologically speaking, such that they are much more knowledgeable than the supposed Neanderthal, "Dark Age," and non-Enlightened men of old. Yet the opposite is true. Since the fear of God in Western culture (and also in the Church) has decreased over time, so too have our reservoirs of true knowledge and wisdom been depleted over time. One simply has to compare the amount of true knowledge and wisdom contained within a sermon from a great Puritan (say, for example, Jeremiah Burroughs, 1599-1646) with the striking dearth of true knowledge and wisdom in a typical contemporary sermon.

math are still quite elementary, perhaps on the level of basic addition and subtraction, compared to the higher math of an all-knowing Creator. With all of our structural engineering knowledge, our best building construction projects remain flimsy houses of cards, able to be knocked over by a mere breath from the One who is too big to be contained by the heavens. We, who presume to understand the created order with all of our theories of physics, chemistry, astronomy, and geology, really understand very little of it.

God, who, according to the Bible, created the world approximately six thousand years ago,[6] looks down from Heaven upon the scholars of this age who go to great lengths (and distortions) to argue that the universe is billions of years old. He laughs at them, and then asks them, *"Where were you when I laid the foundations of the earth?"* (Job 38:4). They think that they know so much. But since they refuse to fear God and thus reject the doctrine of His breath-taking omniscience, they, in reality, know little.

This same God listens in on the literature professors and philosophers of this age as they debate "the reader's meaning" versus "the author's meaning"—a debate in which both sides agree that any sense of transcendent meaning has been disproved long ago. God graciously withholds from them the logical quip, "Is your conversation about meaning a meaningful one?" Instead, He simply warns them, gravely, *"Everyone who is of the truth listens to My voice"* (John 18:37).

Who, then, is truly wise and knowing? Is it the "liberated" woman who has "chosen" not to have children, so that she can teach, without hindrance, at a local college? Or is it the Christian mother, who in the fear of God has embraced eleven biological children, and adopted three more, and who spends her time homeschooling her children, and reviewing her Scripture memory verses while she changes dirty diapers? Is it the agnostic lawyer who is quite in the know about science, and who has done enough reading in Neo-Darwinian thought to make charismatic speeches on the need for the teaching of Darwinism as scientific fact in the public schools? Or is it

---

[6] For a rigorous defense of why the sole truly-Christian reading of Genesis 1-11 is a young-earth one, see Jonathan Sarfati, *Refuting Compromise: A Biblical and Scientific Refutation of "Progressive Creationism" (Billions of Years), as Popularized by Astronomer Hugh Ross* (Green Forest, AR: Master Books, 2004). Note, especially, Sarfati's chapter on "The History of Interpretation of Genesis 1-11," 107-139.

the Christian mechanic, who never went to college, and who lacks the vocabulary to challenge Darwinism on scientific grounds, but who simply chooses to refute Darwinism with the profoundly theological reply, "God hates death—and Darwinism teaches that there was animal bloodshed and death prior to the Fall of Adam—so if Darwinism were true, the pre-Fall creation could not be the 'vegetarian' (Genesis 1:29-30) and 'very good' (v. 31) creation that God said that it was in the first chapter of the Bible"?

Let the wisdom of this age be seen to be the foolishness that it really is. *"Yes, let God be found true, but every man a liar"* (Romans 3:4). Let the faithful, believing, God-fearing children of the Father hear the Father's Son exclaim, *"I thank You, O Father, Lord of heaven and earth, that You have hidden these things from the wise and understanding, and revealed them to little children. Yes, Father, for so it was well-pleasing in Your sight"* (Luke 10:21). And regarding abortion, let the omniscience of God humble the political proclamations of men. If He knows all things, and sees all things, then He alone has the right to decide the question of the sanctity of life in the womb. Since the omniscient God has declared preborn children, from conception onwards, to have full personhood, full human rights, and full status as His image bearers, let us humbly and joyfully embrace His infinitely wise declaration.

OMNISCIENCE, OMNIPRESENCE, AND THE MOTHER'S WOMB

In Psalm 139, God is not merely omniscient. He is also omnipresent. That is, He is present everywhere. He is not "one with the creation," being identified with the creation, as in Hindu or New Age thought.[7] Rather, He, being infinite, is infinitely distinct from the finite creation, yet still is present everywhere within it, and outside of it. God fills all space with His presence, and also transcends all space with His presence. Too big to be contained by the heavens and the earth, He nevertheless has a divine presence in every square inch of the creation.

According to Psalm 139, the omnipresence of God is just as glorious as His omniscience. He is not only all-knowing, but also all-present. Therefore, the famous riddle posed to us by Eastern mysticism, in which a tree falls in the woods, but no human is present

---

[7] The proper term for this wicked and idolatrous system of thought is "pantheism."

to hear the sound of its falling—and so the question is forced on us about whether or not there was any true sound made at all (for what is the meaning of sound if there is no one present to hear it?)—turns out to be a riddle of great, idolatrous folly. God hears the sound of every tree falling in every acre of the unpopulated woods. He hears it because He is an all-present Creator and Ruler.

Thus, in Psalm 139, the God who knows all things is also present everywhere. His presence searches our hearts and thoughts. It also invades the hidden and dark places of the world. Therefore, nothing escapes His attention or His gaze:

Where could I go from Your Spirit? Or where could I flee from Your presence? If I ascend up into heaven, <u>You are there</u>. If I make my bed in Sheol, behold, <u>You are there</u>! If I take the wings of the dawn, and settle in the uttermost parts of the sea; <u>even there</u> Your hand will lead me, and Your right hand will hold me. If I say, "Surely the darkness will overwhelm me; the light around me will be night"; even the darkness does not hide from You, but the night shines as the day. The darkness is like light to You. (Psalm 139:7–12)

God is simultaneously present in all places, at all times. This is true because of His infinite size. He does not dwell in a house or temple. He cannot be confined within a physical space, no matter how large that space is. Therefore, though the Temple, in the Old Testament, is His meeting place with His people, it certainly cannot be said to contain Him:

But who is able to build Him a house, since <u>heaven and the heaven of heavens cannot contain Him</u>? Who am I then, that I should build Him a house, except just to burn incense before Him?...But will God indeed dwell with men on the earth? Behold, <u>heaven and the heaven of heavens cannot contain You</u>; how much less this house which I have built! (2 Chronicles 2:6; 6:18)

And,

The God who made the world and all things in it, He, being Lord of heaven and earth, <u>does not dwell in temples made with hands</u>, neither is He served by men's hands, as though He needed anything, seeing He Himself gives to all life and breath, and all things. (Acts 17:24–25)

The presence of God is everywhere. It is thus inescapable. The wicked have no place to hide from God, since He is all-present. False prophets cannot presume to hide where God cannot find them. They will not be able to escape His judgments against them:

"Am I a God at hand, says the LORD, *and not a God afar off? Can any hide himself in secret places so that I shall not see him?" says the* LORD. *"<u>Do I not fill heaven and earth</u>?" says the* LORD. (Jeremiah 23:23–24)

God is both omniscient and omnipresent. He neither lacks knowledge, in any way, nor has any lack of presence in any part of the universe. Thus God, who is all-present, and from whose Spirit even our minds and hearts are not hidden, sees all, hears all, and knows all.

David praises both God's omniscience and His omnipresence. To do so, he draws upon the example of God's omniscience and omnipresence in his own mother's womb.[8] In Psalm 139, David is known by God with a deep, personal, and intimate knowledge. God knows David wholly and completely. He even knows David's previous formation in the womb, in its entirety. Yet He not only knows this, but He also was *present with* the baby, David, in the womb. In fact, the Lord was the master Craftsman who built David's physical frame in the womb. God *knows* life in the womb, and, at the same time, His industrious *presence* in the womb fashions the baby's living, growing body in the womb:

For You formed my inmost being. You <u>knit me together</u> in my mother's womb. I will give thanks to You, for I am fearfully and wonderfully made. Your works are wonderful. My soul knows that very well. My frame was not hidden from You when I was made in secret, <u>woven together</u> in the depths of the earth. Your eyes saw my [unformed substance]. In Your book they were all written, the days that were ordained for me, when as yet there were none of them. (Psalm 139:13–16)

---

[8] Edwards, *Works of President Edwards*, 4:502, rightly says of Psalm 139 in relation to God's omniscience, "Then [David] represents [God's omniscience] by the knowledge which God had of him while in his mother's womb." Yet the womb is related to both God's omniscience and His omnipresence in the Psalm.

There are two different "textile" verbs present in these sacred verses. David was *"knit together"* by God in his mother's womb (v. 13); he was also *"woven together"* by God in his mother's womb (v. 15). Both of these verbs, the *"knitting"* one and the *"weaving"* one, are found in an important command in the book of Exodus concerning the construction of God's Tabernacle. Thus the human body in the womb, much like the Tabernacle, itself, is created to be a Temple of God's Holy Spirit:

"You shall make a [knitted-screen] for the door of the Tent, of blue, and purple, and scarlet, and fine twined linen, the work of the [weaver]." (Exodus 26:36)

God is a master Craftsman. He knows how to *"knit"* and *"weave"* us together in our mother's wombs. The force behind the wonder of human growth and development in the womb is not genetics. It is not biochemistry and physiology. Rather, it is the personal, Triune God of Scripture, Himself. *He* knits us and weaves us together in the womb. *He* creates and knits together our intricate frames, with His own magnificent artistry and design.[9] As Charles Haddon Spurgeon (1834-92), seeing God behind the artistic craftsmanship of the human body, so poetically puts it, "What tapestry can equal the human fabric?"[10] To slaughter a baby in the womb, at any time during pregnancy, from conception onwards, and no matter the method of the slaughter (be it chemical or be it surgical), is thus to destroy God's holy handiwork:

Have You not poured me out like milk, and curdled me like cheese? You have clothed me with skin and flesh, and <u>knit me together</u> with bones and sinews. (Job 10:10–11)

Still, how do we know that Psalm 139 is describing God's knitting and weaving together of a *person* in the womb, and one who

---

[9] That is, God authors and employs genetics, biochemistry, physiology, etc., in the womb. But He does so actively, rather than passively. Just as the Bible wars against a deistic view of cosmology, so too does it war against a deistic view of embryology.
[10] Charles H. Spurgeon, *The Treasury of David*, Commentary on Psalm 139:15, n.p. [cited 2 September 2013]. Online: http://www.spurgeon.org/treasury/ps139.htm.

is already fully alive, with *full personhood*, from conception onwards? That is, what of the "Christian" skeptics who argue that the grand handiwork of God that takes place in the womb (as described in Psalm 139) is merely the preparation for life, and not the actual existence of life? Theologically, how do we know that the baby in the womb has a soul? Is this a mere shell being formed in the womb, which will, upon birth, be infused with a human soul? Or is the soul of the baby united with his body, in the womb, the whole duration of pregnancy, from conception onwards?

Those who argue that these difficult questions are unanswerable from Psalm 139 are missing something very important in the Psalm: the presence of God's *"thoughts"* for David in verse 17. God not only knows David, intimately, and is present with David, even in the womb. He also has *"thoughts"* concerning David, which are too many to be counted:

How precious to me are <u>Your thoughts</u>, O God! How vast is their sum! (Psalm 139:17)

What *"thoughts"* of God are these, which are so precious to David? Is David pondering God's mighty thoughts about the physical composition of stars, or His sovereign thoughts about the rising and falling of kingdoms? No, this is not likely. For, the context of Psalm 139 is too personal and intimate for this. Since God, in verse 2, has already been praised for understanding David's own *"thought"* from afar, the *"thoughts"* of God in verse 17 must be specifically focused on David, himself. They are relational thoughts of David, which demonstrate God's omniscient, yet quite personal knowledge of David. Thus David says while God's thoughts are *"more in number than the sand,"* they nevertheless remind him of the truth that, *"When I wake up, I am still <u>with You</u>"* (v. 18). These are highly relational thoughts. They are too numerous to be counted, and yet Jesus says to us that they are very personal and loving thoughts, *"But the very hairs of your head are all numbered."* (Matthew 10:30).

God's thoughts of David are highly relational ones. Yet this means that His thoughts of the baby, David, while he is being *"knitted"* and *"woven"* in his mother's womb, are also highly relational ones. That is, God, through His omniscience and omnipresence, is *relating to* the baby, David, in the womb.

This is exactly how Matthew Henry (1662-1714), the great Bible commentator, reads Psalm 139. He sees David's formation in the womb as a highly relational time with God. The womb is the place where God hides us from the world, in our weakest and most vulnerable state, but He nevertheless relates to us, God-to-person, in the womb. Thus Henry says, "...when He hid us from all the world He did not intend to hide us from Himself."[11] He goes on to state that God's *"thoughts"* of David in verse 17, thoughts which include His thoughts of the baby, David, in the womb (vv. 13-16), are highly relational thoughts. David, from conception onwards, is a person. For, God's *"thoughts"* of him are loving thoughts, and *loving thoughts require personhood*. As Henry puts it, "God, who knew him, thought of him, and His thoughts towards him were thoughts of love...."[12]

The Lord God, then, is present with babies in their mother's womb in highly relational ways. He actively knits and weaves together their bodies, such that He causes their hearts to beat three weeks after conception.[13] From nine to ten weeks after conception, He teaches their mouths to yawn, encourages them to suck their thumbs, and causes their fingerprints to appear.[14] From thirteen to fifteen post-menstrual weeks, God starts watching babies do somersaults in the womb.[15] He delights in all of these things, for He is present in the womb with these children, and He knows them in the womb, relationally.

We must think, then, upon God's own relation to the baby in the womb. The child is His handiwork. He, Himself, carves the child's fingerprints in the womb. Yet the child is also His relational delight. God knows the specific personality of the baby in the womb. He teaches the baby, saying, "Know Me." He also encourages the baby, saying, "Do you hear that rhythmic sound? That is your

---

[11] Matthew Henry, *Matthew Henry's Commentary on the Whole Bible: Complete and Unabridged in One Volume* (Peabody, Mass.: Hendrickson, 1991), 748.
[12] Ibid., 748.
[13] Gary R. Fleisher and Stephen Ludwig, eds., *Synopsis of Pediatric Emergency Medicine* (4th ed.; Philadelphia, PA: Lippincott Williams & Wilkins, 2002), 255.
[14] The Endowment for Human Development, "Prenatal Form and Function: The Making of an Earthly Suit; Unit 10: 9 to 10 Weeks," n.p. [cited 23 September 2013]. Online: http://www.ehd.org/dev_article_unit10.php.
[15] Stanley J. Ulijaszek, Francis E. Johnston, and Michael A. Preece, eds., *The Cambridge Encyclopedia of Human Growth and Development* (Cambridge: Cambridge University Press, 1998), 164.

mother's heartbeat. Do you hear that singing sound? That is your mother's voice."

In return, preborn children respond to God's relational presence with them in the womb *with worship*. He knows them, omnisciently, but He is also with them, omnipresently, in the womb. And when babies sense God's holy presence with them in the womb, they praise Him. The womb becomes their chapel of worship.[16] Responding with worship to God's relational presence with them, these children participate in the fulfillment of the words of Jesus:

> *"Yes. Did you never read, <u>'Out of the mouth of babes and nursing babies you have perfected praise?'</u>" (Matthew 21:16)*

If God is present, intimately and relationally, with the little babies in the womb, then who are abortionists to intrude upon that sacred space? How dare a physician, who is called to protect life, push his murderous chemicals, or insert his murderous instruments into the womb, where God is present! If birth-control pills, prescribed by a doctor, prevent the tiny, "hatching" baby, who has just left the uterine tube, from being able to latch onto the wall of his mother's uterus, does not God, who is present to see this, weep over this murderous process? If the baby in the womb screams a silent scream of torture at the start of a surgical abortion, is not God present to hear that scream? If the little one in the womb, whose heart God has formed, begins to sob, along with his mother, in the abortion clinic, does not God gather those precious preborn tears into His wineskin (Psalm 56:8)? And when the blood of His beloved little one is poured out on the ground of the abortion clinic, does not that blood cry out to Him for vengeance? And will not the God of justice repay such murderous crimes, if the perpetrators remain obstinate and unrepentant, with the full fury of His divine retribution?

---

[16] Luke 1:41, 44 is the ultimate fulfillment of this principle, since the baby, John the Baptist, praises not only the spiritual presence of God with him in his mother, Elizabeth's womb, but also the incarnational presence of God the Son, in Mary's womb, that has come near to him through Mary's visitation of Elizabeth.

Such is the wrathful side of God's omnipresence, as it relates to the abortions that take place within the sacred confines of the womb. There is, however, a very hopeful application, for Christian mothers, of God's omnipresence, as it relates to the womb. Namely, Psalm 139 encourages mothers not merely to marvel at the beauty of life in the womb, but to *worship Christ*, who so skillfully knits and weaves together their children in the womb.

This means, for Christian mothers—the ones who are born of the Holy Spirit, and who thus have died to the sinful cravings of the flesh, and live according to the Spirit—that pregnancy is a time of discipleship. Mothers should not wait until their children can read children's Bibles before beginning the discipleship process. Instead, the mother-child discipleship relationship, which trains the child in the fear of the Lord, begins as soon as the mother realizes that she is pregnant. Discipleship starts with the time of growth and exploration that takes place in the womb.

A truly Christian mother, then, will go through pregnancy pondering the wonder of how God is present with her child in the womb. She will say often, and out loud, to her preborn little one, "You, my sweet baby, are being fearfully and wonderfully made by God." She will sing the praises of God, out loud, so that her baby can hear the songs, hymns, and spiritual songs of the Church echoing off of the walls of the womb. As a mother, she will pray over her baby, with her hand on her womb, asking God to show His magnificent glory to her child throughout the pregnancy. She will tell her baby, often, that Jesus, too, was once a baby in the womb. And (in the case of a Christian mother who is also married to a godly man) she will entreat her husband to read Scripture over both mother and child, so that the Scriptures are the very first words to which the baby is exposed. The little one will not, of course, understand the sacred Word that is read to him, but the act of reading the Scriptures over him will set a crucial pattern for his parents to follow with regard to their lifelong, biblical, and primarily *parental* training of him in the ways of the Lord.

GOD'S OMNISCIENCE SEARCHES OUR HEARTS

We return, once again, to the doctrine of God's omniscience, but now as it relates to our own hearts. Psalm 139 is not a "safe" Psalm. It is not an easy prayer to pray. No one can read Psalm 139 and walk away from it unchanged. Either the reader shall finish Psalm 139 with a greatly chastened heart, and find himself closer to God, or else, having read the Psalm in a posture of pride, he shall finish reading it in a state of being further away from God than when he had begun. This is because God Himself uses the Psalm to *"search"* our hearts:

O L<small>ORD</small>, You have <u>searched</u> me, and You know me. (Psalm 139:1)

When God's Spirit uses Psalm 139 to *"search"* our hearts regarding abortion, what does He find? Does He discover a compassionate, holy heart that weeps for the children in the womb who are being killed through abortion? Or does He find, instead, large amounts of selfishness, worldliness, cowardice, and moral compromise, all of which prevent us from loving our preborn neighbors as ourselves?

Under the searchlight of God's omniscience, the depths of our hearts are exposed. And, surprisingly, one of the greatest exposures of the contents of our hearts comes through examining our posture towards the wicked. How we respond to God's enemies (and God has many, many enemies in this world) says volumes about the state of our hearts.

For example, verse 19 of the Psalm is not the kind of prayer that one would expect to hear prayed on a typical Lord's Day, at a peaceful congregation of believers:

If only You, O God, <u>would kill the wicked</u>. Get away from me, <u>you bloodthirsty men</u>! (Psalm 139:19)

This prayer is a bit shocking to our ears. And yet it is sacred Scripture. How, then, do we handle it? In specific, how do we handle it with regard to abortion?

The way in which we view this prayer exposes the spiritual state of our own hearts. For example, those who have lived rich and selfish lives amidst their prosperous surroundings may not understand the depths of these sentiments. But those who truly commiserate with the preborn child who is murdered through abortion (along with all other persecuted Christians who are murdered for their faith in Christ), should be able to understand this prayer a little bit better. Perhaps we, ourselves, who have never faced the threat of martyrdom (Hebrews 12:4), do not feel compelled to say, *"Get away from me, you bloodthirsty men!"* However, if we can hear the preborn child saying this, in his little preborn way, to the abortion doctor who looms, murderously, over his mother's womb, then we understand the verse a little bit better than we formerly did.

Again, our response to God's enemies says an awful lot about our own spiritual posture before God:

> *For they speak against You wickedly. Your enemies take Your name in vain. O LORD, do I not <u>hate those who hate You</u>? Am I not grieved with those who rise up against You? <u>I hate them with perfect hatred</u>. They have become my enemies. <u>Search me, O God</u>, and know my heart. Try me, and know my thoughts.* (Psalm 139:20–23)

Is David a wicked man for hating wicked people? Is this "hate speech" of his an evil form of speech? Is he an ancient Pharisee? Does David lack grace, and thus reject the Gospel of grace?

It is true that the Gospel of the Kingdom empowers Christians to live under a new, even more difficult kind of "law." Rather than being governed by the Law of Moses, which Christ has fulfilled on our behalf, we are governed by the Law of Christ.[17] This is the Perfect Law of Liberty,[18] and the Royal Law of the Gospel.[19] It is the Law of Love,[20] which includes the command to bless, rather than curse, one's enemies.[21] In this New Covenant Law, however, we are not to abolish the Old Covenant Scriptures,[22] for the Word of our God, both Old and New Testaments, stands forever.[23] Rather, we are to *obey the Old Testament*, but only *as fulfilled in the Gospel of Christ*. This

---

[17] 1 Corinthians 9:21.
[18] James 1:25.
[19] James 2:8.
[20] Romans 13:9.
[21] Romans 12:14.
[22] Matthew 5:17.
[23] Isaiah 40:8.

requires a much higher righteousness,[24] accomplished solely by the imputed righteousness of Christ—through faith alone—and the power of God's Spirit at work within us.[25] By the grace of God, it raises the standards of biblical love to the level of perfection:

> *Therefore you shall <u>be perfect</u>, just as your Father in heaven <u>is perfect</u>.* (Matthew 5:48)

Therefore, David's hatred of God's enemies is not the Gospel fulfillment of the Law. It does not have the ripe maturity and glorious clarity of the full revelation of God's nature that comes to us through Christ Jesus:

> *For if, while <u>we were enemies</u>, we were reconciled to God through <u>the death of His Son</u>, much more, being reconciled, we will be saved by His life.* (Romans 5:10)

That is, now that Jesus has come preaching the Kingdom of God, we are expected to understand, more fully, the import of loving all people, even *our enemies*:

> *You have heard that it was said, "You shall love your neighbor and <u>hate your enemy</u>." But I tell you, <u>love your enemies</u>, bless those who curse you, do good to those who hate you, and pray for those who mistreat you and persecute you.* (Matthew 5:43-44)

Nevertheless, we would be slandering David if we were to portray him as a man who hates, with dark hatred, those who are his enemies. For, is it not David who mercifully chooses to spare the life of King Saul, even after Saul has unjustly hunted him, seeking to kill him, and treated him like a dog (1 Samuel 24:11)? Is it not David who shows mercy towards Absalom, even after Absalom, his own son, has started a revolt against him, and sought to kill him (2 Samuel 18:5)?

---

[24] Matthew 5:20.
[25] Romans 8:7-10.

Instead of slandering David, then, let us remember that his hatred is not directed against *his own* enemies,[26] but rather against *God's own* enemies:

> *For they speak <u>against You</u> wickedly. Your enemies take <u>Your name</u> in vain. O LORD, do I not hate those who <u>hate You</u>? Am I not grieved with those who rise up <u>against You</u>? I hate them with perfect hatred. They have become my enemies. Search me, O God, and know my heart. Try me, and know my thoughts.* (Psalm 139:20–23)

Again, Christians, who live under the Royal Law of Christ, are not permitted to hate anyone, even the enemies of God. We are to love them, and pray for their repentance. Like God, our Father, we should take no pleasure in the death of the wicked. We should desire that they repent, and be saved from the wrath to come. When they persecute us, and even kill us,[27] we ought to pray with the blessed martyr Stephen, *"Lord, do not hold this sin against them!"* (Acts 7:60).

Still, David teaches us that our zeal for God's glory does, indeed, put us in a state of enmity with those who hate God. To embrace God's enemies as our closest friends, or to flatter God's enemies as if they were admired by us, would be to betray our love for God. If they hate God, they must also hate us. If they spit at God, then let them also spit at us. For, we are yoked to Him by His love for us, and by our love for Him. Therefore, to wound Christ is to wound us.

In this sense, only, can we say that David is right to "hate" God's enemies. They take God's name in vain. They hate God. Therefore, we, as Christians, must hate their *deeds*:

> *…and some save, snatching them out of the fire with fear, <u>hating even the clothing stained by the flesh</u>.* (Jude 23)

---

[26] Interestingly, it is God who *"hates"* all *"workers of iniquity"* in Psalm 5:5. And while David, in the Psalms, never claims to hate *his own* enemies (rather than God's enemies), it is, instead, David's enemies who hate him *"with cruel hatred"* (Psalm 25:19).

[27] William Tyndale, who gave his life for the Gospel as a valiant martyr, says of Christian love in *Obedience* (emphasis added), 150, "We are now ready to suffer with Christ and to lose life and all *for our very enemies to bring them to Christ.*"

Also,

> *But this you have, that you <u>hate the works of the Nicolaitans</u>, which <u>I also hate</u>.* (Revelation 2:6)

We live in a liberalized world, in which "love" is no longer biblical love. God is love, indeed. But our liberalized society wants to turn this around and claim that "love is God." This destroys the nature of love. It takes it out of its biblical context, and turns it into the spiritual affirmation of all people, in all of their deeds, whether good or evil. If we can affirm the statement, "All are welcome into the membership of the Church, regardless of their lifestyles," then we are applauded by the world as being true disciples of love. Yet if, due to conscience, as informed by our loyalty to the God of Scripture, we refuse to affirm such a statement, then we are told by liberalized Christianity that we have no share in the "love of Jesus."[28]

Therefore, our hearts' posture towards the wicked deeds of wicked men reveals our spiritual condition. God *"searches"* our hearts through this test of loyalty. Do we love Him more than others? Are we hurt, through our love for Him, when His enemies take His name in vain? Do we align ourselves with the wicked, or is there an ongoing spiritual enmity between us and them?

John Calvin, whom many non-Calvinists claim was a scathing, hateful Christian Reformer, was, to the contrary, an extremely loving man. He understood Christ's call to love one's enemies. Also, as a pastor, he threw himself into the visitation of the sick, even during seasons when such visitations were to those who had been smitten by the contagious and deadly bubonic plague. This warm-hearted pastor loved people, summoning his flock to bless their enemies. Still, Calvin also understood that a man's heart is thoroughly searched and tested, according to Psalm 139, by his response to those who hate God:

---

[28] Wong Ming-dao (1900-1991), the father of the Underground Church in China, admonishes us in this regard in his *A Call to the Church: 20 Pre-Prison Messages of Conviction and Courage* (Fort Washington, PA: Christian Literature Crusade, 1983), 161: "We should never accept the carnal love offered by others; nor should we love others with this fleshly, human kind of love....Believers should love people with the kind of love expressed in the Word of God. Only this kind of love is genuine love."

It is a proof of our having a fervent zeal for God when we have the magnanimity to declare irreconcilable war with the wicked and them who hate God, rather than court their favor at the expense of alienating the divine layout.[29]

How, then, do we feel about those who wage war against God, through the unblushing practice of abortion? Do we approach them with the false love of liberalized Christianity? Do we speak against abortion at the morning press conference, and yet flatter the proponents of abortion at the afternoon schmoozing party? Do we view them as being innocently misguided, or do we recognize the evil of their enmity towards God (and towards His preborn children) for what it really is? And if we do allow our loyalty to God to expose the evil of their hearts and actions, do we love them enough to warn them of the coming wrath, and to bless them with the invitation of the Gospel of repentance and faith in Christ?

How, too, do we feel about those who are active in the Abortion Abolitionist movement, but who simultaneously deny and reject our Lord Jesus Christ? Is our loyalty to the Abolitionist cause one that trumps our loyalty to the revelation of God in Christ? Or, does our loyalty belong, first and foremost, to the God of Scripture, even if that loyalty causes strong tensions, or even enmity, between us and other Abolition-minded people? Are the enemies of God really to be our closest friends, so long as they hold to Abolitionist principles? Or do we let the whole world know that all people, whether for or against abortion, who hate the Gospel of Christ, must also, by definition of our loyalty to Christ, hate us?

May the Spirit of God use Psalm 139 to search our own hearts. The fact that the omniscient and omnipresent God knows children in the womb *in a relational way* gives a definitive "Yes!" to the question of their personhood, from conception onwards. Yet these little image bearers, who are fearfully and wonderfully made by God and who, today, are being slaughtered by the millions in our world, are martyrs of the Gospel of life. As such, they themselves will not allow any "sanctity of life" rhetoric to represent them if that rhetoric fails to give glory to the God of Scripture. The preborn martyrs are our

---

[29] John Calvin, Commentary on Psalm 139:22, *Calvin's Commentaries, Vol. 12: Psalms, Part V*, tr. by John King, [1847-50], n.p. [cited 2 September 2013]. Online: http://www.sacred-texts.com/chr/calvin/cc12/cc12022.htm.

friends if and only if we honor their God, who is the God of David, and who revealed Himself in the God-man, Jesus Christ, to the Apostles. But if we deny the one, true God His proper glory, and in spiritual rebellion war against Him, then we make the preborn martyrs of the womb out to be our own enemies. For they, the martyrs of the womb, are, like David, zealously loyal to their God.

Dear Reader, is your Abortion-Abolitionist zeal a God-centered zeal, or does it stem from some other kind of zeal? Are your Abolitionist labors calculated to make a name for yourself, or are they aimed at proclaiming the exclusive Lordship and glory of Jesus Christ to all nations? Are they self-interested and self-centered, or are they sacrificial and Cross-centered? What are your motives for wanting to defend the lives of children in the womb? Do your Abolitionist labors exalt the very God who formed you, in fearful and wonderful ways, in your own mother's womb?

Let us expose our own hearts to the spiritual searchlight of Psalm 139:23-24. Let us pray, with David:

> *Search me, O God, and know my heart. Try me, and know my thoughts. See if there is any wicked way in me, and lead me in the everlasting way.*

9

SHE DID NOT REMEMBER:
God's Fatherhood and Preborn Children

(Ezekiel 16:1-63)

Again the LORD's Word came to me, saying, "Son of man, cause Jerusalem to know her abominations; and say, 'Thus says the Lord GOD to Jerusalem: Your ancestry and your birth is of the land of the Canaanite; the Amorite was your father, and your mother was a Hittite. As for your birth, in the day you were born your navel was not cut, neither were you washed in water to cleanse you; you were not salted at all, nor swaddled at all. No eye pitied you, to do any of these things to you, to have compassion on you; but you were cast out in the open field, for that your person was abhorred, in the day that you were born.'"
(Ezekiel 16:1–5)

God weeps for orphans. He looks upon the helpless children who have been bereaved of their fathers and mothers, and has great compassion upon them. If their parents have died, He grieves over such little children, who are not yet able to understand why the very ones whom they need the most—especially their mothers, whose warmth they have known so fondly, even from the womb—do not respond to their lonely, pleading cries for parental comfort. Or, if their parents have abandoned them out of selfish callousness, God's own heart is pained by the ways in which parental sin has crushed the hearts of young and tender children.

True Christians, therefore, also weep for orphans. Our faith, if it lacks a great love for orphans, is a dead faith: *"Pure religion and undefiled before our God and Father is this: to visit the fatherless and widows in their affliction, and to keep oneself unstained by the world"* (James 1:27). We love orphans, since our God loves them so much. We care, sacrificially, for all children in need. As Christians, we do all that we can to protect the preborn children of the world. Yet as Christians, we also do all that we can to care for the post-born children who are in need. We visit orphans with the love of Jesus Christ.

When an Orphan Girl Becomes a Prostitute

Victor Hugo, the famed nineteenth-century French author, introduced the world, in his classic novel *Les Misérables*, to a fictional orphan with whom the world has since fallen in love:

> [She] was one of those beings which are brought forth from the heart of the people. Sprung from the most unfathomable depths of social darkness, she bore on her brow the mark of the anonymous and unknown....Who were her parents? None could tell; she had never known either father or mother. She was called Fantine—why so? Because she had never been known by any other name. She could have no family name, for she had no family; she could have no baptismal name, for then there was no church. She was named after the pleasure of the first passer-by who found her, a mere infant, straying barefoot in the streets. She received a name as she received the water from the clouds on her head when it rained. She was called Little Fantine. Nobody knew anything more of her. Such was the manner in which this human being had come into life.

An orphan girl, she grows up to become a prostitute. Little Fantine matures out of toddler-hood, into childhood, and on into adulthood. Once the delicate flower of this little orphan girl has ripened into a woman in search of a lover, she makes her way to Paris and develops an immoral relationship with a university student. He takes her, belittles her, and abandons her, leaving her pregnant and alone.

Several years flitter away. Fantine has named her baby Cosette and has intended to take her back to her hometown, which is under the benevolent government of a certain Mayor Madeleine. However, she fears that the stigma of having a child out of wedlock will prevent her from getting a job, so she unhappily leaves Cosette in the care of a couple in a town somewhere between Paris and her destination.

This conniving couple promises to take good care of Cosette, but instead abuses Fantine's little girl. They deprive her of her belongings, neglect her, and threaten to put her out into the winter streets—unless Fantine will satisfy their exorbitant demands for money. Fantine does manage to land a job at Mayor Madeleine's factory, but she is fired when her secret about having a daughter is discovered.

Therefore, it is out of desperation to pay off her loans and to appease the monetary demands of Cosette's caretakers that she first sells her hair, and then proceeds to sell her two front teeth. Finally, enraged by her poverty and despair, she turns to prostitution. Little Fantine, the orphan girl, has become a prostitute.

The benevolent Mayor Madeleine, however, is a gracious man. He rescues Fantine because he sees her need for grace. She has not chosen prostitution out of lust, or even out of a desire to get rich. She has, instead, made a horrible and sinful decision in response to a desperate situation. She and her child are, at least as Hugo would have us see them, pitiful victims of poverty and social ostracism.[1]

Les Misérables helps us to have compassion for this orphan girl, turned prostitute. Though we do not condone her sinful decision to become a prostitute, we nevertheless hurt for her, and long for her repentance, and redemption. When she dies of panic, still without Cosette, we weep for her.

There is, then, a beautiful way in which the Gospel of Christ summons prostitutes to spiritual cleansing and redemption.[2] We rightly pity the impoverished orphan girl who, in her desperation, sells herself into such a degrading form of slavery to sin. But what would we think of an orphan girl, turned prostitute, who had no apparent reason at all to prostitute herself out to the world? What if this orphan girl, turned prostitute, was adopted into riches, not self-raised in poverty? And what if she had given birth to children within wedlock, and not outside of it? What if she was, in fact, the very wife of God?

---

[1] If Fantine's story were true, and not just fictional, the Bible would simultaneously defend Fantine as one of the weak and vulnerable members of society that ought to be protected by the righteous (Proverbs 29:7), and also warn her, with the loving severity of God's holy commandments, to trust in God to help her (Genesis 21:16-17), and never to turn to prostitution, no matter her desperation (1 Corinthians 6:9-10).

[2] The blood of Jesus Christ has the power to wash away all sins (Isaiah 1:18). For those who will turn away from filth and wickedness, and believe upon His name as God and Christ, there is life-transforming power in the Gospel. The giving of the Holy Spirit to those who believe has the power to transform former prostitutes into holy, pious, and sober-minded women of faith. There is, in the Gospel, much hope for a new, transformed life. The one whom God has forgiven much, will love God much (Luke 7:47).

WHEN AN ORPHAN, TURNED QUEEN, BECOMES A PROSTITUTE

The prophet Ezekiel loves to tell parables. In Ezekiel 16, he is ready to tell us a parable, this time a scandalous tale about an orphan girl who grew up, married God, and then became a prostitute:

> *Again the* LORD's *Word came to me, saying, "Son of man, cause Jerusalem to know her abominations; and say, 'Thus says the Lord* GOD *to Jerusalem: Your ancestry and your birth is of the land of the Canaanite; the Amorite was your father, and your mother was a Hittite. As for your birth, in the day you were born your navel was not cut, neither were you washed in water to cleanse you; you were not salted at all, nor swaddled at all. No eye pitied you, to do any of these things to you, to have compassion on you; but you were cast out in the open field, for that your person was abhorred, in the day that you were born.'"* (Ezekiel 16:1–5)

She is an orphan, and her father is an Amorite and her mother is a Hittite. This is not the way that Queen Jerusalem likes to remember her national history. She likes to think of herself as the beautiful child of Abraham, her father, and Sarah, her mother. But Ezekiel will not let the truth go untold. Before the time of Joshua, Jerusalem was, in fact, a Canaanite city. Her birth is thus described as an ugly, Canaanite birth.

What is more, Jerusalem, the orphan, was abandoned in the wilderness by her Canaanite parents. She was left there to die of exposure. With no mother to nurse her and clothe her, and with no father to protect her, both the harsh elements and the wild beasts were ready to kill her.

Infanticide was commonplace in the ancient world. Aristotle, the preeminent Greek philosopher and tutor of Alexander the Great, taught that those infants who are born with physical deformities, or those who are born into large families ought to be left outside to die of exposure. Such is the case of little infant Jerusalem. Unlike the Egyptian princess who had compassion on baby Moses, there is no one having compassion on the little, dying baby, named Jerusalem.

God, however, sees the little baby girl, exposed and dying, and decides to have compassion on her:

"When I passed by you, and saw you wallowing in your blood, <u>I said to you, 'Though you are in your blood, live'; yes, I said to you, 'Though you are in your blood, live.'</u> I caused you to multiply as that which grows in the field, and you increased and grew great, and you attained to excellent ornament; your breasts were fashioned, and your hair was grown; yet you were naked and bare. Now when I passed by you, and looked at you, behold, your time was the time of love; and I spread My [wing] over you, and covered your nakedness: yes, I swore to you, and entered into a covenant with you," says the Lord GOD, "and you became Mine." (Ezekiel 16:6–8)

The key phrase in verse 6, which is repeated twice, is, *"I said to you, 'Though you are in your blood, live.'"* This is a phrase not so much of well wishing, but rather of legal adoption. God is granting the rights of adoption to this dying infant. *She has been adopted by the Creator of the universe.*

And yet she is ugly and naked. The word *"naked"* in verse 7 is the same word used to describe Eve after she ate from the tree of the knowledge of good and evil. Eve was ugly and naked in her sin. So too has Jerusalem been born into ugliness and nakedness. And even after she has grown into maturity and become a woman, she remains naked and depraved.

The striking thing, then, is that God decides to marry her. He sees her helpless state, naked and bare, and brings her under the legal protection of engagement. Just as Boaz "spread his wing over" Ruth (see Ruth 3:9), so too does God "spread His wing" of engagement over Maiden Jerusalem. And when God marries her, He clothes her, and makes her a most beautiful bride:

"Then I washed you with water; yes, I thoroughly washed away your blood from you, and I anointed you with oil. I clothed you also with embroidered work, and shod you with sealskin, and I dressed you about with fine linen, and covered you with silk. I decked you with ornaments, and I put bracelets on your hands, and a chain on your neck. I put a ring on your nose, and earrings in your ears, and a beautiful crown on your head. Thus you were decked with <u>gold and silver</u>; and your clothing was of <u>fine linen, and silk, and embroidered work</u>; you ate fine flour, and honey, and oil; and you were exceeding beautiful, and you prospered to royal estate. Your renown went out among the nations for <u>your beauty</u>; for it was perfect, through My majesty which I had put on you," says the Lord GOD. (Ezekiel 16:9–14)

She used to be quite ugly in her sin. Yet now God has chosen her, married her, and clothed her with the finest of clothes. Her clothes are, in fact, things that represent Solomon's Temple in Jerusalem. It was the Temple, itself, that had *"gold and silver"* adorning it and *"fine linen, and silk, and embroidered work"* within it. And that Temple, Solomon's, was given such extravagant gifts in order to make a Name for God among the nations. It was all for the glory of God's Name.

Yes, but Lady Jerusalem has made her clothing all about the glory of her own name. She has not remembered her former ugliness, but has taken God's nuptial gifts and used them for her own fame. The former orphan has now grown haughty and proud.

What is worse, the *"beauty"* that God gave Queen Jerusalem is the very beauty that she now takes and uses to seduce other lovers. God, and no other, gave her beauty. But now she takes her beauty, not remembering her former ugliness and who it was that made her beautiful, and uses it to commit adultery. She goes whoring after the nations. *She even becomes a prostitute*, for no other reason than that she is so addicted to her lustful adulteries.

Do we hear the horror of this? God gave Jerusalem her beauty so that she could proclaim His Name to the nations. She was supposed to worship her Husband and to adore Him with such fervor that the nations would see her beauty, and come and worship Him, too. But instead she forgets her former ugliness, idolizes her own beauty, and plays the harlot, cheating on God, Himself.

The biblical truth is that God, alone, made her beautiful. She used to be ugly, but God made her beautiful, for His own glory. When people saw her beauty, they were supposed to give glory to God for it:

Out of Zion, <u>the perfection of beauty</u>, <u>God shines out</u>. (Psalm 50:2)

God made Jerusalem beautiful, so that the nations would see His glory. Jerusalem becomes, in Scripture, the very symbol of beauty:

You are <u>beautiful</u>, my love, <u>as Tirzah</u>, <u>lovely as Jerusalem</u>, awesome as an army with banners. (Song of Solomon 6:4)

Still, beauty can be ever so dangerous. It can lead to idolatrous pride. Thus the beauty of Tyre, mirroring Satan's own angelic beauty (before his fall from Heaven), also becomes the city's downfall:

> *<u>Your heart was lifted up because of your beauty</u>; you have corrupted your wisdom by reason of your brightness: I have cast you to the ground; I have laid you before kings, that they may see you.* (Ezekiel 28:17)

Whenever this occurs, God will debase the proud. If He has granted beauty to Jerusalem, He can also take it away from her, on account of her idolatrous pride. She, who has been made beautiful, also can be brought down from her throne of beauty:

> *All that pass by clap their hands at you. <u>They hiss and wag their head at the daughter of Jerusalem</u>, saying, "Is this the city that men called '<u>The perfection of beauty</u>, the joy of the whole earth'?"* (Lamentations 2:15)

Here, then, is the sequence of the parable. Jerusalem is born ugly and depraved, the daughter of Canaanite parents. She is, at birth, abandoned by her Canaanite parents, left kicking in her own blood, to die of exposure. God, then, sees her and has compassion on her. In His grace, He saves her, marries her, and makes her beautiful. But in her beauty Jerusalem forgets both her former ugliness and the subsequent kindness of God, her Husband. Instead of honoring Him, she uses her beauty to attract foreign lovers. She prostitutes herself out to the nations. The judgment from God, then, is to hand her over to her lovers for torture and punishment, so that she will become ugly again.

Queen Jerusalem does not remember her former ugliness. She forgets that she was once an ugly, helpless orphan, and, in her willful forgetting, she becomes a prostitute. What, then, about those of us who were, formerly, Gentiles who worshipped idols? Have we, too, forgotten our former ugliness?

> *Therefore <u>remember</u> that once you, the Gentiles in the flesh, who are called "uncircumcision" by that which is called "circumcision" (in the flesh, made by hands); that you were at that time separate from Christ, alienated from the commonwealth of Israel, and strangers from the covenants of the promise, <u>having no hope and without God in the world</u>.* (Ephesians 2:11–12)

Think upon the history of England. Before the Gospel came to England, she was an ugly nation. She was steeped in sin and full of filth. It was only *the Gospel* that made her *beautiful*. But after so many centuries with the Gospel, England has not remembered her former, pre-Gospel ugliness. She has taken the beautiful blessings of the Gospel for herself, but has rejected the Gospel, itself. So now, when we look at England, what do we see? Do we see a beautiful nation? Well, the nations may still be found lusting after her universities and her wealth, but spiritually speaking England is on the brink of massive judgment from God. In the eyes of Christ, England has become ugly again.

Have we forgotten how ugly we were before Christ saved us? Do we remember that we, ourselves, were born steeped in sin and hating God? Do we remember the ugliness of our youth? Do we recall that we were once children of wrath, loving wickedness and abhorring righteousness? Have we taken the blessings of God and used them for spiritual adultery?

We must remember our former ugliness. If we do not cling to the doctrine of depravity, recalling how wretched we were prior to Christ, then we, the Church, will become worse than Queen Jerusalem. She committed adultery against the God who took her out of her own blood. But we, the Church, are on the brink of committing adultery against the Christ who gave His own blood for us. Thus Ezekiel's parable teaches us that whenever the Church neglects the doctrine of human depravity, she will quickly drift towards false teaching, spiritual adultery, and spiritual destruction.

THE COST OF NOT REMEMBERING: "BLOOD"

There is, however, something that God hates even more than His own wife taking His nuptial gifts and using them for adulterous prostitutions. But can that possibly be true? Can God actually hate something even more than His own bride, taking His own nuptial gifts, and prostituting herself out with them? Yes, there is something that He hates even more than this. That something is child sacrifice:

Moreover you have taken your sons and your daughters, whom you have borne to Me, and you have <u>sacrificed these to them to be devoured</u>. Was your prostitution a small matter, that you have slain My children, and delivered them up, in <u>causing them to pass through the fire to them</u>? In all your abominations and your prostitution you have not remembered the days of your youth, when you were naked and bare, and were wallowing in your blood.
(Ezekiel 16:20–22)

Child sacrifice is strictly forbidden in the Law of Moses. God hates idolatry, but He hates child sacrifice even more. And, in the Bible, idolatry and child sacrifice are almost always found together:

You shall not do so to the LORD your God; for every abomination to the LORD, which He hates, have they done <u>to their gods</u>; for they even <u>burn their sons and their daughters in the fire to their gods</u>. (Deuteronomy 12:31)

Again, idolatry, which is the worship of demons, goes hand in hand with child sacrifice:

Yes, they <u>sacrificed their sons and their daughters to demons</u>.
(Psalm 106:37)

King Manasseh's reign is the quintessential example of the link between idolatry and child sacrifice. Jerusalem will be burned, says God. Moreover, due to Manasseh's great wickedness, her judgment is irrevocable. Manasseh's great wickedness mixes gross idolatry with the horrific practices of child sacrifice:

He <u>made his son to pass through the fire</u>, <u>practiced sorcery</u>, <u>used enchantments</u>, and <u>dealt with those who had familiar spirits, and with wizards</u>. He did much evil in the LORD's sight, to provoke Him to anger. He set the engraved <u>image of Asherah</u> that he had made in the house of which the LORD said to David and to Solomon his son, "In this house, and in Jerusalem, which I have chosen out of all the tribes of Israel, will I put My name forever."
(2 Kings 21:6–7)

Where, then, did abortion, which is a form of child sacrifice, come from, both in ancient and in modern times? Where, also, did the contemporary, yet murderous scientific field of human embryonic stem cell research (commonly known as hESCR) come from? Did these practices come from noble-minded individuals who simply made grave ethical miscalculations? No, the Bible says that these practices came from spiritually-minded people (for, even agnostics and atheists are quite spiritual about their agnosticism and atheism) whose hearts were fixed on idolatry. People worshipped demons. Then, in their demon worship (through idols), they were led into the dark realms of philosophical and political advocacy for child sacrifice.

But why does Queen Jerusalem sacrifice her children to foreign gods? How can Queen Jerusalem, who herself was abandoned by her parents, and left to die of exposure, possibly be so cold as to sacrifice her own children? She does it because she *has not remembered* the days of her own childhood:

> *In all your abominations and your prostitution <u>you have not remembered</u> the days of your youth, when you were naked and bare, and were wallowing in your blood.* (Ezekiel 16:22)

There is a strong link in verse 22 back to the pathetic infancy of Jerusalem. It is the word, *"blood."* Ezekiel says to Jerusalem: *"…you have not remembered the days of your youth, when you were naked and bare, and were wallowing in your <u>blood</u>."* This word, blood, is a link back to verse 6:

> *When I passed by you, and saw you wallowing <u>in your blood</u>, I said to you, "Though you are <u>in your blood</u>, live"; yes, I said to you, "Though you are <u>in your blood</u>, live."* (Ezekiel 16:6)

What, then, did Queen Jerusalem willfully and wickedly fail to remember? She did not remember her own pathetic infancy, in which she almost died of exposure, struggling in her blood. However, what does this have to do with child sacrifice? How does the blood of Jerusalem's own infancy relate to child sacrifice? The *blood* of the baby, Jerusalem, and the horror of child sacrifice do relate, without ambiguity, in verse 36:

> *Thus says the Lord GOD, "Because your filthiness was poured out, and your nakedness uncovered through your prostitution with your lovers; and because of all the idols of your abominations, and <u>for the blood of your children</u>, that you gave to them…."* (Ezekiel 16:36)

SHE DID NOT REMEMBER

Jerusalem almost died in *her blood*. And yet because she does not remember her own infancy, she now brazenly sacrifices her own offspring and pours out *their blood* on the altars of foreign deities.

It has already been stated that God hates child sacrifice even more than the horrific sin of adultery. There are degrees of sin. Adultery against God is among the worst of sins. Yet child sacrifice is even worse. This is true because of verse 20:

Moreover you have taken your sons and your daughters, whom you have borne to Me, and you have sacrificed these to them to be devoured. <u>Was your prostitution [not enough]</u>...? (Ezekiel 16:20)

The *"not enough"* at the end of verse 20 is a statement from the lesser to the greater sin. It is the same in Isaiah 7:13:

He said, "Listen now, house of David. Is it <u>not enough</u> for you to try the patience of men, that you will try the patience of my God also?" (Isaiah 7:13)[3]

So the *lesser sin* in Ezekiel 16 is spiritual adultery. It is hard to believe that there could be a *greater sin* than God's own wife prostituting herself out with God's own nuptial gifts, but there is. And the reason why child sacrifice is a *greater* sin than spiritual adultery is contained in a small, yet almost nuclear-powered word in verse 21:

...that you have slain <u>My</u> children, and delivered them up, in causing them to pass through the fire to them? (Ezekiel 16:21)

When this present author used to read Ezekiel 16 during his personal Bible reading times, he would briskly and carelessly pass over that little word, *"My."* But one morning in his study, when he was preparing to preach Ezekiel 16 to his congregation, he finally noticed it.

This tiny word *"My"* has nuclear power packed into it. For any Christians who are waffling over the abortion debate, this little word in verse 21 is a nuclear bomb that will explode and annihilate any

---

[3] In Hebrew, the *"not enough"* argument, from the lesser to the greater, is made in both Ezekiel 16:20 and Isaiah 7:13 by employing the phrase *ham'aṭ min*.

argument that sets itself up against true, biblical, Abolitionist theology. It carries in itself that much energy.

God says of Queen Jerusalem's child sacrifice, *"You have slain **My** children."* This author, as has been mentioned already, encountered the word *"My,"* in verse 21, one morning in his pastoral study. He read, in Hebrew, that little word *"My"* and he put down his translation pen, and began to weep. And then he wept, more and more. He burst into tears and wept, and wept, and wept. He had to stop his translation work and set it aside for quite a long time. All he could do was weep!

Here is why he wept. He wept, uncontrollably, because it became so Scripturally clear to him that the little babies who are victims of abortion, the slaughtered ones, are *God's* children! They are not ours to kill. They are *God's* babies!

And, of course, the present author immediately thought of Luke 1:41, which tells us of John the Baptist leaping in Elizabeth's womb because Jesus, in Mary's womb, has come near to him. God's Baby, His Son, Jesus, is in the womb! And Jesus is a Person in the womb! The Son of God in the womb is the second Person of the Trinity, in the womb. Fully God and fully Man, He has full Personhood in the womb. Thus if anyone were to have performed a forced abortion on Mary (not that God would have allowed it, but just hypothetically speaking, for the sake of argument), he would have been murdering the Son of God.

In Ezekiel 16, all babies are not the same as the Baby Jesus. They are fully human, but they are not the same as the Baby Jesus, who alone possesses a divine nature. Nevertheless, in Ezekiel 16, all babies are *God's* babies! All little ones who are murdered, either in the womb or outside of the womb, are *God's* children! They are *His* children! If we love God, we shall love His children. If we do not love His children, we do not love God.

Shall we, then, claim to worship God, and yet not weep for upwards of 4,000 of *His* children who are murdered in America every day? Shall we say that we worship Jesus Christ, and yet not be willing to speak up for, and even risk our lives on behalf of *His* children? They are *Jesus'* children. If we do not weep for them, and speak for them, then our claims to worship Jesus are false claims. For we cannot worship the Jesus of Gethsemane, and the Jesus of Golgotha, if we do not first worship the Jesus who was in Mary's womb. And in worshipping the Jesus who was in Mary's womb, we cannot help but weep for *His* children who are being slain in the womb.

SHE DID NOT REMEMBER, BUT GOD WILL REMEMBER

She did not remember. Jerusalem did not remember her former ugliness, so she used her beautiful wedding gifts for ugly acts of prostitution, and so fell under God's holy judgment. Next, she did not remember her own desperate infancy, so she murdered God's children. And this act of child sacrifice was deserving of Hell. (It will do no good for us to lie to others by saying that child sacrifice, including abortion, does not deserve Hell. According to Ezekiel, child sacrifice is an even greater sin than committing adultery against God, since it is the slaughter of God's own children. It does deserve Hell.)

So is there any hope for Queen Jerusalem? Is the orphan girl, turned Queen, now such a prostitute and a murderer that her only thought should be of her future execution? Should she only be mindful of the Tower of London?

God is not a merciless Monarch. He is, rather, a King of such great mercy that there is yet much hope for Lady Jerusalem. There is much hope because although Jerusalem *"did not remember,"* God *does remember*; He is a covenantal God. This is the hope of the Glad Tidings of Christ. He causes us, through the Gospel, to remember our shame, and to see that His work of atonement, which He has provided on our behalf, is the only hope that we have for being rescued out of our shame:

> *In all your abominations and your prostitution <u>you have not remembered</u> the days of your youth, when you were naked and bare, and were wallowing in your blood....<u>Because you have not remembered</u> the days of your youth, but have raged against Me in all these things; therefore, behold, I also will bring your way on your head, says the Lord GOD: and you shall not commit this lewdness with all your abominations....<u>Then you shall remember</u> your ways, and be ashamed, when you shall receive your sisters, your elder sisters and your younger; and I will give them to you for daughters, but not by your covenant...<u>that you may remember</u>, and be confounded, and never open your mouth anymore, because of your shame, <u>when I have [provided atonement for] you [for] all that you have done</u>, says the Lord GOD.*
> (Ezekiel 16:22, 43, 61, 63)

But why does God choose to remember His faithless, adulterous wife? If Queen Jerusalem, in her lusty adulteries, has willfully decided not to remember God's former graciousness towards her, and if she has gone so far as to slay His own children on the sacrificial altars of her pagan lovers, why does not God simply decide to forget her, and to move on from her? Why would the Lord God choose to graciously remember such a wicked, adulterous, and murderous wife?

This brings us to the glorious mystery of God's covenantal love. The God of Scripture is a covenantal God. He makes covenants with His people. He has entered into a marriage covenant with Israel. And as a covenantal God, He keeps His covenant with His people, even when His people violate their covenant with Him:

> *Nevertheless <u>I will remember My covenant with you</u> in the days of your youth, and I will establish to you <u>an everlasting covenant</u>.* (Ezekiel 16:60)

Jerusalem was unfaithful because she did not remember her former ugliness, and how it was God who had made her beautiful. She was murderous towards her own children because she did not remember her own desperate infancy, and how it was God who had saved her. She did not remember. She is now condemned as an adulteress, a harlot, and a murderer, and all because she did not remember her covenant with God.

And yet, amazingly, there is hope for Jerusalem because God *does remember*. He has a covenant with His people that He remembers. He has a marriage covenant with Israel, which He made long ago, that He chooses to remember. He will never forget it:

> *Do not be afraid; for you will not be ashamed. Do not be confounded; for you will not be disappointed. For you will forget the shame of your youth; and the reproach of your widowhood you shall remember no more. For <u>your Maker is your Husband</u>; the* LORD *of Hosts is His name. The Holy One of Israel is your Redeemer. He will be called the God of the whole earth.* (Isaiah 54:4–5)

In specific, God's covenant with Israel is a covenant of forgiveness. In the wondrous, breathtaking mercy of God, the Lord promises the people of Israel that He will never turn away anyone from among them who will come to Him with a broken, trembling, repentant heart, crying out to Him for forgiveness. He shall always remember His covenant with repentant sinners who call upon His name. And He shall do so by seeing to it that their sins, from which they have turned, shall be remembered no more:

Again, when I say to the wicked, "You shall surely die"; if he turn from his sin, and do that which is lawful and right; if the wicked restore the pledge, give again that which he had taken by robbery, walk in the statutes of life, committing no iniquity; he shall surely live, he shall not die. <u>None of his sins that he has committed shall be remembered against him</u>: he has done that which is lawful and right; he shall surely live. (Ezekiel 33:14–16)

Can we not hear the criminal, who is hanging on his cross beside Jesus' own Cross, crying out for Jesus to forgive him? The other criminal is heaping insults on Jesus, but not this one. He remembers his own sinful ugliness, but when he looks at Jesus, bleeding and suffering on the Cross next to him, he does not see an ugly sinner. Rather, he sees a sinless Lamb, being slain for the sins of the world. And so he cries out:

"Lord, <u>remember me</u> when You come into Your Kingdom!" (Luke 23:42)

Jesus does remember. He remembers the New Covenant, made with His own blood, poured out for ugly sinners, such as us. We did not remember Him, but He remembered us. In the New Covenant, we, the Bride of Christ, come to love Him only because He first loved us.

Therefore, if you, beloved Reader, have had an abortion, or have counseled someone to have an abortion, and you feel the weight of Hell bearing down upon you for your murderous crime, you can be completely forgiven by God, through faith in the atoning blood of Christ. When He carried the Cross to Calvary, He bore the weight of your sin for you! You need not bear it any longer! If you will repent of your crimes against Him, and believe upon His Lordship, surrendering your soul to His kingly authority and entrusting it to His loving care, you shall be saved from your sins. And when you stand before God on Judgment Day, *He will not remember your sins against you, but instead will remember the blood of His Son that has cleansed you, and pardoned you.*

Or, dear Brother or Sister, if, in selfish cowardice, you have been shirking your Christian duty to speak out, publicly, against abortion, and you have come to see your shameful nakedness in this glaring sin of omission, remember that there is amazing hope for you. Your sins can be forgiven. If you will allow Jesus to carry these sins for you, on His own back, and in His own body on the Cross, then all shall be forgiven. Then, following your confession and prayer before the Throne of Grace, the Spirit of Christ will embolden you to go forth and speak, without any fear of man, on behalf of God's children in the womb.

Lady Jerusalem did not remember. Yet God always will remember His covenant with His children. If you are truly washed in the blood of the Lamb and sealed with the promised Holy Spirit, you are clean. He will remember His covenant with you. You need not fear the everlasting curse of Hell.

God always remembers. He remembers His covenant; He also remembers His children. The Lord God never forgets His children, who to this day are being slaughtered in the womb. They are His little ones. They are constantly on His mind and heart.

Will you remember? Will "Sanctity of Human Life Sunday" come and go ever so briskly once a year, and will you remember God's children, who are being sacrificed to the gods of this age, for only one day out of the year? Will you forget about them for all of the days in between such yearly reminders? Or will you remember them, constantly? Will you pray for them, at least weekly, if not daily? Will you ask in prayer, with trembling reverence, for God, our Father, to abolish abortion in our world?

<u>*Remember Jesus Christ*</u>, *raised from the dead, of the seed of David!* (2 Timothy 2:8).[4]

Remember Jesus Christ. Remember that He was *God's* Child in Mary's womb. Remember Him on Rome's barbaric Cross, dying for the sins of the world. Remember that it is God, the God of Israel, who always remembers His covenant with us because He loves His only-begotten Son, and He loves His own, precious children.

---

[4] The present author's translation.

Part Three:

The New Testament Heartbeat

DIVINE HEARTBEAT

10

THE BABY LEAPED!
Elizabeth, Mary, and Preborn Children

(Luke 1:39-45)

Mary arose in those days and went into the hill country with haste, into a city of Judah, and entered into the house of Zacharias and greeted Elizabeth. When Elizabeth heard Mary's greeting, the baby leaped in her womb, and Elizabeth was filled with the Holy Spirit. She called out with a loud voice, and said, "Blessed are you among women, and blessed is the fruit of your womb! Why am I so favored, that the mother of my Lord should come to me? For behold, when the voice of your greeting came into my ears, the baby leaped in my womb for joy! Blessed is she who believed, for there will be a fulfillment of the things which have been spoken to her from the Lord!" (Luke 1:39–45)

The Gospel of God brings glad tidings to a suffering, believing people. It also brings great blessings to a humble, faithful people. That is, the goodness of the Good News is only understood by the meek and lowly. It is only those who are hungry for righteousness that are able to recognize the sweetness of the bread of the Gospel. Also, it is only those who mourn over sin and death that are able to hear the comforting notes of the music of the Gospel.

Yet the preaching of the Gospel can be mimicked and distorted by false teachers. These spiritual charlatans, who have a form of godliness, but deny its power, preach an altogether different gospel than the one that was preached by the Apostles. They speak of faith, comfort, goodness, justice, righteousness, kindness, and love, but they pour into these biblical terms a meaning that contradicts the biblical Gospel, itself. They are pretenders of mercy, whose false claims to Agape-love only result in immorality and violence. In the end, as the blessed Paul warns, they shall *"be accursed"* (Galatians 1:9).

A specific instance of this hijacking of Gospel terms for evil purposes comes in the conflict over abortion. There are, in this world, professing Christians who fight for pro-abortion ends under the banner of "the Gospel." Shockingly, some of them are even professing-Christian pastors.

This is backwards to a most sinister degree, that the professing-Christian wing of the current pro-abortion militancy calls its work a Gospel work. It is not unlike *"worshiping the sun toward the east"* within the very precincts of the Temple of God (Ezekiel 8:16). This is, most assuredly, a false gospel.

Still, the proponents of the "pro-choice gospel" come replete with their own evangelists and theologians. Indeed, their message is oftentimes heeded, and converts are frequently made of it because of its appeals to human sympathies. It toys with human compassion by calling the attention of its hearers to the woes of young, pregnant mothers, who have been abandoned by their lovers and left to live on the streets, without means. It highlights the incessant sorrows of victims of rape and incest. Thus the "pro-choice gospel" draws people into a compassionate consideration of the plight of the impoverished, battered, and neglected pregnant women of the world.[1] Then, once it has caught people on its "compassionate" hook, it reels them into its murderous message.

It is most fitting, then, for this false gospel of "choice" to be exposed as such by *two pregnant women* in Scripture. Neither of these women are women of privilege. At least one of them is poor. Both of them are women who undergo great social ostracism and familial persecution on account of their pregnancies. Neither of their pregnancies are "planned," and both of their pregnancies are biologically "ill-timed." However, despite their great sorrows, and despite the great dangers to which they are exposed on account of their pregnancies, these women are unequivocal in their biblical conviction that *all* life in the womb is sacred, from conception

---

[1] Christians, in particular, are commanded by Scripture to exercise great, Christ-like compassion towards such women. The entire crisis-pregnancy-center movement, which is largely Christian-based, is fueled by such compassion. But the irony here is that the pro-abortion message, which is a murderous message, not only fails to alleviate the sorrows of such women, but actually increases them exponentially. The inevitable guilt that comes from murdering their own offspring is more than many of these already downtrodden mothers are able to bear.

onwards, and ought to be protected as such. We speak, of course, of Elizabeth, the wife of Zacharias, and of her close relative, Mary.

ELIZABETH AND MARY: WOMEN OF HUMILITY

In the Gospel of Luke, these two women, Elizabeth and Mary, experience tremendous sufferings, both leading up to, and concurrent with the incalculable blessings of their pregnancies. They are women who know how to prepare their sons for godly suffering, since they, themselves, are familiar with such suffering. Their own sorrows carve a deep outline of the Cross into their hearts, even as the Cross overshadows them. Thus it is the presence of the Cross in their lives that works to shape and form their magnificent humility.

In specific, the sufferings of Elizabeth and Mary come in the forms of severe social stigmas, prophetic foreknowledge of their sons' future persecutions, and the hardships of womanhood, itself. Such trials are, for them, cumulatively tremendous, even as they are concomitant with the blessings of God in their lives. Yet both women endure these great sufferings with such a Scripture-saturated faith in God that their humility is only deepened on account of them.

The Social Stigmas of Elizabeth and Mary

Elizabeth's sorrows are all tied up in her barrenness. Like Sarah of old, she is righteous before God, and well advanced in years, and yet knows the unrelenting pain of a barren womb:

> *There was in the days of Herod, the king of Judea, a certain priest named Zacharias, of the priestly division of Abijah. He had a wife of the daughters of Aaron, and her name was Elizabeth. They were both <u>righteous before God</u>, walking blamelessly in all the commandments and ordinances of the Lord. But they had no child, because Elizabeth <u>was barren</u>, and they <u>both were well advanced in years</u>.* (Luke 1:5–7)

If any Israelite woman's life ought to be marked out for blessing, it should be Elizabeth's. She is married to a godly priest. She, herself, is the daughter of a priest. She *"walk[s] blamelessly in all the commandments and ordinances of the Lord"* (v. 6). Due to her righteous faith before God, she, more than all women, ought to know the blessings of the Covenant:

<u>No one will miscarry or be barren in your land</u>. I will fulfill the number of your days. (Exodus 23:26)

And yet Elizabeth's womb is not marked out for the blessings of a fruitful womb, whence comes an abundance of children. Rather, her life has been painfully marked by the social stigma of barrenness. Surely, her neighbors—the other Israelite women around her who are much less interested in faithful piety than she is—appear to be much more blessed by God. Each one of their homes is filled with a boisterous brood. But Elizabeth's home is silent, and empty.

Therefore, when God performs His mighty miracle and causes Elizabeth to conceive a son in her old age, Elizabeth gives glory to Him for *"tak[ing] away my reproach among men"* (Luke 1:25). Her stigma of barrenness, and all of the personal pain that has gone with it, has been removed by the gracious hand of God. Her great suffering has marked her out for an even greater blessing.

Mary, too, has her social stigmas, but of entirely different kinds. Firstly, she is poor. The idea that Jesus, in the Gospels, is born into wealth is a heresy that has been invented by greedy false teachers in the Church in order to justify their own greed. The truth is that Jesus' family is poor. Thus when Joseph and Mary go to the Temple to offer the sacrifices of purification, as prescribed in the Law of Moses, they bring their sacrifices *"according to that which is said in the Law of the Lord, 'A pair of turtledoves, or two young pigeons.'"* (Luke 2:24). Yet Leviticus 12:8, which is the verse to which Doctor Luke here refers, makes it clear that only *the poor* are allowed to bring such an offering (in place of a more expensive lamb).

Mary is poor. God *"raises up <u>the poor</u> out of the dust. He lifts up the needy from the dunghill, to make them sit with princes, and inherit the throne of glory"* (1 Samuel 2:8). He has chosen *"those who are <u>poor</u> in this world to be rich in faith, and heirs of the Kingdom which He promised to those who love Him"* (James 2:5). Mary is chosen to be the mother of our Lord partly because of her poverty. Christianity, then, is not a religion of health and prosperity. It comes most readily to the poor. The Abortion Abolitionist cause, therefore, is not to be equated, ever so blindly, with a brand of Christianity that trumpets excessive wealth, on the one hand, and neglects the plight of the poor, on the other. Rather, on account of the impoverished family of Jesus, the Abortion Abolitionist cause is forever tied to God's own heart for the poor and the needy.

Secondly, Mary is a virgin. Christ Jesus is one Person, the Son of God, consisting of two separate, full, and unconfused natures, one of man and one of God. Therefore, the miraculous conception of Christ Jesus in Mary's womb is both of Mary, as to Christ's human nature, and of the seed of God, as to His divine nature. This means that the Holy Spirit overshadows Mary before she has ever known a man. It is a most wondrous wonder. But it also is a great social stigma.

Mary's miraculous conception, as a virgin, causes her great pain. Joseph, her fiancé, being a righteous man, thinks of seeking to divorce her, with mercy, in secret. Providentially, Joseph is prevented from doing so when an angel of the Lord appears to him in a dream and explains the nature of the miracle to him. Still, Mary will carry this pregnancy-out-of-wedlock stigma with her the rest of her life. Thus Jesus' enemies will taunt him by saying, *"We were not born of sexual immorality…"* (John 8:41). The pain of this false accusation will be, for Mary, a pain that is lifelong, and deep.

The Prophetic Sufferings of John and Jesus

Why does God choose Elizabeth and Mary for such miraculous pregnancies? Why does His favor rest upon them in such a way that they will be recognized, in Heaven, as the mothers of John and Jesus? Surely, God's sovereign choice is mysterious. Still, we must notice that Elizabeth and Mary are uniquely faithful, and uniquely righteous, so much so that they are willing, out of their intense love of God, to draw near to the pain and horror of the Cross of salvation. Neither of them shirks the colossal suffering that awaits them, and that awaits their precious sons.

Elizabeth's sufferings, of course, are less than those of Mary. Elizabeth's husband, Zacharias, has been told by the angel of the Lord to give the name "John" to the boy in her womb. Yet this untraditional naming of the baby boy causes a great rift between Elizabeth and her own family members:

They said to her, "<u>There is no one among your relatives who is called by this name</u>." (Luke 1:61)

    We do not want to read too much into this family dispute, but it is certainly possible that the family friction caused by John's name foreshadows the coming sufferings of John. He will preach against the hypocritical traditions of the Scribes and the Pharisees. John will condemn the "family traditions" of Israel, insofar as they neglect God's Word in favor of power, lust, and greed. For doing so, John will be beheaded. Elizabeth's "miracle baby" will, one day, suffer a terrible martyrdom at the hands of his own people.

    Yet if the life of John the Baptist draws Elizabeth towards the Cross, at least spiritually speaking (in the Gospels, it seems safe to assume that Elizabeth most likely dies before the time of John's public ministry and Jesus' subsequent crucifixion), it is the life of Jesus that brings Mary, literally, to the Cross. At Golgatha, *"there stood by the Cross of Jesus <u>His mother</u>…"* (John 19:25, NKJV). She, as His mother, carries Him in the womb. He, as her Son, carries her to the Cross.

    The great sufferings of Mary, as she watches her blessed Son bleed and suffocate at Calvary, are prophesied to her while Jesus is yet a baby:

Simeon blessed them, and said to Mary, His mother, "Behold, this Child is set for the falling and the rising of many in Israel, and for a sign which is spoken against. Yes, <u>a sword will pierce through your own soul</u>, that the thoughts of many hearts may be revealed." (Luke 2:34–35)

    Those who know Christ best have the deepest fellowship with Him in His own sufferings, even *"being conformed to His death"* (Philippians 3:10). They *"die daily"* (1 Corinthians 15:31). Mary's faith is such a suffering faith. Her unique calling is to go through physical labor pains in order to bring forth Baby Jesus into our world of air, pollen, and dust. Afterwards, however, she is to follow Him, as His disciple, even to the point of witnessing *His* physical labor pains of death and resurrection.

THE BABY LEAPED!

The Womanhood of Elizabeth and Mary

Despite what the twisted psychological theories of our day have to say about "transgender identity," motherhood is exclusive to women. Furthermore, a large part of feminine identity is tied to motherhood. The tenets of feminism may rage against this fact, calling, as they do, for a strong separation between femininity and motherhood, but the tie between the two remains unbroken.

Now, it is true, as feminism loves to point out, that throughout the centuries women have been mistreated and oppressed by men. And while this historical truth in no way justifies the feminism that has come to dominate Western society (even as it neglects the many ways in which women have seduced, manipulated, and displaced men throughout history), it nevertheless must be known. The history of humanity, which has oftentimes been filled with great male hubris and violence towards women, has, more often than not, forced women into very lowly positions.

The triumph of Elizabeth and Mary, therefore, is an exaltation of womanhood, *through motherhood*, back to its original, glorious status. That is, the very *womanhood* of Elizabeth and Mary marks them out for lowliness. This, in turn, prepares them for the great exaltation of womanhood that oftentimes comes *through motherhood*, and that comes to them, specially, through the miraculous nature of their pregnancies.

Women in ancient Rome were not treated with the same kind of dignity that they are given in the Law and the Prophets. Rather, they were born into a degraded societal status. Therefore, it seems that Jesus first appears, in His resurrected body, *to the women* in order to demonstrate how the Gospel comes most readily to the lowly, the oppressed, and the humble. Even if a woman's testimony was less credible to the ears of the Romans than that of a man's testimony, Jesus would exalt the humble faith of pious women by making women the first eyewitnesses to His resurrection:

> *[The women] remembered His words, <u>returned from the tomb, and told all these things to the eleven</u>, and to all the rest….These words seemed to them to be nonsense, and <u>they did not believe [the women]</u>.* (Luke 24:8-9, 11)

Doctor Luke must have this lowly societal status of women in mind when writing the first chapter of his Gospel. He portrays, with great detail and intentionality, the humility of Elizabeth and Mary. Part of this humility involves their womanhood. They, the lowly women, have more faith than Zacharias, the proud and self-confident man:

The Angel Gabriel to <u>Zacharias</u>: *"Behold, you will be silent and not able to speak, until the day that these things will happen, because <u>you did not believe my words</u>, which will be fulfilled in their proper time."* (Luke 1:20)

Elizabeth to <u>Mary</u>: *"Blessed is <u>she who believed</u>, for there will be a fulfillment of the things which have been spoken to her from the Lord!"* (Luke 1:45)

In fact, the literary structure of Luke 1:8-79 is one that highlights the strong faith of Elizabeth and Mary, in contrast with the weaker faith of Zacharias:[2]

Zacharias (vv. 8-23)
    Elizabeth (vv. 24-25)
        Mary (vv. 26-38)
            Mary & Elizabeth Together (vv. 39-45)
        Mary (vv. 46-56)
    Elizabeth (vv. 57-61)
Zacharias (vv. 62-79)

What, then, do Elizabeth and Mary have to say to a contemporary Church that is plunging headlong into feminism? Do their lives, as recorded in Holy Scripture, endorse egalitarian models of Christian living? Should women no longer be submissive to men in the home and in the Church?

Given the intimate friendship between Doctor Luke and the Apostle Paul, we can imagine the former responding to these

---

[2] The present author owes this insight to Richard Bauckham, *Gospel Women: Studies of the Named Women in the Gospels* (Grand Rapids: Wm. B. Eerdmans, 2002), 49. Bauckham himself gives a more complete and detailed summary of the chiastic narrative structure of Luke 1:5-80, including the voice of the "Narrator" in vv. 5-7, 80 and the voice of the "People" in vv. 21-23, 62-66.

questions by employing the latter's patented exclamation, "Certainly not!" To the contrary, it is the *lowliness* and *submission* of Elizabeth and Mary, as women, which marks their great humility. They were humble and content in the glory of their submissive womanhood.

Ironically, then, in an age in which even church women are seeking to abandon the blessings of motherhood in exchange for the perceived delights of the workforce, we find such feminists warring against the very thing that brought about the exaltation of Elizabeth and Mary. The glory of womanhood lies neither in corporate-world leadership, nor in political leadership, nor in the leadership offices of the Church, but rather in the mysteries and wonders of pregnancy and motherhood. Once again, the great Apostle Paul puts it this way:

> *…but she will be saved <u>through her childbearing</u>, if they continue in faith, love, and sanctification with sobriety.* (1 Timothy 2:15)

The Word-centeredness of Elizabeth and Mary

The lives of both Elizabeth and Mary, are, then, marked out for great suffering. But why? What is it about them that brings the favor of God's miraculous hand upon them? Again, God's calling is sovereign and mysterious. However, the Gospel of Luke wants it to be known that both Elizabeth and Mary are very special servants of God. And it is their Word-centered humility that makes them so special.

How does Elizabeth respond to her great sufferings, and also to the miraculous news of the two boys, John and Jesus? She responds, humbly, with a Bible-saturated faith:

> *"Why am I so favored, that <u>the mother of my Lord</u> should come to me?"* (Luke 1:43)

And what, exactly, does Elizabeth mean by the phrase *"the mother of my Lord"*? Surely, hers is not a biblically-ignorant faith, based only on raw spiritual experience. Rather, Elizabeth, who is much older than Mary, is nevertheless humbled by Mary's presence for the very reason that she sees in Mary the fulfillment of Isaiah's magnificent prophecy:

Therefore the Lord himself will give you a sign. Behold, <u>the virgin</u> will conceive, and bear a son, and shall call his name Immanuel. (Isaiah 7:14)

    Elizabeth's humility is thus a Word-centered humility. Her faith is a Scriptural faith. She clings to Scripture both as a woman of affliction, and as a daughter of Abraham.

    In the same way, Mary faces her own great sufferings with a Scripture-saturated faith. She believes not only in the power of God, but also in the Word of God:

Mary said, "Behold, the servant of the Lord; let it be done to me <u>according to your word</u>." The angel departed from her. (Luke 1:38)

    Again, Mary exercises great faith, and the object of her great faith is God's holy Word:

"Blessed is she who believed, for there will be a fulfillment of <u>the things which have been spoken to her from the Lord</u>!" (v. 45)

    Yet there is more. After Mary receives the blessing from Elizabeth, she utters a song of praise to the Lord. This song has since been called Mary's *"Magnificat,"* which is Latin for the verb "to magnify" that appears in its opening line:

"My soul magnifies [Latin: magnificat] the Lord…." (v. 46)

    What makes the *Magnificat* so magnificent, however, is not just Mary's spontaneous eruption of worship. It is the Scriptural saturation of the song that causes the Christian reader of it to pause, in great awe and wonder. Mary obviously has large sections of the Bible put to memory, for every line of the *Magnificat* contains either a direct quotation from Scripture, or else a clear allusion to Holy Writ. Much of it is modeled after Hannah's song of praise in 1 Samuel 2:1-10. But many other verses of Scripture are woven into it, as well. For example, verse 49, alone, contains direct quotations from two different Psalms:

THE BABY LEAPED!

"For He who is mighty <u>has done great things</u> for me. <u>Holy is His name</u>." (Luke 1:49)

Your righteousness also, O God, reaches to the heavens; You <u>have done great things</u>. O God, who is like You? (Psalm 71:19)

He has sent redemption to His people; He has ordained His covenant forever: <u>His name is holy and awesome!</u> (Psalm 111:9)

Also, the Magnificat ends with a Messianic reference *"to Abraham and his [seed] forever"* (Luke 1:55). This reference demonstrates, concerning Mary, both her amazing ability to allude to the Messianic fulfillment of Psalm 105, and a very deep and mature understanding of the nature of the Baby in her womb as the Messianic *"seed"* of Abraham:

…<u>you [seed] of Abraham</u>, His servant, you children of Jacob, His chosen ones. (Psalm 105:6)

Now the promises were spoken to Abraham and <u>to his [seed]</u>. He does not say, "To [seeds]", as of many, but as of one, "<u>To your [seed]</u>", <u>which is Christ</u>. (Galatians 3:16)

This is the mark of Mary's deep humility. She is a woman of God who is humble and contrite, and who knows how to tremble, joyfully, at God's holy Word. Hers is a biblical faith. Hers is a biblically-saturated form of worship. Her mind and heart are filled with the Scriptures. Therefore, God has chosen her very womb to be filled with His Word, incarnate.

THE BLESSEDNESS OF THE VIRGIN MARY

Mary is very blessed by God. All of those who believe the Gospel know that Mary is the recipient of a blessedness that is so filled with grace and wonder that it leaves people, who meditate upon it, both breathless and speechless. Yet when we consider the blessedness of Mary, we must not forget what, exactly, it is that makes her so blessed. Her blessedness is found not externally, in the works of her hands, but internally, in the fruit of her womb:

> *[Elizabeth] called out with a loud voice, and said, "<u>Blessed are you</u> among women, and <u>blessed is the fruit of your womb</u>!" (Luke 1:42)*

    Women, today, are turning away from the very thing that made Mary so blessed. They are using contraception and employing abortion in order to prevent the fruitfulness of their wombs and to destroy the very fruit of their wombs. Their wombs are made, by God, to bear much fruit. Yet they are calling this blessing of God a curse—a great, obstructive boulder on their jogging path towards slim bodies and lucrative careers. In doing so, they are rejecting the blessings of the fruit of the womb in exchange for the curse of a self-centered life, bereft of such sweet, plentiful fruit.

    Let us not be vague and ambiguous on this critical point. Rather, let us affirm, wholeheartedly, that Scripture describes God's blessing upon women in terms of bountiful procreation.[3] Let us also, then, affirm, with much conviction, that every child, from the very moment of conception, no matter his physical health, nor the circumstances of his conception, is a blessing from God:

> *Joseph is <u>a fruitful vine</u>....The Almighty...<u>will bless you</u>, with blessings of heaven above, blessings of the deep that lies below, <u>blessings of the breasts, and of the womb</u>. (Genesis 49:22, 25)*

And,

> *They will <u>not labor in vain, nor give birth for calamity</u>; for they are <u>the offspring of the LORD's blessed</u>, and their descendants with them. (Isaiah 65:23)*

    Why, then, is Mary so blessed? Her blessedness is inseparable from the fruit of her womb. Thus Elizabeth says not only, *"Blessed are you among women,"* but also, *"and blessed is the fruit of your womb!"* (Luke 1:42). It is the "fruit" of Mary's womb that makes her so blessed. As it is written:

---

[3] However, the converse of this is not true. It is *not* true that women who lack bountiful procreation in their lives necessarily lack God's blessing. Rather, many of the most blessed women of Scripture had to carry a personal cross of barrenness or bereavement. See note 5 in Chapter 2, "God's Great Blessings."

The Baby Leaped!

Behold, children are a heritage of the LORD. *<u>The fruit of the womb is [a] reward</u>.* (Psalm 127:3)

Would it, then, have been ethical for Mary to have attempted to abort the Baby in her womb? If she had chosen not to "practice her religion," so to speak, would it have been wrong for her to attempt an abortion, say, early on in her first trimester of pregnancy? (It is approaching insanity for our society to have reached such a morally deplorable state that such questions are actually relevant to the ethical discourse of our day). The stakes, here, are infinitely high, for the *"fruit"* of Mary's womb is both *Messianic* and *divine* fruit:

The LORD *has sworn to David in truth. He will not turn from it: "<u>I will set the fruit of your body on your throne</u>."* [4] (Psalm 132:11)

If Mary is truly the mother of God,[5] then her pregnancy with Jesus ought to be the decisive factor in the debate that rages over abortion. Skeptics (of the ilk who nevertheless profess a belief in the Bible) are far too quick to dismiss questions such as, "Since Mary had an unplanned pregnancy, would it have been ethical [anachronistically

---

[4] Most English translations say, *"the fruit of your body,"* so as to make the metaphor match David's masculinity. But the Hebrew is strongly connected to the language of *"the fruit"* of the *"womb,"* which makes the Psalm 132:11/Luke 1:42 connection quite Messianic, indeed!

[5] The Greek term *Theotokos*, or "Mother of God," is applied to Mary not merely to emphasize the humanity of Christ (that He was in the flesh, having a human mother). Rather, it is a much more comprehensive "Christological" term. It describes the *one* Person, Jesus Christ, as having both a fully divine and a fully human nature, and it teaches that those two natures exist without confusion, without change, without division, without separation, etc. Thus Cyril of Alexandria uses *Theotokos* to describe the full *deity* of Christ, "If any one does not acknowledge that Emmanuel is in truth God, and that the holy virgin is, in consequence, 'Theotokos,' for she brought forth after the flesh the Word of God who has become flesh, let him be anathema" (qtd. in Henry Bettenson and Chris Maunder, eds., *Documents of the Christian Church* [Oxford: Oxford University Press, 1999], 50), while the Symbol of Chalcedon employs *Theotokos* to describe Christ as "born of the virgin Mary, the *Theotokos, according to the Manhood"* (trans. in Schaff, *Creeds of Christendom*, 2:62, emphasis added). Thus the true focus of *Theotokos* is not on Mary (and, therefore, the church-historic title, "Mother of God," in no way supports Roman Catholic views on Mary!), but on the one Person, Christ Jesus, having two separate and distinct natures, one of God and one of man, who became incarnate and was born of the virgin.

speaking, of course] for Mary to have taken the morning-after pill as soon as she discovered that she was pregnant?" or, "Since Mary was impoverished, would it have been ethical for her to have had an early first-trimester abortion?" by appealing to her special calling as the mother of God. When these skeptics reply, hastily, "Well, Mary was spoken to directly by God, and hers was a miraculous conception, and she was carrying the Son of God in her womb, etc.," they are entirely missing the point of these questions. The point is that Mary's pregnancy answers, with great lucidity, the question of the "personhood" of babies in the womb (from conception onwards).

In the Gospel of Luke, Jesus Christ is the Son of God in Mary's womb, *from conception onwards*. This is proved by the fact that Elizabeth is, at a minimum, in her *"sixth month"* of pregnancy when Jesus is conceived in Mary's womb (Luke 1:36). That means that when Mary visits Elizabeth, with Baby Jesus already in her womb, Mary must be *in her first trimester*, since Elizabeth is still pregnant with John upon Mary's arrival (v. 44). Therefore, since Baby John obviously acknowledges the "Personhood" of Baby Jesus upon Mary's arrival,[6] the "Personhood" of Jesus is established *within His first trimester of growth in the womb*.

Of course, it could not be otherwise. For, the very conception of Jesus happens when the Holy Spirit comes upon Mary, and *"the power of the Most High"* overshadows her (v. 35). To claim that the newly conceived Baby in Mary's womb (even just seconds after conception) is not the actual Person of the Son of God, is more than theologically reckless. It is downright blasphemous.[7] It also undermines the Gospel.[8] The Personhood of the Son of God does not develop or

---

[6] See the section entitled, "Two Pregnancies and Two 'Babies,'" below.

[7] Who, for example, would dare to say that the newly conceived Baby in Mary's womb is not the Person of the Son of God? Does not the mere thought of such an assertion evoke the wrath of Almighty God? Does it not reek of heresy, albeit in a different manner, but with a similar potency and foulness as that of the ancient heresy of Arius?

[8] The technical theological argument for this undermining of the Gospel is as follows. First, human beings are *conceived in sin* (Psalm 51:5), which means that they have a sin nature (inherited from Adam), even *from conception*. Second, the Son of God assumed humanity in order to recapitulate humanity in sinless perfection (that is, He sanctified humanity by His sinless life, from conception to death). Third, if the Son of God did not assume humanity (as the Second *Person* of the Trinity) until sometime after conception, then He could not have fully recapitulated humanity in sinless perfection.

evolve in Mary's womb. Jesus is not less of the Son of God early on in the pregnancy, and more of the Son of God later on in the pregnancy. To the contrary, Jesus has full Personhood, as the Son of God in Mary's womb, from conception onwards.

This is what makes Mary so blessed among women. It is also what makes the pro-abortion case so preposterous. The Second Person of the Godhead, having taken up residence in Mary's womb, as a Baby, settles the debate over abortion with sovereign and divine finality. The Baby Jesus testifies loudly against abortion. He condemns it as an abomination, and He does so with His own divine and kingly presence in the womb. Thus the Word of God gets the last word on abortion. God, of course, would have it no other way.

Two Pregnancies, and Two "Babies"

The present author recently had a softly-spoken, yet still very serious debate with a professing-Christian pastor over the issue of abortion. In the course of the debate, the "pastor" made the claim that the Scriptures are virtually silent on the issue of "the personhood of the 'thing' in the womb." He even went so far as to boast of having gone through a miscarriage with his wife without ever having grieved for the "tissue" lost from his wife's womb, and without once having thought to conduct a memorial service for "it," or to bestow upon "it" a personal name.

Such an experience impresses upon the mind of a Christian Abolitionist the diabolical nature of the act of seeking to silence the Scriptures on the personhood of the baby in the womb. To say, "The Bible is unclear, or vague on the personhood of the child in the womb," is just as evil as if one were to say, "The Bible is pro-choice regarding abortion," for both are murderous lies. The personhood of the baby in the womb is firmly established in Scripture, as the entirety of this present volume testifies. This fact is nowhere more transparent than in the case of Elizabeth's and Mary's pregnancies.

"For behold, when the voice of your greeting came into my ears, <u>the baby leaped in my womb for joy!</u>" (Luke 1:44)

In 1534, William Tyndale translated the Greek word *bréphos* in this verse as *"babe,"* and he did so very judiciously.[9] This is not a potential human, but an actual person. John the Baptist is the preborn *"babe"* [*bréphos*] in Elizabeth's womb in Luke 1:44, and this Greek word for *"child"* or *"babe"* is the exact same word that Doctor Luke employs in chapter 2 to describe the *post-born* Baby Jesus:

For lo, as soon as the voice of thy salutation sounded in mine ears, the babe sprang in my belly for joy. (Luke 1:44, Tyndale's 1534 New Testament)

And take this for a sign: ye shall find the child swaddled and laid in a manger. (Luke 2:12, Tyndale's 1534 New Testament)

And they [the shepherds] came with haste, and found Mary and Joseph and the babe laid in a manger. (Luke 2:16, Tyndale's 1534 New Testament)

The clarity of Scripture on this point is divinely intentional. God has spelled out for us, in clear Greek letters, the personhood of the baby in the womb. John the Baptist is a *bréphos*, a *"babe,"* in Elizabeth's womb. Jesus Christ is a *bréphos*, a *"babe,"* while swaddled and lying in a manger. The *"babe"* is a full person, both inside and outside of the womb. There may be a change of environment for the baby (the one environment cozy and warm, the other exposed and vulnerable to the elements), but there is, in God's mind, absolutely no change in personhood.

In fact, the Greek term *bréphos*, used to describe John the Baptist as the *"babe"* in Elizabeth's womb, also describes other *post-born infants* in Doctor Luke's writings:

They were also bringing their babies to him, that he might touch them. But when the disciples saw it, they rebuked them. (Luke 18:15)

---

[9] Luther chose to translate *tò bréphos* into German as *"das Kind,"* while the Vulgate (Latin) chose *"infans"* for *bréphos*.

Also,

> *The same [Pharaoh, king of Egypt] took advantage of our race, and mistreated our fathers, and <u>forced them to throw out their babies</u>, so that they would not stay alive.* (Acts 7:19)

Furthermore, not only does Doctor Luke establish the personhood of Baby John in the womb through his use of the term *bréphos*, but he also, in his account of the meeting of the two mothers, establishes the Personhood of the Baby Jesus. For, the "babe" in Elizabeth's womb leaps for joy *because of the nearness of the other Babe in the room*. Mary, too, carries a Babe in her womb (and, again, note that her Babe is in His first-trimester),[10] and it is the Personhood of this Babe that causes Baby John to leap in the womb with exceeding joy.

Holy Scripture, then, does not differentiate between the personhood of a baby within the womb, versus the personhood of a baby outside of the womb. If infants, nursing at their mothers' breasts, have full personhood, then so too, in Scripture, do babies inside of the womb possess full personhood. In the Bible, to kill a baby in the womb, at any stage of pregnancy, is as much an act of murder as it is for Pharaoh to force the male Hebrew infants to be cast into the Nile River. In Scripture, a baby is a baby, whether inside or outside of the womb.

Predictably, however, what Holy Scripture makes clear, Satan seeks to make ambiguous. If abortion is murder, as Scriptures says that it is, then it is a black-and-white matter. Yet Satan likes to blur lines and blend colors. He wants moral lines to be made quite fuzzy, and black-and-white matters to become gray. Therefore, Satan works hard to deceive pastors through the means of liberalized Bible commentaries on Luke's Gospel (or through other, even "Evangelical" expositions of Luke), that completely ignore the Abortion-Abolitionist implications of its first two chapters. Also, Satan pressures physicians, professors, lawyers, and politicians into following academic protocol in employing medical nomenclature, so that they feel obligated to use the ambiguous Latin term *"fetus"* in place of the more definitive English term "baby." In all of these

---

[10] For the evidence that Mary is in her first trimester of pregnancy, see above, in the section entitled "The Blessedness of the Virgin Mary."

crafty and wily ways, the truth is not contradicted, but simply smeared, and, therefore, cast into doubt.

Yet God's Word remains plain and perspicuous in the hearts of those who fear Him. The mind of Christ does not equivocate on the personhood of the baby in the womb. In the mind of God, a *bréphos* is a baby, with full personhood, and a preborn child, from conception onwards, is, indeed, a *bréphos*. The words of Holy Scripture declare this to be so. Therefore, let not the words of man contradict it.

THE JOY OF BABY JOHN AND THE JOY OF THE GOSPEL

To remember the personhood of Baby John, in Elizabeth's womb, is a mournful thing—for how many babies have been murdered in their mothers' wombs this very day?—but it is also a most joyful practice. For, to meditate upon the personhood of Baby John is to discover the marvelous link between personhood and joy. It takes *personhood* for a human being to be able to experience *joy*. And Baby John, in Elizabeth's womb, is found leaping for *joy*:

> *For behold, when the voice of your greeting came into my ears, the baby <u>leaped in my womb for joy</u>!* (Luke 1:44)

Elizabeth, the joyful mother of John, feels her son *"leap"* in her womb. She thus recalls the joyful, miraculous pregnancy of Rebekah, wife of the patriarch Isaac, who, in her pregnancy, has become the mother of twin boys, one of whom is the patriarch Jacob:

> *And Isaac prayed to the Lord concerning Rebekah his wife, because she was barren; and the Lord heard him, and his wife Rebekah conceived in her womb. <u>And the babes leaped within her</u>; and she said, "If it will be so with me, why is this to me?" And she went to inquire of the Lord.* (Genesis 25:21-22, LXX)[11]

Still, John the Baptist's leaping in his mother's womb is less like Jacob and Esau, wrestling over the birthright, and more like the mountains of Israel, leaping like rams. For, according to the Psalmist,

---

[11] This is from the English text of the ancient Greek translation of the Old Testament known as the Septuagint (Latin for "Seventy"), which is commonly referenced by the Roman-numeral abbreviation LXX.

it is the *"presence of the God of Jacob"* that causes those mountains to leap:

> *The sea saw it, and fled. The Jordan was driven back. The mountains <u>[leaped] like rams</u>, the little hills like lambs. What was it, you sea, that you fled? You Jordan, that you turned back? You mountains, that you <u>[leaped] like rams</u>; you little hills, like lambs? Tremble, you earth, <u>at the presence of the Lord</u>, <u>at the presence of the God of Jacob</u>.* (Psalm 114:3–7)

This is an awe-striking Scriptural connection. John the Baptist leaps in Elizabeth's womb, much as the mountains of Israel leap before the presence of the God of Jacob. This means, that when Mary draws near to greet Elizabeth, little Baby John senses, through the Holy Spirit (Luke 1:15), the very presence of the God of Jacob. The presence of the Lord is in Mary's womb! God-the-Son is in the virgin's womb, and so Baby John leaps, like a ram, or like a little lamb!

"Ahah!" the skeptics will say, "but are not mountains inanimate, non-personal objects? And so could not the leaping of John the Baptist in Elizabeth's womb be merely a poetic image, and not a truly animate and personhood-demanding event?"

Ah, but these skeptics miss, entirely, the point that the Holy Spirit is making here. The account of the opening chapter of Luke's Gospel is written as history, not as poetry (see vv. 1-4). These are real, animate, *personal* beings described in this historical account. Elizabeth and Mary are not poetic figures of righteous principles, personified. They are, rather, actual persons living in actual history. In the same way, Baby John the Baptist, in the womb, is not a righteous motif, personified. He is a real, living, human being.

The Gospel of Luke stands or falls on the historical nature of these events. Their historicity is inextricably tied to the truth of the Gospel, itself. Therefore, unlike Psalm 114, the leaping of John the Baptist in the womb is not a personification of a non-personal object. Rather, the historicity of this event ensures that Baby John's leaping is a real, historical leaping. It is done by a real human being, in real human history. That means that his joy is a real, *personal* joy:

> *For behold, when the voice of your greeting came into my ears, the baby <u>leaped in my womb for joy</u>!* (Luke 1:44)

Joy abounds in the historical account of the opening chapter of the Gospel of Luke. Persons, not inanimate things, experience much joy during the miraculous events that surround the births of Baby John and Baby Jesus. The entire account is, in fact, soaked with joy. Thus the angel, Gabriel, foretells the joy that the birth of John the Baptist will bring into the world:

"You will have <u>joy</u> and <u>gladness</u>; and many will <u>rejoice</u> at his birth." (Luke 1:14)

Also, once Mary receives the blessing from Elizabeth, and hears that the Baby in her womb has caused the baby in Elizabeth's womb to leap for joy, she, too, is filled with joy:

"My spirit has <u>rejoiced</u> in God my Savior." (Luke 1:47)

Why is this? Why is John such a joyful babe in Elizabeth's womb? What evokes in him such joy that he leaps in his mother's womb?

As a man who is filled with the Holy Spirit, even from his mother's womb, John is overwhelmed by the joy of the Gospel. It is his great joy and unique privilege to be the first man to herald the arrival of Christ, in the flesh, in the world. As the forerunner of Christ, he blazes the trail of Kingdom proclamation for his Lord to tread upon. John's joyful calling is that of the King's messenger, announcing the long-expected arrival of the King:

The voice of one who calls out, "<u>Prepare the way of the</u> LORD <u>in the wilderness! Make a level highway in the desert <u>for our God</u>." (Isaiah 40:3)

He is the Elijah who was to come *"before the [coming of the] great and terrible day of the* LORD*"* (Malachi 4:5). As such, his joyful calling—though it is quite dangerous, too, and shall cost him his own life—is that of the friend of the Bridegroom, announcing the glorious arrival of the Bridegroom, Himself:

The Baby Leaped!

"He who has the bride is the bridegroom; but the friend of the bridegroom, who stands and hears him, <u>rejoices greatly</u> because of <u>the bridegroom's voice</u>. This, <u>my joy</u>, therefore is made full." (John 3:29)

John is the herald of the joy of the Gospel. His joy is nothing other than pure, Gospel joy. His act of leaping in Elizabeth's womb (and we can imagine his tiny, little baby body leaping with all of its might!) is a harbinger of the Gospel of Christ. The Gospel, itself, causes men to leap for joy, just as the babe, John, leaps in Elizabeth's womb:

Then the lame man will <u>leap like a deer</u>, and the tongue of the mute will sing; for waters will break out in the wilderness, and streams in the desert....Then the LORD*'s ransomed ones will return, and come with singing to Zion; and <u>everlasting joy</u> will be on their heads. They will obtain <u>gladness and joy</u>, and sorrow and sighing will flee away.* (Isaiah 35:6, 10)

But what, specifically, causes such joy? Why is the babe in Elizabeth's womb a leaping babe? What is it about the Gospel that produces such joy? Whence comes this joy? From what spring does it gush with such rapid, bubbling movement?

The source of the river of the Gospel, whose flowing rapids clothe river rocks with the pure, white sprays of Gospel joy, is Christ Himself. Immanuel means "God with us." To see Christ Jesus is to see the Father in Heaven (John 14:9). The very presence of the Son of God, in human flesh, is what Baby John senses in Elizabeth's womb, and this is the wellspring of Gospel joy that causes him to leap.

The heart of the Gospel is God Himself. It is proclaimed by the Prophet Isaiah in the words, *"Behold, your God!"* (Isaiah 40:9). It is foretold by the Prophet Zechariah with the words, *"Behold, your King comes to you!"* (Zechariah 9:9). Thus, as the last of the Prophets, John the Baptist shall announce the Gospel with the words, *"Behold, the Lamb of God!"* (John 1:29). The joy of the Gospel springs from the knowledge of God that is obtained through the revelation of Christ Jesus to the world. God *"has at the end of these days spoken to us by his Son"* (Hebrews 1:2).

What can be more joyful than the unutterable grace of knowing God? What could possibly bring more joy to a human heart than the nearness of God's glory to man through the incarnation of His only-begotten Son? The nearness of God's presence to man, through the incarnation of the Word of God, is the wellspring of all Gospel joy. As Baxter puts it, so plainly, "If you had the word of God, and not 'the Word,' which is God…this were a poor happiness."[12]

Yes, but we must not neglect the Gospel joy, that powerfully flowing joy, of the forgiveness of sins. That all sins stain badly, like blood, and are as heavy as lead, dragging one's soul down towards Hell, is a mightily sobering biblical truth. That the fierce and jealous God of Scripture is at the same time gracious and compassionate, slow to anger and abounding in covenantal love, and thus willing to forgive sins, by way of atonement, is an incredibly joyful biblical truth. Here is true joy: *"…that Christ Jesus came into the world to save sinners; of whom I am chief"* (1 Timothy 1:15).

Baby John, in Elizabeth's womb, senses the presence of Baby Jesus in Mary's womb. In sensing this, he knows that the Lamb of God has come near to him. Mary's Babe, once born into the world and having grown a bit, will learn to walk, much like a newborn lamb, through an innocent cycle of rising and stumbling. He shall be an infinitely adorable Toddler. But like an unblemished, prized, *sacrificial* lamb, Mary's Babe is predestined for the slaughter. He is, according to John, not only the Lamb of God, but also *"the Lamb of God, who takes away the sin of the world!"* (John 1:29).

The Babe in Mary's womb will be born as the Firstborn Son of God (Hebrews 1:6). Unlike Isaac, who was Abraham's firstborn son, and who, in God's mercy, was spared the blade of his father's raised knife, Jesus will not be spared. The Father in Heaven will allow the knife of sacrifice to be lowered upon His only-begotten Son. God's Firstborn shall give His own blood in order to cover our sins and thus make atonement for them.

When we remember the darkness of our sin, displayed through the darkness of Calvary, we do not leap for joy. Rather, we beat our breasts and mourn. We grieve, mourn, and wail. We exchange our laughter for mourning, and our joy for gloom. We repent, and humble ourselves before this Lamb of God on the Cross, who was willing to be slain in our stead.

The joy, unspeakable, does not come until dawn on the first day of the week. Then is the Son of God raised from the dead in power

---

[12] Baxter, *Saints' Everlasting Rest*, 185.

(Romans 1:4). Then is the Firstborn of God declared to be *"the Firstborn of the dead"* (Revelation 1:5). Only then do His disciples know true rejoicing, like the rejoicing of a mother who has just given birth, *"for the joy that a human being is born into the world"* (John 16:21). At the resurrection of Christ Jesus from the dead, the disciples leap for joy!

Therefore, by faith in the Gospel promises of God, wretched sinners can know the joy of full forgiveness from God. And this amazing atonement for sins, brought about by Mary's Babe, can be applied to all the sins related to abortion. Once murderous physicians can, by repentance and faith in God, receive a full pardon for their crimes against Him, and against His children. Pro-abortion activists can be converted, by the Gospel, into God-fearing and humble Abortion Abolitionists. Once murderous fathers can have their scarlet-stained garments washed in the blood of the Lamb and made as white as snow. Mothers who willingly allowed their wombs to become dens of murder can have their wombs touched, healed, and cleansed by the Gospel. For, Jesus' blood was not shed in the womb, but it was shed for those sinners who have shed blood in the womb.

The forgiveness of sins, by the washing of regeneration through the Holy Spirit, brings with it ineffable joy. "Amazing Grace" is not only available to former slave traders.[13] It is also available, in abundant supply, to former abortionists and post-abortive parents who have repented of their evil deeds. "'Full atonement,' can it be?" asks the old Philip Bliss hymn. The resounding Gospel shout is, "Yes!" and this "Yes!" causes liberated sinners to leap for joy!

It is no wonder, then, that Jesus speaks of Abraham's prophetic insight into the Gospel as a very joyful one:

"Your father Abraham rejoiced to see My day. He saw it, and was glad." (John 8:56)

In fact, the joy of the Gospel is so permanently abiding, through the indwelling Holy Spirit, that not even the greatest of sufferings and persecutions can snatch it from the heart of a true Christian:

---

[13] The Rev. John Newton, the author of the masterful hymn, "Amazing Grace," was once, in what he still considered to be his pre-conversion years, the captain of various slave-trade ships.

But because you are partakers of Christ's sufferings, rejoice; that at the revelation of His glory you also may <u>rejoice with exceeding joy</u>. (1 Peter 4:13)

As the disciples of our Lord Jesus Christ, His promise to us is never failing: *"…your heart <u>will rejoice</u>, and <u>no one will take your joy away from you</u>"* (John 16:22). This is because our joy is not dependent upon temporal pleasures or temporal things. Ours is a joy that is fully invested in the everlasting realities of Heaven:

Let us <u>rejoice</u> and <u>be exceedingly glad</u>, and let us give the glory to Him. For the marriage of the Lamb has come, and His wife has made herself ready. (Revelation 19:7)

The babe, John, who leaped for joy in Elizabeth's womb, grew up to become the friend of the Bridegroom. He rejoiced to see the Bridegroom, face to face. In the same way, as we anticipate, with full assurance of faith, the Second Coming of the Bridegroom, with His holy angels accompanying Him, our hearts rejoice with great joy. Like the babe in Elizabeth's womb, we, too, sense the nearness of Immanuel, so we, too, leap for joy!

11

CHRIST'S TEMPLE:
The Physical Body and Preborn Children

(1 Corinthians 6:13b-20)

But the body is not for sexual immorality, but for the Lord; and the Lord for the body. Now God raised up the Lord, and will also raise us up by His power. Do you not know that your bodies are members of Christ? Shall I then take the members of Christ, and make them members of a prostitute? May it never be! Or do you not know that he who is joined to a prostitute is one body? For, "The two," He says, "will become one flesh." But he who is joined to the Lord is one spirit. Flee sexual immorality! "Every sin that a man does is outside the body," but he who commits sexual immorality sins against his own body. Or do you not know that your body is a temple of the Holy Spirit which is in you, which you have from God? You are not your own, for you were bought with a price. Therefore glorify God in your body and in your spirit, which are God's.
(1 Corinthians 6:13b–20)

    If Christ Jesus had not come in a physical body, we could not be saved from our sins. To be sure, the Man Christ Jesus is divine. Without His divinity, the ransom price for the sins of the world could not have been paid. And yet He is also human, fully human. He came *in the body* in order to be a substitutionary sacrifice for sins, which we, as humans, have committed *in the body*.

    It was the ancient heresy of Gnosticism[1] that denied the teaching that God the Son has come to us *in the body*. Stemming, at least in part, from the disdain that Plato, the ancient Greek philosopher, had for the material world (in contrast to his worship of immaterial "ideas"), Gnosticism interpreted the creation of the material universe as an evil event. Therefore, the Gnostics' dual considerations of matter as evil, on the one hand, and of salvation as an escape from matter, on the other, forced them to deny the physical body (and thus the human nature) of Christ Jesus.

---

[1] Gnosticism's name is derived from the Greek term *gnōsis*, meaning "knowledge," which, in turn, refers to the "secret knowledge" of the Gnostic cult.

According to Gnosticism, the creation of matter was not the act of a sole, infinitely-wise Creator. Rather, in Gnostic mythology, a female member of the thirty originally begotten gods and goddesses (the so-called "thirty Æons" of Gnostic theology), whose name was Sophia, broke hierarchical ranks and consequently suffered passion (by sinfully desiring to search into the nature of the unknowable Father). In her passion, her terror and sorrow over what she had done produced the corporeal elements of the world. For instance, "from her tears all that is of a liquid nature was formed."[2]

Since the Gnostics viewed all corporeal elements as evil, they related to the human body in one of two ways (both of which were the logical out-workings of their disdain for material substance). Some of them became extreme ascetics, refusing to marry, to enjoy the pleasures of food, etc.[3] Others among them became extreme hedonists, indulging the body with all manners of vice and dissipation. Having an "it's all going to perish, anyway" attitude towards the body, these false teachers were first in line to watch gladiators spill blood in the arena (a spectacle that orthodox Christians felt forbidden, by the Gospel, to attend), and were so licentiously bold as to "seduce [women] away from their husbands, and contract marriages of their own with them."[4] These Gnostic hedonists reasoned that their spiritual natures were, through Gnostic enlightenment, made to be as gold, and that no bodily actions, however filthy they might be, could corrupt that gold.

In response, historic Christianity rightly identifies Gnostic teachings on the body as "a tissue of falsehoods."[5] It condemns these Gnostic teachings as being Satanic, to the core. It points out that

---

[2] Irenaeus (120-202), in *Against Heresies* 1.4.4 (*ANF* 1.321), counters this mythical creation story via a whimsical and prophetically mocking rebuttal: "But it is probable that [Sophia], in her intense agony and perplexity, was covered with perspiration. And hence, following out their notion, we may conceive that fountains and rivers, and all the fresh water in the world, are due to this source. For it is difficult, since we know that all tears are of the same quality, to believe that waters both salt and fresh proceeded from them. The more plausible supposition is, that some are from her tears, and some from her perspiration."

[3] In the New Testament, we meet the prototypes of these Gnostic ascetics in Colossians 2:21 and 1 Timothy 4:3. Also, Irenaeus, *Against Heresies*, 1.24.2 (*ANF* 1.349), describes the Gnostic teachings of a certain Saturninus as declaring "that marriage and generation are from Satan."

[4] Irenaeus, *Against Heresies* 1.6.3 (*ANF* 1.324).

[5] Irenaeus, *Against Heresies* 1.9.5 (*ANF* 1.330).

Gnostic doctrine denies both the "one God, the Father Almighty, *Maker of heaven, and earth, and the sea, and all things that are in them*" and also the "one Christ Jesus, the Son of God, who *became incarnate* for our salvation."[6] Historic Christianity thus exposes Gnostic thought on the nature of the body as nothing less than Anti-Christ in its nature (1 John 4:3).

What, then, is the historic Christian view of the "body"? If Gnostic views of the body lead either to legalistic asceticism or to unabashed licentiousness, where does a Christian view of the body lead? And how does a Christian view of the human body help to safeguard the "Church Body" from the spiritual virus of pro-abortion thought?

The Body is for the Lord

But the body is not for sexual immorality, but for the Lord; and the Lord for the body. (1 Corinthians 6:13b)

God made the body. Therefore, the body does not belong to the individual, but to God. It is His creation, and, therefore, His property. The Apostle Peter calls it a *"tent"* (2 Peter 1:13), and this "tent" is only given us to "rent." At the end of our lives, we must give an account to its Owner of how well we took care of it, and *for what means* we exercised the use of it.

Yet unbelievers delude themselves into thinking that they, themselves, possess complete ownership of their bodies. Thus at a "pro-choice" rally in a major urban center in America, women of various ages and skin shades shout chants that champion their desire to keep abortion-on-demand a legal possibility. At the rally, a heavily-tattooed woman holds up a sign that reads, "My Body, My Choice." It is clear whom this woman thinks is the owner of her

---

[6] Irenaeus, *Against Heresies* 1.10.1 (*ANF* 1.330), emphases added.

body. She is her own god. She thinks that she, and not God, owns her body.⁷

Now, it is true, as the Abortion Abolitionist response likes to point out to such women, that pregnancy involves not just one body, but two.⁸ The baby, too, must be allowed to make a "choice" concerning his own body. However, an even deeper issue involved in this debate over "a woman's body" is whether or not there is a God who has *full ownership rights over every single human body*. If such a God does not exist, then, of course, the debate devolves into the inevitable power-struggle of moral relativism. But if such a God does exist, then the slogan can no longer be, "My Body, My Choice," but rather must be, "God's Body, God's Holy Law Concerning the Body."

Reverence for the Body

Since God creates the body, and thus has divine ownership rights over it, historic Christianity has always exercised a deep reverence for the body. This explains why the earliest Christians were against the practice of cremation. The great church father Tertullian, for example, calls cremation "a cruel custom" that should be averted "in the interest *even of the body*; since being human, it is itself

---

⁷ On January 22, 2014, President Barack Obama issued the following statement, in which he lauds the 41ˢᵗ anniversary of the *Roe v. Wade* decision: "Today, as we reflect on the 41st anniversary of the Supreme Court decision in *Roe v. Wade*, we recommit ourselves to the decision's guiding principle: that every woman should be able to make her own choices about *her body* and her health" n.p. [cited 22 January 2014, emphasis added]. Online: http://www.whitehouse.gov/the-press-office/2014/01/22/statement-president-roe-v-wade-anniversary. Obviously, the President does not believe that the God of Scripture, and not a woman, is the rightful Owner of her body.

⁸ Randy Alcorn, *Why Pro-Life?* (Sisters, OR: Multnomah, 2004), 37-38, explains, "A body part is defined by the common genetic code it shares with the rest of its body. Every cell of the mother's tonsils, appendix, heart, and lungs shares the same genetic code. The unborn child also has a genetic code, but it is distinctly different from his mother's. Every cell of his body is uniquely his, each different from every cell of his mother's body. Often his blood type is also different, and half the time his gender is different....In prenatal surgeries, the unborn, still connected to [his] mother by the umbilical cord, is removed, given anesthesia, operated on, and reinserted into [his] mother. The child is called a patient, is operated on, and has [his] own medical records, indicating blood type and vital signs."

undeserving of an end which is also inflicted upon murderers."[9] Also, while commenting on pagan banquets given in honor of the dead, Tertullian issues forth the following scathing condemnation of the practice of cremation:

> I on my side must deride [the pagan custom of hosting banquets for the dead] still more, especially when it *burns up its dead with harshest inhumanity*, only to pamper them immediately afterwards with gluttonous satiety, using the selfsame fires to honor them and to insult them. What piety is that which mocks [its victims] with cruelty? Is it sacrifice or insult (which the crowd offers), when it burns its offerings to those it has already burnt [Latin: *Cum crematis cremat*]?[10]

This disavowal of the practice of cremation makes much biblical sense, for in the Bible every pious Israelite knows that burial, and not cremation, is what best honors the body and shows reverence for it. Thus King David does not condemn, but rather honors the actions of Rizpah, the daughter of Aiah, when she courageously protects the exposed bodies of her two sons and the five sons of Michal:

> *Rizpah the daughter of Aiah took sackcloth, and spread it for herself on the rock, from the beginning of harvest until water poured on [the bodies] from the sky. <u>She allowed neither the birds of the sky to rest on [the bodies] by day, nor the animals of the field by night</u>.* (2 Samuel 21:10)

In the New Testament, the disciples of John the Baptist, even though their teacher has been beheaded, make sure to bury his body, thus treating it with great reverence:

> *His disciples came, and took the body, and <u>buried it</u>; and they went and told Jesus.* (Matthew 14:12)

---

[9] Tertullian, *A Treatise on the Soul* 51 (*ANF* 3.228), emphasis added.
[10] Tertullian, *On the Resurrection of the Flesh* 1 (*ANF* 3.545), emphasis added. Note also the argument employed by Minucius Felix, *Octavius* 34 (*ANF* 4.194): "Every body, whether it is dried up into dust, or is dissolved into moisture, or is compressed into ashes, or is attenuated into smoke, is withdrawn from us, but it is reserved for God in the custody of the elements. Nor, as you believe, do we fear any loss from [burning/cremation], *but we adopt the ancient and better custom of burying in the earth*" (emphasis added).

The Jews favored burial, when at all possible, and their reverence for the body was bequeathed to the early Christian communities. That is, the Christians understood respect for the body to be an issue of godliness and piety, and not simply a Jewish custom that could be discarded with the dawning of the New Covenant age.[11] Thus, in the face of the common Roman practice of cremation, they turned burial into an evangelistic ministry (e.g. the vast network of Christian catacombs underneath the city of Rome). This ministry was so powerful that it eventually turned medieval Europe away from the "pagan" practice of cremation, altogether. It is no surprise, then, that in the Reformation and Post-Reformation ages, Protestants upheld the Catholic tradition of erecting church buildings with adjacent plots of land to be used as church *burial* grounds.

Why, then, have Christians, throughout the centuries, paid so much attention to the need to show reverence towards the body of the deceased? And why do Christians, today, insist on burying the bodies of their deceased loved ones, including the dismembered bodies of the victims of the Abortion Holocaust? Certainly, since respectful burial is the normative pattern given to us in Scripture, we defy any secular or pagan mistreatment of the body that goes against this pattern. Yet there is more. As Christians, we reverence the body because Jesus came to us *in the body*. In the Gospel, the glory of God is *embodied* in Jesus Christ:

The Word <u>became flesh</u>, and lived among us. (John 1:14a)

Also,

For in Him all the fullness of the Godhead dwells <u>bodily</u>.... (Colossians 2:9)

---

[11] Thus Al Mohler, in "Cremation Gains Ground in Colorado—Why?" (June 6, 2005), n.p. [cited January 20, 2014]; online: http://www.albertmohler.com/2005/06/06/cremation-gains-ground-in-colorado-why/, says, "The primary issue [concerning the Christian custom of burial and the Christian disavowal of cremation] was and is *a proper Christian respect for the body as the temple of the Holy Spirit*" (emphasis added).

Concerning our redemption, it is the *bodily* death of Christ Jesus that provides substitutionary atonement for our sins:

> *...who His own self bore our sins <u>in His body</u> on the tree.* (1 Peter 2:24a)

Moreover, the treatment of the deceased body is central to the Gospel because, in the Gospel accounts, Jesus' post-crucifixion body, though horribly marred and pierced, is reverenced by His disciples. The way in which the disciples show reverence towards Jesus' body is inseparable from the Gospel, itself:

> *Behold, a man named Joseph, who was a member of the council, a good and righteous man...went to Pilate, and asked for Jesus' body. He took it down, and wrapped it in a linen cloth, and laid Him in a tomb that was cut in stone, where no one had ever been laid....The women, who had come with Him out of Galilee, followed after, and saw the tomb, and how His body was laid. They returned, and <u>prepared spices and ointments</u>.*
> (Luke 23:50, 52-53, 55-56a)

Of course, if, historically speaking, Jesus merely died, and was not truly raised from the dead, raised in the body, then the Gospel, itself, is worthless. We who believe the Gospel *"are of all men most pitiable"* if Christ has not been raised physically, in His very body (1 Corinthians 15:19). But now Christ is, indeed, *"raised from the dead"* (v. 20), and dwells in a resurrected, *"glorious body"* (Philippians 3:21). That His resurrected body is physical is proved by the fact that He ate broiled fish and honeycomb after His resurrection (Luke 24:42). That it is glorious is evidenced by its ability to cause even the greatest of Christians to fall down at Jesus' feet *"as dead"* (Revelation 1:17).

The Resurrection of the Body

Jesus' resurrection, then, speaks to us of our own, coming resurrection. His resurrection is the firstfruits, and we, who fear Him, shall be raised, in turn. At the sounding of the trumpet, with a loud shout from the Lord, and the voice of an archangel, He shall return on the clouds with all of the holy angels. And *"the dead in Christ will rise first"* (1 Thessalonians 4:16). Then, *"we who are alive, who are left, will be caught up together with them in the clouds, to meet the Lord in the air"* (v. 17a). And we, in our resurrected bodies, *"will be with the Lord forever"* (v. 18b).

Christians, then, live with the great and powerful hope of the resurrection of the body:

Now God raised up the Lord, and <u>will also raise us up by His power</u>. (1 Corinthians 6:14)

Why does the body matter? Why do the deeds that we do in the body, whether good or evil, really matter? What should cause us to tremble when we think about giving an account to God of the ways in which we have stewarded and employed our bodies? It is the resurrection of the body that answers these questions for us:

For we must all be revealed before the judgment seat of Christ; that each one may receive the things <u>in the body</u>, <u>according to what he has done</u>, whether good or bad. (2 Corinthians 5:10)

This is terrifying news for the unregenerate, but good news for us, who believe. If, through repentance and faith, we have been born from above, born of the Holy Spirit, and thus, by the Spirit, continually put to death the deeds of the flesh, so that we now walk according to the Spirit, and not according to the flesh, then we can have confidence on the Day of Judgment. Therefore, when our flesh is raised immortal and imperishable, for us, as true believers, it shall be a most joyful event:

After my skin is destroyed, then <u>in my flesh shall I see God</u>. (Job 19:26)

And,

Not only so, but ourselves also, who have the first fruits of the Spirit, even we ourselves groan within ourselves, waiting for adoption, <u>the redemption of our body</u>. (Romans 8:23)

As Christians, we show reverence towards the body because we believe in the coming resurrection of the body. Our bodies are not evolutionary products of natural selection, soon to be eclipsed by newer and higher forms of evolutionary beings. Also, they are not cosmic accidents that are soon to be discarded and turned back, forever, into star dust. Rather, our bodies are specially and individually created by God to make us what we are—and what we are is essentially human—and since they bear the seal of their Creator and His promise of future resurrection upon them, we rightly reverence them.

Sins against the Body

It is, therefore, a very grave thing to commit sins against the body. If the body is *"for the Lord, and the Lord for the body"* (1 Corinthians 6:13), then to sin against the body is to defile the Lord's desired abode. We cannot dedicate our bodies wholly unto the Lord God, nor invite His glory to dwell within our bodies, if we are simultaneously defiling them through sin. And, in specific, the blessed Apostle says that it is the sin of sexual immorality that so greatly defiles the body:

> <u>*Flee sexual immorality*</u>*! "Every sin that a man does is outside the body," but <u>he who commits sexual immorality sins against his own body</u>.*
> (1 Corinthians 6:18)

Now, to be sure, the Apostle Paul is not saying that sexual immorality is the *only* kind of sin that one can commit against his own body. In the Old Testament, for example, there are abusive sins against the body, including tattooing, cutting, and mutilation, that are dark sins against the body—the body which is made in God's image:

> *You shall not make <u>any cuttings in your flesh</u> for the dead, nor <u>tattoo any marks on you</u>. I am the LORD.* (Leviticus 19:28)[12]

Also, God gives the following commandment concerning the priests, the sons of Aaron:

---

[12] That this prohibition against both cutting and tattooing is timeless, and not culture-bound, is clear from the context of verse 28. For, only two verses prior to it, God warns, *"You shall not eat any meat with the blood still in it. You shall not use enchantments, nor practice sorcery"* (v. 26). In other words, these pagan practices are to be abhorred, and are timelessly condemned.

They shall not shave their heads or shave off the corners of their beards[13] *or make any cuttings in their flesh.* (Leviticus 21:5)

Nevertheless, sexual sins are uniquely defiling to the body because they violate the one-flesh-ness principle of marriage. The Lord designed marriage to bring about the exclusive union of husband and wife, under the sacred covenant of marriage. It is a covenant of the body, of one flesh, in order to demonstrate its relational intimacy, no doubt, but also its jealous exclusivity:

Therefore a man will leave his father and his mother, and will join with his wife, and they will be one flesh. (Genesis 2:24)

In turn, the union of the bodies of husband and wife in *"one flesh"* is for the purpose of procreation. That is, God sanctions and blesses the exclusivity of the marriage bed (Hebrews 13:4) by making its *télos* (its purpose or end goal) the means of His creation of new human life (Genesis 1:28). The marriage covenant is thus a living illustration of God's exclusive covenant with His people (there shall be no other gods before Him), on the one hand, and a loud proclamation of God's desire for godly offspring (see Malachi 2:15), on the other. The one-flesh-ness of marriage is to produce the joyful fruit of the womb.

This means, therefore, that contraception is a sin against the body that defiles the body. It severs the one-flesh-ness of marriage from its procreative purpose. In doing so, it wages war against the body's intended design. It also defiles the sanctity of the one-flesh-ness of marriage, since it robs it of its God-ordained commission. This is why God judges the contraceptive sin of Onan so severely:

---

[13] Gordon Wenham, *The Book of Leviticus* (NICOT; Grand Rapids: Eerdmans, 1979), 272, 291, sees the "shaving" of the edges of the beard as, more specifically, a form of *cutting* or *disfiguring* the face: "This is usually taken to be simply a prohibition of pagan mourning rites, but there is more to it than this....Man is not to disfigure the divine likeness implanted in him by scarring the body....Defacement of the human body is incompatible with holiness." See also: 1 Kings 18:28 and Jeremiah 41:5.

Judah said to Onan, "Go in to your brother's wife, and perform the duty of a husband's brother to her, and raise up offspring for your brother." Onan knew that the [seed] would not be his; and when he went in to his brother's wife, he <u>spilled [the seed] on the ground</u>, lest he should give [seed] to his brother. The thing which he did was evil in the LORD's sight, and <u>He killed him also</u>. (Genesis 38:8–10)

Yet the sin of contraception is only a specialized instance (oftentimes occurring within marriage, rather than outside of its confines) of the more general category of sins against the body known as sexual immorality. And sexual immorality is a uniquely devastating sin, since it is a sin against the body. It is this sin, that of sexual immorality, from which the Apostle commands us to *"flee"* (1 Corinthians 6:18). And this is for good reason, since sexual immorality destroys the exclusive one-flesh-ness of the marriage covenant.

God has made marriage—that is, exclusively between one man and one woman—and nothing outside of marriage, for the sharing of one's body with another:

The wife does not have authority over her own body, <u>but the husband</u>. Likewise also the husband does not have authority over his own body, <u>but the wife</u>. (1 Corinthians 7:4)

All sexual sins violate this exclusive nature of the marriage covenant.[14] Whether by lusting with the eyes, flirting with the mouth, or sinfully touching with the body, they defile the marriage covenant. A sexually-immoral virgin thus defiles his or her future marriage covenant (or his or her exclusive spiritual vows to God), while a married person, through lust and sexual sin, defiles his or her living marriage covenant. In both cases, the body of the sexual sinner is defiled because the exclusive one-flesh-ness of marriage is defiled. In other words, the body, which is solely to be joined with one's spouse (or, in the case of a vowed singleness, solely to be given over to the service of the Lord), has now been joined with another.

---

[14] Even the use of contraception within marriage can be said to violate the exclusive nature of the marriage covenant in that it introduces a foreign element (an element which works against the covenant, as God designed it) into the purity of the covenant: that of desiring physical intimacy without procreative purpose.

Wisdom warns us about the way in which sexual immorality harms the body by sinning against the body. If a man commits sexual immorality, he is damaging his own body:

> *Do not lust after [the immoral woman's] beauty in your heart, neither let her captivate you with her eyelids. For a prostitute reduces you to a piece of bread. The adulteress hunts for your precious life. Can a man scoop fire <u>into his lap</u>, and his clothes not <u>be burned</u>? Or can one walk on hot coals, and <u>his feet</u> not <u>be scorched</u>? So is he who goes in to his neighbor's wife. Whoever touches her will not be unpunished.* (Proverbs 6:25–29)

Furthermore, if sexual immorality is a uniquely devastating sin against the body, then all forms of homosexuality are among the worst of such devastations. For, not only is the marriage covenant (both for the unmarried and for the married) defiled by homosexuality, but the very use of the body is grossly defiled. If the one-flesh-ness of marriage is illustrative of God's exclusive covenant with His people (of Christ [masculine] wedded to His Bride [feminine]), then homosexuality is so deeply sinful as to be illustrative of the worship of demons. It twists and perverts the doxological parable of marriage and, through so-called "gay marriage," turns it into a parable about the worship of *Bēlial*.

Thus, speaking first of sexual offenders, in general, and then of homosexuals, in particular, the Apostle writes:

> *Therefore God also gave them up in the lusts of their hearts to uncleanness, that <u>their bodies should be dishonored among themselves</u>....For this reason, God gave them up to vile passions. For their <u>women changed the natural function into that which is against nature</u>. Likewise also the men, leaving the natural function of the woman, burned in their lust toward one another, <u>men doing what is inappropriate with men</u>, and receiving in themselves the due penalty of their error.* (Romans 1:24, 26–27)

All of this, then, has a lot to say about the reasons why our society has devalued the human body to the great extent that it has. If sexual immorality harms the body, then those who love sexual immorality must also learn to love the degradation of the body. It comes as no surprise, then, that with so much rampant pornography on men's laptops and other electronic devices, there also exist, in our culture, the horrors of rampant rape and domestic violence. When our society encourages immodest dress and licentious seduction as means of empowerment for women, it should not come as a shock to us that it also is plagued by fornication and adultery. Immorality and tattoos go hand in hand. Obscene body piercings and a culture of fornication go hand in hand. Homosexuality degrades the body, and thus increases the lack of respect for the body in society. Contraception robs the body of its God-given procreative mandate, and thus an abortion mentality, which dehumanizes the body of the baby in the womb, easily and inevitably follows on its heels.

THE BODY IS NOT TO BE JOINED WITH A HARLOT

One of the sins of the body that is most often condemned in Scripture is that of a man uniting himself with a prostitute. This particular sin, of joining one's body with a harlot (from the man's side), or of giving one's body over to harlotry (from the woman's side), is important for understanding the Gospel of Christ because it is often used in the Bible as a spiritual metaphor. In the Old Testament, Israel is the Bride of God. But Israel makes herself out to be a *"harlot"* whenever she goes after foreign gods (Ezekiel 23:5, 11). In the same way, the New Testament teaches that the Church is the Bride of Christ. But She, too, possesses the sinful propensity to play the harlot with *"another Jesus…or a different Gospel"* (2 Corinthians 11:4).

The Body of Christ

The metaphor in the sixth chapter of 1 Corinthians, however, is slightly different. In this chapter, the Church is not the Bride of Christ—who is tempted to commit adultery against Him by playing the harlot with false gospels and false gods. Rather, in the sixth chapter of 1 Corinthians, the Church is Christ's very "Body," and is warned by the Apostle Paul not to unite the Body of Christ with a prostitute.

There is, in fact, much teaching in the New Testament about the Church as Christ's own Body. For example:

> *For even as we have many members <u>in one body</u>, and all the members do not have the same function….* (Romans 12:4)

Also,

> *He is the head of <u>the body, the [Church]</u>, who is the beginning, the firstborn from the dead; that in all things He might have the preeminence.* (Colossians 1:18)

Yet this "Body" metaphor for the Church, as distinct from the "Bride" metaphor, still includes with it the symbolism of marital fidelity. The one-flesh-ness of the marriage covenant ensures this. For, just as husbands ought to love their wives *"as their own <u>bodies</u>"* (Ephesians 5:28), so too does Christ love the Church as His own Body:

> *...because we are members of <u>His body</u>, of <u>His flesh and bones</u>. "For this cause a man will leave his father and mother, and will be joined to his wife. The two will become <u>one flesh</u>." This mystery is great, but I speak <u>concerning Christ and [the Church]</u>.* (Ephesians 5:30–32)

Therefore, as the "Body" of Christ, we are obligated, as members of the Body, to protect the marital fidelity and moral purity of the Body. Practically speaking, this means that we need to keep our own, individual bodies pure, so that the larger, Church Body may also be pure:

> *Do you not know that <u>your bodies are members of Christ</u>?* (1 Corinthians 6:15a)

One-flesh-ness with a Harlot?

But if our bodies are all members of Christ's larger Body, then how can we ever contemplate uniting them with the body of a prostitute? That is, if a Christian's individual body is really part of Christ's Body, then would not the uniting of the former with a prostitute also mean that the latter has, in some way, been united with a prostitute? Shall we not shudder at the thought of it?

Christ's Temple

Shall I then take the members of Christ, and <u>make them members of a [harlot]</u>? May it never be! Or don't you know that <u>he who is joined to a [harlot] is one body</u>? For, "The two," He says, "will become one flesh." (1 Corinthians 6:15b–16)

Of course, the soft dough of the metaphor is not to be kneaded too thin. Christ, Himself, shall never be united with a harlot, spiritual or otherwise. The sins of Christ's people cannot actually compel Christ to commit sin. Yet the power of the metaphor remains. The point is that those who are members of Christ's body should be utterly repulsed by the thought of giving over one of Christ's members to become "one flesh" with a prostitute.

And yet, this is exactly what sexual immorality does! The sin of sexual immorality, if committed by a true Christian, unites a member of the Body of Christ with a whore! It consents to one-flesh-ness with the adulteress. It unites oneself to a harlot, and gives one of Christ's own members over to such an idolatrous union.

The "harlot" side of this metaphor is, no doubt, a scathing rebuke to immoral women. Sexual immorality, committed by a Christian woman, is likened to prostitution. Nevertheless, the Lord God is actually harder on His sons, whenever they commit sexual sins, than He is on His daughters, when they do so:

I will <u>not punish your daughters when they play the [harlot]</u>, nor your brides when they commit adultery; <u>because the men consort with [harlots]</u>, and they sacrifice with the shrine prostitutes; so the people without understanding will come to ruin. (Hosea 4:14)

Furthermore, as is often the case in the Bible, the physical sin of immorality is indicative of an even greater spiritual sin. Sexual immorality, committed by a member of the Body of Christ, is, indeed, a form of harlotry. Yet that physical harlotry, disgusting and abominable as it is, is nevertheless a lesser sin, when compared with the greater sin of the spiritual harlotry that accompanies it:

How can I pardon you? Your children have <u>forsaken Me</u>, and <u>sworn by what are no gods</u>. When I had fed them to the full, they committed adultery, and assembled themselves in troops <u>at the [harlots'] houses</u>. (Jeremiah 5:7)

Sexual sin and spiritual adultery almost always come as a pair. They are twin harlots, who are never far apart from each other. Where one is, the other is close by. Therefore, those who have committed physical acts of sexual immorality are deluding themselves if they do not also recognize that they have indulged in severe acts of spiritual adultery along the way. A man's wife is robbed of her husband's marriage vows when he unites himself with a prostitute, the thought of which is heart-rending enough. Yet if that husband is also a member of the Church (he may even be a pastor or a deacon), he is guilty of uniting himself, *a member of Christ's Body*, with an evil woman. In other words, he is guilty of *spiritual adultery*, which is an even greater sin.

Apocalyptically speaking, the *"Harlot"* is the great Temptress. She offers her immoral favors in exchange for one's own soul. She loves to bait and seduce those who call themselves men of God. And she uses lust and fornication as one of her favorite lures:

> *...for true and righteous are His judgments. For He has judged <u>the great [Harlot], who corrupted the earth with her sexual immorality</u>.* (Revelation 19:2)

Do we, then, truly understand the *severity* of sexual sins? Have the loose morals of the culture around us also loosened the morals of Christ's Body, the Church? After hearing these fearful words from the Holy Bible, do we still think that it is permissible for Christians to view movies that depict sexual immorality before our watching eyes, even if only in suggestive form? Should we not flee from such immorality on the silver screen, refusing to watch any film that contains even a hint of its seductive lure?

And should we not guard the Body, as a whole, from the terrors of sexual immorality? Should not the *men* of the Church rebuild and guard the walls of *propriety* in the Church, such that inappropriate relational and physical familiarity between themselves and those women who are not their wives is altogether precluded? Should not the *women* of the Church reestablish distinctly Christian forms of feminine dress, such that a noticeable *modesty* and *simplicity* prevail in their wardrobes (including their beach attire), even if such modesty and simplicity cause them to be scorned and mocked by the fashionable women of the world?

If the Body of Christ desires to be truly Abolitionist in its posture towards abortion, it must first be a sexually-pure Body. It cannot fight abortion, while simultaneously embracing pornography and contraception. Rather, the Abolitionist call to the Body is a call to moral purity. It is a summons to the jealous guardianship and stewardship of Christ's Body on earth. Only a chaste Body can be an Abolitionist Body. Only a Body of covenantal fidelity to Christ, our Head, can be a submissive Body, gracefully directed, powered, and moved by His Spirit to abolish abortion in this world.

THE BODY IS A TEMPLE

Thus we have seen that the "Body" metaphor for the Church, wherein the Church is the Body of Christ, demands moral purity in the Church. For, who shall dare to unite one of the members of Christ's Body with a harlot?

Yet *the human body is also depicted in Scripture as Christ's own temple*. It is fearful, no doubt, to think of the Church as Christ's Temple (Ephesians 2:21), for do we not commonly turn this Temple, this House of Prayer, into a den of robbers? Do we not commonly cry, *"The Temple of the LORD, the Temple of the LORD, the Temple of the LORD"* (Jeremiah 7:4), with regards to the Church, when, in fact, we are simultaneously filling it with idols? Yet if the truth of the Church as Christ's Temple is a fearful one, how much more the thought of the individual human body as Christ's own temple? Do we honor the body as the temple of the Holy Spirit?

> *Or do you not know that your body is a temple of the Holy Spirit which is in you, which you have from God? You are not your own, for you were bought with a price. Therefore glorify God in your body and in your spirit, which are God's.* (1 Corinthians 6:19–20)

Here, however, is no Christian universalism. Not all—really only few—are truly born of the Holy Spirit. Our Lord says that the multitudes will enter the afterlife through the wide gate of idolatry (even the kind of idolatry that professes to worship Jesus, but in reality worships a false Jesus), and perish, consciously and everlastingly, in Hell. Only a small remnant will enter the afterlife through the narrow gate of repentance and faith in Christ, and find salvation. Therefore, we are not saying that every living human body is a true temple of the Holy Spirit—being indwelt by the Spirit of Christ. Far from it! Rather, we are saying that this is the purpose for which God created every living person: to repent of their wickedness and wretchedness; to call upon the name of the Lord Jesus Christ, alone, for salvation; to be born anew in the Holy Spirit; and thus to become, through faith, a new creature in Christ, and a temple of the Holy Spirit.

The Apostles are genuine examples of those whose bodies were given over to Christ as little temples of the Holy Spirit. For, just as fire came down from Heaven to consecrate the dedicatory sacrifices of the Temple in Israel (Leviticus 9:24; 2 Chronicles 7:1), so too the Apostles dedicated themselves, by prayer, to Christ as living sacrifices, and, supernaturally, experienced fire from Heaven falling down upon their own bodies:

> *Tongues like fire appeared and were distributed to them, and one sat on each of them. They were all filled with the Holy Spirit, and began to speak with other languages, as the Spirit gave them the ability to speak.* (Acts 2:3–4)

The body is made to be the temple of the Holy Spirit. It is in the body and by the body that we, as members of a royal priesthood, offer sacrifices of praise to God. With our lips, we *"proclaim allegiance to His name"* (Hebrews 13:15). With our hands, we do good works and share with others, as a means of sacrifice to Christ (v. 16). With our feet, we take the liberating, light-filled message of the Gospel to sinners imprisoned in darkness (Romans 10:14-15). And by our suffering, in the body, for the sake of righteousness, we bear the reproach of Christ *"outside of the camp"* (Hebrews 13:13), identifying with Him in His scorn. In all of these things, the Holy Spirit purifies us, consecrates us, beautifies us, and fills our bodies with the cloud of His glory.

The Defilement of the Temple

It only remains, then, to meditate, with deep sobriety and sadness, on how the act of abortion is a defilement of the body—the very body that is designed by God to be *a temple of the Holy Spirit*. For, the very sobering fact is that the Israelites, living with the glorious

Temple of God in their midst, oftentimes defiled that Temple with the horror of child sacrifice:

> *[King Manasseh] did that which was evil in the LORD's sight, after the abominations of the nations whom the LORD cast out before the children of Israel. For he built again the high places which Hezekiah his father had destroyed; and he raised up altars for Baal, and made an Asherah, as Ahab king of Israel did, and worshiped all the [hosts] of the sky, and served them. He built altars <u>in the LORD's house</u>, of which the LORD said, "I will put my name in Jerusalem." He built altars for all the [hosts] of the sky <u>in the two courts of the LORD's house</u>. He* **made his son to pass through the fire**, *practiced sorcery, used enchantments, and dealt with those who had familiar spirits, and with wizards. He did much evil in the LORD's sight, to provoke Him to anger. He set the engraved image of Asherah that he had made <u>in the house</u> of which the LORD said to David and to Solomon his son, "In this house, and in Jerusalem, which I have chosen out of all the tribes of Israel, will I put My name forever."* (2 Kings 21:2–7)

Defiling the Temple of God, especially with the blood of child sacrifice, is a sin of unspeakable proportions. In the Bible, idolatry and child sacrifice go hand and hand. And when they are brought into the House of God, the wrath of God is kindled against the idolaters in its hottest measure:

> *"For the children of Judah have done that which is evil in My sight," says the LORD. "They have set their abominations <u>in the house which is called by My name</u>, to defile it. They have built the high places of Topheth, which is in the valley of the son of Hinnom, <u>to burn their sons and their daughters in the fire</u>; which I did not command, nor did it come into My mind."*
> (Jeremiah 7:30–31)

Not only that, but as Psalm 106 catalogues the sins of Israel that led up to the destruction of Jerusalem and the desecration of His Temple in Jerusalem (vv. 40-41), it is child sacrifice that is listed last. This seems to mean that child sacrifice is the "last straw" or ultimate sin[15] that provokes the judgment[16] of the destruction of the Temple in Jerusalem:

> *Yes, they <u>sacrificed their sons and their daughters to demons</u>. They shed <u>innocent blood, even the blood of their sons and of their daughters</u>, whom they sacrificed to the idols of Canaan. <u>The land was polluted with blood</u>. Thus were they defiled with their works, and prostituted themselves in their deeds.* (Psalm 106:37–39)

In the New Testament age, all of this now applies to the Church. If the Church is the new Temple of God, then we dare not defile the Church by bringing ideas into the Church that are sympathetic to the legalization of abortion in society:

> *Do you not know that you are a temple of God, and that God's Spirit lives in you? <u>If anyone destroys God's temple, God will destroy him</u>; for God's temple is holy, which you are.* (1 Corinthians 3:16–17)

Also,

> *<u>What agreement has a temple of God with idols</u>? For you are a temple of the living God. Even as God said, "I will dwell in them, and walk in them; and I will be their God, and they will be My people."* (2 Corinthians 6:16)

However, what is most sobering about all of this is the way in which it applies to the sanctity of a mother's womb. That is, if the mother's body is designed by God to be a temple of the Holy Spirit, then does not abortion bring the bloodshed of child sacrifice into that temple? Is not the womb the sanctuary of God? Shall children be sacrificed, in cold blood, in that sanctuary?

---

[15] Note also Deuteronomy 12:31: *"You shall not do so to the LORD your God; for every abomination to the LORD, which He hates, have they done to their gods; for <u>they even burn their sons and their daughters in the fire to their gods</u>."*

[16] It is interesting to ponder here the extent to which modern, globalized abortion, happening daily on such a massive, global-Holocaust scale, may prompt the Second Coming of Christ and the ultimate Day of the Lord's Wrath.

> *Or do you not know that <u>your body is a temple of the Holy Spirit</u> which is in you, which you have from God? <u>You are not your own</u>....*
> (1 Corinthians 6:19)

If the body is intended to be the temple of the Holy Spirit, then abortion defiles that temple in uniquely diabolical ways. First, it simultaneously destroys one temple (that of the baby's body, which is uniquely different than the mother's body),[17] while harming another (that of the mother's body, which suffers violence). Secondly, it defiles the mother's womb with the blood of the innocent—that of her own child. Thirdly, it combines self-idolatry (namely, the idolatry of self-choice) with murder in the very sanctuary of God. Fourthly, it introduces a foreign sacrifice (that is, the kind of sacrifice [child sacrifice] that pays homage to demons) into the temple of God. Lastly, it commits this act of child sacrifice within the "most holy place" of the mother's body—the womb—the very sanctuary where Jesus dwelt in Mary's body.

<u>The Cleansing and Sanctifying of the Body</u>

The breathtaking power of the Gospel, however, is that even this sin, the sin of abortion, which is the worst of the defilements of the body, can be cleansed away and forgiven. For, Jesus' earthly body was not simply another temple of the Holy Spirit, being one among many. It was, rather, *the* Temple (capital "T") of the Holy Spirit. And yet this Temple, being as it was completely undefiled by sin (Hebrews 4:15), was defiled and destroyed by both unbelieving Jews and unbelieving Romans alike. They flogged His back until it was shredded. They twisted a crown of thorns upon His head until it bled. They marred His visage beyond recognition (Isaiah 52:14). In short, they utterly desecrated the body—which is the Temple—of the Son of God.

Yet when Jesus Christ suffered for our sins, He took the judgment of our own temple defilements in our stead. We desecrated the body, which is God's temple, but the Son of God allowed His own body, which is God's very Temple, to be desecrated for the forgiveness of our sins. He willingly and sacrificially gave His holy Temple to be defiled, so that our utterly defiled temples could be

---

[17] See note 8 of this chapter, above.

cleansed and made holy (cf. 2 Corinthians 5:21). Therefore, the bodies of men who have joined themselves with prostitutes, and the bodies of women who have given themselves over to fornication, can be cleansed and purified through the washing of regeneration in the Gospel. Moreover, even the wombs of women who have had an abortion, or the murderous hands of doctors who have performed abortions, or the coercive lips of boyfriends who have pressed their girlfriends into abortions, can be cleansed. If such defiled people will repent of their crimes, and believe the Gospel of salvation in Christ, their bodies, their temples, can be made new, and clean, in Christ.

Oh, what spiritual cleansing would take place in our world if fathers and mothers would see the womb as the temple of the Holy Spirit! If they would cleanse their own souls with tears of repentance, combined with faith in Christ, then they would be enabled, by the grace of God, to see procreation for the miracle that God designed it to be. Living lives of chastity and honoring the sacred covenant of marriage (for example, committing to get married if they have been cohabiting outside of marriage), they would come to purify their bodies and to consecrate them, in holiness, to Christ. Washed in the cleansing waters of Christian baptism (first having been regenerated through the baptism and rebirth of the Holy Spirit), they would sanctify marriage, as unto the Lord, and thus sanctify the fruits of marriage as amongst the greatest gifts of the Lord.

Then, when experiencing pregnancy as a husband and wife *in Christ*, and no longer outside of Him, they would understand the temple-nature of the womb. Witnessing, together, God's creation and growth of a new human life in the womb, they would come to understand that children do not merely cry out, spontaneously, *"Hosanna to the Son of David!"* in the outer Temple courts (Matthew 21:15). Rather, they would rejoice in learning that little children know how to cry out, *"Hosanna to the Son of David!"* even in the inner temple courts of the womb. From the mouths of babes, even babes in the womb, He has ordained praise. Therefore, the womb is a blessed sanctuary, a holy haven for God's smallest image bearers. And the very bodies of children in the womb, even when they are at their smallest stages of development, are meant to be temples of the Holy Spirit.[18]

The Lord, speaking of Zerubbabel's small, fragile Temple—that is, small and fragile when compared with Solomon's grand, robust Temple—asks, *"Indeed, who despises the day of small things?"* (Zechariah 4:10). The small, fragile bodies of newly conceived and first-trimester babies in the womb are tiny, indeed. At first, they are too small to be seen with the naked human eye. Yet preborn children possess bodies that are designed by God to be little temples of the Holy Spirit. They are, in fact, designed to be the smallest of temples. Yet they are magnificently glorious.

Could it be that we, in the modern world, have so despised the day of small things that we have failed to treasure and to protect some of the most glorious temples of the Holy Spirit in existence? For, in God's eyes, a newly-conceived baby is His image-bearer, and the baby's microscopic body, so fearfully and wonderfully designed, is crafted to be His temple. And, in God's wondrous design, that little, ever-so-delicate temple is meant to be filled with the cloud of the glory of the Holy Spirit, which is an exceedingly brilliant glory.

---

[18] This is not to suggest that such babies are "regenerate" from the womb, nor to suggest that human depravity is not fully present from conception onwards. Rather, it is to say that God relates to children in their pre-accountable state differently than He relates to adults in their accountable state. Whenever He reveals Himself to children in the womb, He prompts them to worship Him in the womb.

12

THE HEAVENLY WAR:
Spiritual Conquest and Preborn Children

(Revelation 12:1-6)

A great sign was seen in heaven: a woman clothed with the sun, and the moon under her feet, and on her head a crown of twelve stars. She was with child. She cried out in pain, laboring to give birth. Another sign was seen in heaven. Behold, a great red dragon, having seven heads and ten horns, and on his heads seven crowns. His tail drew one third of the stars of the sky, and threw them to the earth. The dragon stood before the woman who was about to give birth, so that when she gave birth he might devour her Child. She gave birth to a Son, a male Child, who is to rule all the nations with a rod of iron. Her Child was caught up to God, and to His throne. The woman fled into the wilderness, where she has a place prepared by God, that there they may nourish her one thousand two hundred sixty days. (Revelation 12:1–6)

There is a great battle taking place in the unseen, heavenly realms of this world. The angels of the Omnipotent God are fighting a war against a great, fiery-red dragon. This is a cosmic war. It is a war that we must familiarize ourselves with, for it has cosmic consequences—the kind of consequences which will reach unto everlasting ends.

In this great war, our arch-enemy is a dragon. This fiery-red dragon, who is the greatest of foes, is not a toothless adversary. His deceptive ways are not straw-man arguments, easily knocked down. His blows are not padded, as with a boxer's gloves. Rather, he fights to kill.

If we could see the dragon, as God sees him, we would not behold him as a radiant, benign, and smooth-talking *"angel of light"* (2 Corinthians 11:14), which is his favorite guise. Rather, we would see him as he is: an ugly, bloodthirsty, monstrous dragon. He has scales that glow like coals in a hot furnace. There is smoke pouring from his nostrils like the smoke from a great forest fire. His bright-yellow, beady eyes, are like the eyes of a black panther when peering out of a dark cave.

However, the most startling thing about this cosmic war between God's holy angels and such a merciless, fiery-red dragon (whose demonic hoards fight alongside of him) is that a seemingly helpless *"Child"* is placed right in the midst of it (Revelation 12:4). Swords clash. Wounded warriors groan in pain. The sounds of the battle are thunderous. Its spectacles are terrifying. This is the fiercest of wars. And yet, right in the center of the battlefield is laid a little baby Boy.

What is this Baby doing on such a ferocious battlefield? Who is He? Who is His mother? Why has He been exposed to the worst of dangers at such a vulnerable, tender age? These questions grip our attention as we read from the holy Apocalypse of the Apostle John.

MOTHERHOOD AS SPIRITUAL WARFARE

We may unravel this mystery by seeking, first, the identity of the Baby's mother. Who is this mysterious mother? If the Child is so special as to be central to the cosmic battle taking place, then who is His mother?

She is simply called *"a woman"* at the beginning of the battle account:

> *A great sign was seen in heaven: a woman clothed with the sun, and the moon under her feet, and on her head a crown of twelve stars. She was with child. She cried out in pain, laboring to give birth.* (Revelation 12:1-2)

Mary, but also "More than Mary"

Who, then, is this woman? Who is the mother? Well, if the Child is none other than Christ Jesus, then the simplest answer to this question is that the mother is Mary, herself. The virgin mother is she who gives birth to Immanuel. Mary, the impoverished Jewish maiden, undergoes labor pains, while yet a virgin, in order to give birth to the Messiah Child.

Nevertheless, the mystery of this cosmic battle account hints at more. The woman *is Mary*, to be sure, but she is also *more than Mary*. The woman is also symbolic of Lady Israel, herself. We know this because she, the woman, wears a *"crown"* of *"twelve stars"* on her head, just as Israel is depicted in the Old Testament as wearing a *"crown"* and consisting of *"twelve stars"* (which represent the twelve tribes of Israel):

A great sign was seen in heaven: a woman clothed with the sun, and the moon under her feet, and on her head <u>a crown of twelve stars</u>. (Revelation 12:1)

Again, it is Queen Israel in the Old Testament who wears a royal crown upon her head:

I decked you with ornaments, and I put bracelets on your hands, and a chain on your neck. I put a ring on your nose, and earrings in your ears, and <u>a beautiful crown on your head</u>. (Ezekiel 16:11–12)

Also, in the prophetic dreams that God gave to Joseph, the twelve tribes of Israel are depicted in the form of twelve stars in the sky:

He dreamed yet another dream, and told it to his brothers, and said, "Behold, I have dreamed yet another dream: and behold, <u>the sun and the moon</u> and <u>eleven stars</u> bowed down to me." He told it to his father and to his brothers. His father rebuked him, and said to him, "What is this dream that you have dreamed? Will <u>I and your mother</u> and <u>your brothers</u> indeed come to bow ourselves down to you to the earth?" (Genesis 37:9–10)[1]

The woman in the twelfth chapter of Revelation, then, is a picture of believing Israel. She is the believing, Messianic community, which has been yearning for the coming of Immanuel. As the faithful remnant of Israel, she first precedes, but then becomes the Church, once the Advent of Christ Jesus is glorified by the events of His death, resurrection, and ascension, and sealed by the miracle of the Holy Spirit given at Pentecost.

This interpretation, of the woman as being equated with Mary, but also as being more than Mary—symbolic of the Church herself, is confirmed by Victorinus (martyred c. 304 under Diocletian's persecution), in our earliest known commentary on the book of Revelation:

---

[1] The reason why there are eleven stars (representing Joseph's brothers), and not twelve, is simply because Joseph himself is the "twelfth star."

> [The woman is] the ancient Church of fathers [i.e. the Patriarchs], and prophets, and saints, and apostles, which had the groans and torments of its longing until it saw that Christ, the fruit of its people according to the flesh long promised to it, had taken flesh out of the selfsame people.[2]

Recognizing this mystery, that the woman is symbolic of both believing Israel and the Church, helps us to understand her place in the great, cosmic battle of the twelfth chapter of Revelation. For, in the Bible, Israel is oftentimes engaged in battles that take on the language of cosmic war:

> *The kings came and fought, then the kings of Canaan fought at Taanach by the waters of Megiddo. They took no plunder of silver. <u>From the sky the stars fought. From their courses, they fought against Sisera</u>.* (Judges 5:19–20)

Also, Israel's prophets oftentimes speak of God's cosmic-sized war against the wicked:

> *The earth quakes before them. The heavens tremble. <u>The sun and the moon are darkened, and the stars withdraw their shining</u>.* (Joel 2:10)

Moreover, Jesus Himself uses the language of cosmic war when referring to His Second Coming. His Second Advent will be marked not by peace and sacrifice, but by war in the heavenly realms. It will be the climactic event in the great, cosmic, Apocalyptic war between God and the fiery-red dragon:

> *"There will be <u>signs in the sun, moon, and stars</u>; and on the earth anxiety of nations, in perplexity for the roaring of the sea and the waves; men fainting for fear, and for expectation of the things which are coming on the world: <u>for the powers of the heavens will be shaken</u>."* (Luke 21:25–26)

---

[2] Victorinus, *Commentary on the Apocalypse of the Blessed John* 12.1 (ANF 7.355).

Giving Birth as Spiritual Warfare

It is wondrous, however, to see that *"the woman"* in Revelation 12 is placed right in the midst of such a fierce, cosmic battle, and yet possesses no weapons of warfare. She is not like Deborah, who once carried shield, bow, and arrow into the battle. Rather, she is helpless—without armor—and nine months pregnant. In fact, not only is she ill-equipped to fight in the battle, but she is actually in the midst of labor pains!

She was with child. She <u>cried out in pain</u>, <u>laboring to give birth</u>. (Revelation 12:2)

The dragon, apparently, hates motherhood. He despises godly women who give birth to godly offspring. In this way, whenever a Christian woman gives birth, this event actually prompts spiritual warfare. The dragon strikes, fiercely, at Christian women who give birth to children who will be raised to follow Christ.

Of course, this is no ordinary mother, and no ordinary Child. The dragon hates this mother and Child with the utmost hatred, for this particular birth puts the writing on the wall for his treacherous reign on earth. Still, it is by *"laboring to give birth"* that this mother defeats the dragon. That is, her labor pains not only prompt spiritual warfare, but also *win the spiritual battle*. Her labor pains defeat the dragon in battle:

His tail drew one third of the stars of the sky, and threw them to the earth. The dragon stood before the woman who was about <u>to give birth</u>, so that when <u>she gave birth</u> he might devour her Child. <u>She gave birth</u> to a Son, a male Child, who is to rule all the nations with a rod of iron. Her Child was caught up to God, and to His throne (Revelation 12:4–5)

In the book of the prophet Isaiah, *"giving birth"* is a way to win the War of the Heavenly Realms. This is, of course, the *"sign"* of victory that wicked King Ahaz so obstinately rejects:

Therefore the Lord himself will give you <u>a sign</u>. Behold, the virgin will conceive, and [<u>give birth to</u>] <u>a son</u>, and shall call his name Immanuel. (Isaiah 7:14)

In fact, as a chosen nation, Israel's very job is to win the cosmic war against evil by *"giving birth"* to salvation. Yet just as Ahaz rejects the victory sign of the virgin birth, so too does idolatrous Israel renege on her task to *"give birth"* to salvation:

Like as a woman with child, who draws near the time of her delivery, is in pain and cries out in her pangs; so we have been before you, O LORD. We have been with child. We have been in pain. We <u>gave birth</u>, it seems, <u>only to wind</u>. <u>We have not worked any deliverance in the earth</u>; neither have the inhabitants of the world fallen. (Isaiah 26:17–18)

However, even if rebellious Israel fails to *"give birth"* to salvation, God will still win the War of the Heavenly Realms. In the future, believing Israel—the true Israel—will, indeed, *"give birth."* She will win the cosmic battle against evil by going into labor pains on behalf of a *"male Child."* She will *"give birth"* to the King of kings:

Before she travailed, <u>she gave birth</u>. Before her pain came, <u>she delivered a Son</u>. (Isaiah 66:7)

This, in turn, tells us that the dragon (of Revelation 12) was that selfsame Serpent who defeated Eve, in battle, in the Garden of Eden. For, in the Garden, the dragon engaged Eve in a cosmic contest. And he won the contest. He dealt a deathblow to Eve, and to her progeny.

In wonderful and ironic fashion, then, God has ordained the ultimate defeat of the Serpent through the labor pains of Eve. If the Serpent's great victory in Eden brought labor pains to Eve, then God has seen to it that Eve's great labor pains will bring about the downfall of the Serpent. She, the woman, and not he, the Serpent or dragon, will win the final contest. And she will do it not with sword and shield, but through her own childbearing:

I will put hostility between you [the Serpent] and the woman, and between your offspring and <u>her offspring</u>. He will [crush] your head, and you will [crush] his heel. (Genesis 3:15)

…but she will be saved <u>through her childbearing</u>, if they continue in faith, love, and sanctification with sobriety. (1 Timothy 2:15)

How, then, is the cosmic battle won? It is won through birth pains. Mary, the virgin, underwent the labor pains of giving birth to Christ Jesus. He, Christ Jesus, underwent the birth pains of torture, crucifixion, death, burial, and resurrection, according to the Gospel. The members of the Church, who are His offspring, follow Him by entering into the birth pains of persecution for His name. In all of these horrific birth pains, Christ is Victor, and the dragon is defeated. In other words, these are the birth pains of the great and cosmic conquest of Christ, and of His Kingdom:

> *A woman, when she <u>gives birth</u>, has sorrow, because her time has come. But when she <u>has delivered the child</u>, she does not remember the anguish any more, for the joy that a human being is born into the world.* (John 16:21)

The cosmic battle, then, is not won with battle-ax and spear. It is, rather, won through the birth pains of persecution and suffering for the name of Jesus Christ. When the woman, Mary, undergoes labor pains, she defeats the dragon by giving birth to the male Child, who is Christ. When the woman, the Church, suffers under the birth pains of persecution, she defeats the dragon by proclaiming, with the voice of suffering that cannot be silenced, the male Child as both Victor and Lord.

Yet the Western Church in our day, and especially the Church in America, has succumbed to a brand of teaching that contradicts this great truth. If the cosmic victory is won through labor pains, and thus through tremendous suffering, then the Western Church has demonstrated that it is no longer interested in engaging in cosmic warfare. Instead, she has gathered to herself the kinds of teachers that her itching ears want to hear—those who proclaim a Gospel devoid of labor pains. These ravenous wolves (who dress in fine wool) teach "the power of positive thinking," and they act as if the War ended long ago.[3] As such, they trumpet prosperity, saying, "Put the birth pains behind you! Think positively, and then the War shall be over! Gather the spoils of the War, and live your best life now!"

---

[3] It is true that the decisive victory was won at Calvary and at the Empty Tomb, but the War will not be over until Christ returns, and, ultimately, until the dragon is cast into the lake of fire.

This is not what Holy Scripture says. It says that the birth pains are not over. It tells us that the War is upon us. It soberly forewarns us that the path to victory is through many tribulations:

> ...<u>*through many afflictions*</u> *we must enter into God's Kingdom.* (Acts 14:22)

Who, then, has truth to share with a Christian mother who has just lost her baby boy? If she woke up from unconsciousness after a car accident—having been blindsided on a major highway—only to find that her baby, who was cozily buckled into his car seat in the rear of the car, had been killed in the accident, to whom will she turn? Will "positive thinking" theology answer the cries of her soul? Or will the twelfth chapter of Revelation ring true in her heart?

Real pain cannot be "positively" thought away. This Christian mother will, no doubt, wake herself up at night with uncontrollable sobbing, even many months after her baby boy was taken away. She will, sadly, be confronted by people in the church lobby who will ask her, recklessly, "Is it hard not being a mother, now, since he was your only child?" She will grieve and mourn, as a Christian, in the depths of sorrow that can only be described, verbally, by an out-loud reading of the book of Job, or of the lamentation Psalms.[4]

Yet if this Christian mother understands the twelfth chapter of Revelation, and thus sees both her motherhood and her tribulations in the light of Christ's cosmic Victory, then there is, for her, a pathway through the pain. She can see that her labor pains were not in vain, but instead were mighty blows landed against the dragon. Also, she can say to her reckless friend in the church lobby, "Excuse me, kindly, but *I am a mother*. My son is in Heaven. And I believe that my suffering for him shall somehow prove to glorify Christ in an eternally valuable way." And in so saying, she will be inflicting wound after wound upon the head of the dragon.

Dear Christian Mother, how painful is your motherhood? Have your labor pains been almost unbearable? Are the demands of Christian motherhood weighing heavily upon your heart? Has your own child wounded you with his selfish sin? Do you feel lonely in your calling? Do you yourself have children who have been taken from you, and into Heaven?

---

[4] See, for example, Psalm 77.

Remember, brave Christian Mother, that your wounds are your weapons. Your labor pains, which you endure for the glory of God, are the means by which the enemy falls. By your tribulations in motherhood, the War shall be won. Through your lonely suffering, the heavenly fellowship of the saints is being prepared. O Christian Mother, cling to the Scriptures that promise you that your tears of loss are Heaven's seeds of joy.

THE DRAGON HATES THE "MALE CHILD"

In this great, cosmic war, there are two main combatants, and each is a *"sign"* of war. There is the *"sign"* of the woman, who fights on the side of God by *"giving birth"* to a *"male Child"* (Revelation 12:1-2, 5). Then, there is the *"sign"* of the dragon, who is fighting, ultimately, to kill the Son of God:

> *<u>Another sign</u> was seen in heaven. Behold, <u>a great red dragon</u>, having seven heads and ten horns, and on his heads seven crowns. His tail drew one third of the stars of the sky, and threw them to the earth. The dragon stood before the woman who was about to give birth, so that when she gave birth he might devour her Child.* (Revelation 12:3–4)

It is time, then, to state, explicitly, that the dragon is none other than Satan. He is *"the old serpent, he who is called the devil and Satan, the deceiver of the whole world"* (v. 9). The dragon is the ultimate foe, for he is the epitome of evil. He is a liar, and a murderer from the beginning. Yet he is also predestined by God to be defeated:

> *In that day God shall bring His holy and great and strong sword <u>upon the dragon</u>, even the serpent that flees, <u>upon the dragon</u>, the crooked serpent: he shall <u>destroy the dragon</u>.* (Isaiah 27:1, LXX[5])

This dragon is to be associated with (perhaps he controls or rules over) the great *"beast"* described in the prophecies of Daniel. For, the dragon has seven heads and *"ten horns"* (Revelation 12:3), just as the *"beast"* in Daniel's prophecies has *"ten horns"*:

---

[5] The LXX is the Greek translation of the Hebrew Old Testament.

After this I saw in the night visions, and, behold, <u>a fourth [beast]</u>, awesome and powerful, and strong exceedingly; and it had great iron teeth; it devoured and broke in pieces, and stamped the residue with its feet: and it was diverse from all the animals that were before it; and it had <u>ten horns</u>. (Daniel 7:7)

Also, similar to the dragon, who *"drew one third of the stars of the sky, and threw them to the earth"* (Revelation 12:4),[6] the *"little horn"* of Daniel's prophecies does, himself, cast down stars from heaven:

The male goat magnified himself exceedingly: and when he was strong, the great horn was broken; and instead of it there came up four notable horns toward the four winds of the sky. Out of one of them came out <u>a little horn</u>, which grew exceeding great, toward the south, and toward the east, and toward the glorious land. It grew great, even to the [host] of the sky; <u>and some of the [host] and of the stars it cast down to the ground, and trampled on them</u>. (Daniel 8:8–10)

Still, the cosmic warfare of the twelfth chapter of Revelation is very much centered upon the little baby Boy, who is placed, helplessly, right in the midst of the battlefield. It is this *"male Child"* whom the dragon is after. Above all else, he wants to kill this Child.

Could it be that the dragon has a very good memory? Could it be that he remembers, all too well, that he failed to slay the baby boy, Moses, during his spiritually-orchestrated pogrom against the Hebrew male babies in ancient Egypt?

Pharaoh commanded all his people, saying, "You shall <u>cast every son who is born into the river</u>, and every daughter you shall save alive." (Exodus 1:22)

And could it be that the dragon's hatred of the *"male Child"* stems from his own fear? Is he not afraid that the sacred prophecy of Genesis 3:15, *"…<u>her seed</u>…shall crush <u>your head</u>…"* shall soon come to pass? Is this not why he hates every baby boy that is born of a believing woman? Is this not why he murders the male infants in Bethlehem?

---

[6] The present author believes that Isaiah 14:12-15 and Ezekiel 28:14-15 are, in fact, allusions (for illustrative purposes, embedded within prophetic denunciation messages to Babylon and Tyre, respectively) to the historic fall of Satan from Heaven.

The Heavenly War

The Apostle Matthew records the murderous work of the dragon, who fears the woman's seed:

> *Then Herod, when he saw that he was mocked by the wise men, was exceedingly angry, and sent out, and <u>killed all the male children</u> who were in Bethlehem and in all the surrounding countryside, <u>from two years old and under</u>, according to the exact time which he had learned from the wise men.* (Matthew 2:16)[7]

What chance, then, does this *"male Child"* of the twelfth chapter of Revelation, this helpless baby Boy, stand in the face of such a foe? If He is lying, helpless, in the center of the cosmic battlefield, with arrows flying to and fro about Him, and with many of the evil archers aiming directly at Him, what chance does He stand? Can a helpless Baby survive the onslaught of a great, fiery-red dragon? Will not such a dragon, whose scales glow like hot embers, and whose nostrils smoke with the smoke of a great forest fire, make short work of the baby Boy?

Here is where the power of God becomes visible amidst this great, cosmic war. It is seen in the fact that the Baby does not fall prey to the dragon, but rather defeats the dragon, Himself! The great, fiery-red dragon is *defeated by* a weak, fragile, and helpless baby Boy!

See how Christ, the Mighty One, defeats the dragon. He is not a legendary figure, like King Arthur, using a magical sword named Excalibur to slay the dragon. Also, Christ is not like William Wallace, whose legendary feats included using his sword to slay a lion, for sport, before the King of France. Rather, Christ is *historical*. In real human history, He takes on human flesh as a baby Boy. He, the historical Christ, humbles Himself to become a Babe. He is dependent and vulnerable, needing the nourishment, warmth, protection, and care of Mary and Joseph. And yet, as a Babe, this Mighty Christ has the power, even as a Babe, to bring down the great, fiery-red dragon. His birth, His incarnation, does not complete the Gospel, but it certainly heralds the beginning of the end for the dragon.

It makes much sense, then, that the dragon hates babies. The baby Moses, once left alive, grows up to become God's great champion. The baby Jesus, having been protected from Herod's

---

[7] This is one of the most deeply mournful verses in all of Scripture.

murderous campaign against the baby boys of Bethlehem, grows up and shows Himself to be the God-man (fully God and fully man). The dragon crushes His heel on the Cross, but He crushes the dragon's head at the Empty Tomb. Thus the dragon has learned that, for his own sake, it is not wise for him to let little babies live. He has always hated babies. But he has learned, over time, to hate babies with an ever-increasing hatred of them.

Therefore, when Christians say that they are fighting a great war against the Morning After Pill, contraception, pornography, prostitution, licentiousness, the redefinition of marriage, and legalized abortion, they do not mean a political war, only. They also mean that they are fighting in the War of the Heavenly Realms. For, it is the dragon who loves these things, since they all lead, in one way or another, towards the killing of babies. Contraception begets sexual immorality. And sexual immorality begets abortion.

Since this is true—since the dragon loves abortion and craves the murdering of God's little ones—it means that the truly God-centered home will never exist, this side of Christ's Second Coming, without intense spiritual warfare being waged against it. Satan will attack Christian couples who desire to have a multitude of children (rather than sinfully desiring to limit the number of children in their family). He will, in fact, attack them with a vengeance. Also, the dragon will fight to destroy the children within a Christian household, knowing that God all too often raises up such children to become Christ's champions for the next generation.

This means, as well, that those who are heavily involved in distinctly Christian efforts to abolish abortion in our world (as opposed to non-Christian or secular Abolitionist efforts) should not be surprised when the dragon attacks them with vehemence. "Satan don't play nice," a friend of the present author once commented to him, and that proverb certainly holds true for those Christians who face his vicious attacks as a result of their defense of preborn children. If they would be silent about the Abortion Holocaust, he might relent and choose to let them live in peace. But if they refuse to stop speaking, boldly, for the sake of those little image bearers who are daily led to the slaughter, he will do everything within his power to silence them.

Dear Christian Fathers, for you this means that your innate protective instincts have found a valiant purpose. You are called, through Christian fatherhood, to protect your families, and especially in a spiritual sense. God summons you to love and nurture your wives. He calls you to pray, daily, with great fervency and with much time spent on your faces before the Throne of Grace, for your wives and children. You are to defeat the dragon on your knees. You are to shield your home with the spiritual shield of fire that is humble faith, and passionate, Scripture-based prayer. And, if need be, you are to place yourself between the dragon and your family, so that you may take the blow of his malice and cruelty in their stead.

Still, be reminded, valiant Christian Fathers, that you are *not* tough and mighty enough, in your own strength, to slay a dragon. Where will your muscles get you, O proud man, once you find yourself facing off against such a fiery-red foe? How many push-ups can prepare you to fight such a giant enemy? No, you will not defeat him by mustering your strength, or by purchasing a higher caliber gun. Rather, in order to fight the dragon, you must fast and pray. As your Lord prayed, *"...keep them from the evil one"* (John 17:15), and taught us to pray, *"...deliver us from the evil one"* (Matthew 6:13), so you must come to God as a spiritual pauper and beg Him—for He alone is able—to protect you and your family from the onslaught of the dragon.

And, Christian Fathers, let your tenderness towards children be evident to all. The dragon hates little babies, and works to murder them. Show the world that you are not like the dragon. Let the world see your many tears for the babies who are being slaughtered through abortion. If you have had children of your own who have gone to Heaven in childhood, let your wives know that your own heart bleeds for them. If you have living babies, hold them in your arms, spend much time with them, counting them as your greatest treasures, and nurture them with fatherly love and compassion. Be *both* "pro-life" *and* "pro-creation." Throw away your selfish hobbies and sports addictions; get to know your Bibles backwards and forwards; *tremble* at God's Word; and thus be ready to bring up your children in the training and admonition of the Lord. If the dragon hates babies, then show the world, through your fatherhood—and even through your fatherly wounds and scars—that Christ loves them with an immeasurable love.

PROTECTION FROM THE DRAGON

The War of the Heavenly Realms centers on a pregnant woman, who is giving birth to a male Child, and a Dragon, who wants to murder that Child. How, then, does God protect the Child, and also protect His mother?

> *She gave birth to a Son, a male Child, who is to rule all the nations with a rod of iron. Her Child was caught up to God, and to His throne. The woman fled into the wilderness, where she has a place prepared by God, that there they may nourish her one thousand two hundred sixty days.* (Revelation 12:5–6)

For the Christian, there is only one sure source of protection. God alone is our one, sole source of perfect protection. There is no other sure safety zone. No other bomb shelter, or safe house will do. Our only safe place of refuge is in God, our Almighty Father.

God, then, miraculously protects this male Child, who is so weak and vulnerable on the battlefield. He is helpless, as an Infant, to protect Himself from the fiery darts of the enemy, and from the cruel claws of the dragon. Still, God comes to His rescue. God, His Father, protects Him. He is *"caught up to God, and to His throne"* (v. 5), where He is kept safe from the dragon.

The twelfth chapter of Revelation, then, does not give us the whole account of the life of Christ—this has already been given to us in the Gospels. Rather, the twelfth chapter of Revelation gives only a "beginning…end" portrait of Christ's earthly battle. At the beginning of His earthly life, He is a helpless Child, attacked by the dragon, but kept safe under the powerful providence of His Father. At the end of His earthly pilgrimage, having conquered death through His resurrection from the grave, He ascends into Heaven. He is thus *"caught up"* to God (v. 5) just as, in the future, the Church shall be *"caught up"* to meet Him in the air—at His Second Coming (1 Thessalonians 4:17).

A Place of Protection

For the Child's mother, however, God provides an altogether different means of protection. Her protection comes in the form of having a place to which she may *"flee"* from the dragon:

The woman fled into the wilderness, where she has a place prepared by God, that there they may nourish her one thousand two hundred sixty days. (Revelation 12:6)

This is often the way in which God protects His people from the persecutions of the dragon. He calls them to *"flee"* from those persecutions. Thus when Jesus is still a Child, God commands Joseph and Mary to escape the dragon's onslaught, through Herod, by *"fleeing"* to Egypt:

Now when [the wise men] had departed, behold, an angel of the Lord appeared to Joseph in a dream, saying, "Arise and take the young Child and His mother, and flee into Egypt, and stay there until I tell you, for Herod will seek the young Child to destroy Him." (Matthew 2:13)

Similarly, Jesus commands His disciples to seek protection from the dragon through the God-ordained means of *"fleeing"* his persecution:

But when they persecute you in this city, flee into the next, for most certainly I tell you, you will not have gone through the cities of Israel, until the Son of Man has come. (Matthew 10:23)

Also, to those who shall face the coming horror of the destruction of Jerusalem (which happened, historically, in AD 70, but which also shall happen again at the time of the end), Jesus gives the admonition to *"flee"* the wrath of the dragon:

"When, therefore, you see the abomination of desolation, which was spoken of through Daniel the prophet, standing in the holy place (let the reader understand), then let those who are in Judea flee to the mountains." (Matthew 24:15–16)

This is how God protects His Church. He calls her to *"flee"* to safety. And in His Fatherly care for her, He also provides a *place* of protection for her. That is, once she flees the onslaught of the dragon, He provides a shelter to which she may go. That shelter is called the *"wilderness"* in Revelation 12:

The woman fled <u>into the wilderness</u>, where she has a place prepared by God, that there they may nourish her one thousand two hundred sixty days....Two wings of the great eagle were given to the woman, that she might fly <u>into the wilderness</u> to her place, so that she might be nourished for a time, and times, and half a time, from the face of the serpent. (vv. 6, 14)

God, then, provides abundantly for the woman's protection. He gives her a means of protection (that of fleeing), a place of protection (that of the wilderness), and even *a provision of sustenance* during her time of protection. That is, if the early Christians ask themselves, "What, then, shall we eat, since God has summoned us into the wilderness?" then God's answer to them is that there will be a miraculous provision of sustenance for them during their time in the wilderness:

The woman fled into the wilderness, where she has a place prepared by God, that there <u>they may nourish her</u> one thousand two hundred sixty days. (v. 6)

Who are *"they"* that feed her in the wilderness? Who are the *"they"* in verse 6 that feed the woman during her lonely exile in the desert? Are *"they"* the ravens, who fed Elijah when he was forced to flee from the dragon, into the wilderness? Are *"they"* the angels who brought down *manna* from heaven, in order to feed the Israelites during their time in the wilderness? We do not know, for the Bible does not explicitly reveal this to us, but we are promised that the Church shall be given miraculous, material provision when she is forced to flee into the wilderness.

Therefore, beloved Christian, do not fear the wrath of the dragon. Do not compromise your bold witness for the Name of Christ simply in order to secure your own food and raiment. If speaking boldly for Christ (not, of course, speaking rudely, contentiously, or provocatively, but with conversation that is full of grace, and seasoned with salt) costs you your employment, so be it. If your parental convictions about providing a God-centered, family-based education for your children force you to flee the government-controlled (thus dragon-controlled) schools, worry not about how you will be enabled to educate them, yourself. God will provide all of your needs in Christ Jesus.

In fact, God's protection of the woman by providing a place for her to flee *"into the wilderness"* is a strong rebuke to those Christians who intentionally immerse their children in the wicked cultures of this world, and who baptize them into the secularism of the surrounding society, all in the name of "socializing" them. Their rhetoric goes that "we should not shelter our children from the world," lest they grow up and be discovered to be "socially awkward," very "incapable of dialoguing with the culture," and "unable to get a job."

O foolish Galatians, who has bewitched you? Is not your parental licentiousness the new legalism? Do you not put out of the Church those who refuse to endorse your licentious practices? Do you really believe that Zacharias and Elizabeth, had they been alive today, would have handed over their five-year old son, John, with intentionality, to the big, yellow school bus? Would they purposefully have allowed him to be discipled by pagan instructors, and socialized by pagan peers, rather than trained him, themselves, to fear God? Who was it that taught John to flee to the desert, and to be content with a diet of *"locusts and wild honey"* (Matthew 3:4)? Was it not John's parents who trained him to be a voice crying out, for the glory of God, *"in the wilderness"* (Mark 1:3)?[8]

By all means, Christian parents, shelter your children from the sinful snares of this world! The dragon is seeking to corrupt your children by any means possible. He will use social media web sites, movie theaters, pagan literary classics, same-age peer groups, shopping malls, amusement parks, and even compromised Christian colleges and compromised Christian churches to do so. Therefore, if you want to protect your children from the dragon, you must love them enough to face, yourself, the social ostracism and social persecution that comes with living holy lives among the pagans. Regardless of the ways in which the world may scorn you, God calls you to shelter your children in the lonely, despised *"wilderness"* of family-based discipleship and radical holiness unto Him.

---

[8] Let it be noted here that although both Moses and Daniel were *forced* (through horrible acts of enemy oppression) into very pagan educational systems, their parents never would have voluntarily endorsed such an upbringing for their sons. Rather, cases such as Moses and Daniel's only prove that God can supernaturally protect the holiness of His children, even when they are so brutally and unjustly wrenched away from their God-fearing parents.

God Prepares It

But how do we know that we will really have a *"place"* to survive once we flee into the wilderness? What if we flee there, only to find no *"place"* for us there? Will we not die of exposure to the harsh elements? Shall not our bodies be food for the wild beasts of the wilderness?

It is faith, alone, that does not fear this necessary flight from the dragon into the wilderness. For, by faith, alone, we know that God has already prepared a *"place"* for us there. We need not fear, for *God, Himself, has prepared it for us*:

The woman fled into the wilderness, where she has a place <u>prepared by God</u>, that there they may nourish her one thousand two hundred sixty days. (Revelation 12:6)

This is what faith sees. It sees that under the real threat of the dragon's rage, God Himself has prepared a place of protection for us. If God Himself has prepared it, then we can count on it. We can be sure that we shall find it waiting for us, for He has prepared it with His own hands.

Historically, this precious promise is quite visible in the lives of many of the believers of the ancient Church who were intensely persecuted by the dragon. One of them was Athanasius, who began his ministry as Bishop of Alexandria in 328. Under the Roman Emperor Constantine, Athanasius enjoyed imperial protection during his doctrinal battle with the Arian heretics. However, once Constantine died in 337, and especially after the murder of Constantine's son Constans in 350, Athanasius was left vulnerable to the dragon's attack. The one remaining son of Constantine, the Emperor Constantius, sided with the Arians and, as a result, criminalized the leadership of Athanasius. The great pastor of Alexandria was thus forced to hide himself away in the wilderness.

It was in the wilderness, perhaps hidden amongst "the numerous cells of the Nitrian desert,"[9] that Athanasius eluded his would be captors. Here, hidden away with the monks in the wilderness, he wrote many substantial works in defense of Christian orthodoxy,

---

[9] Archibald Robertson, prolegomena to *Select Writings and Letters of Athanasius, Bishop of Alexandria* (NPNF² 4), li.

including his *Four Discourses Against the Arians*. He also wrote the biography of his recently-deceased friend and mentor, the widely beloved desert monk named Antony. It was Antony who had taught him both the spiritual benefits and the spiritual power that can be gained by fleeing to the wilderness. Thus God used *"the wilderness"* in literal fashion both to protect His servant Athanasius from the wrath of the dragon, and to produce, through Athanasius' time of exile in the desert, some of the foundational works of the historic Christian Church.[10]

The promise that God has prepared a place for us in the wilderness, to which we can flee, makes much sense in the case of Athanasius. God used the wilderness, literally, to protect Athanasius from being harmed by the evil plots of the Arians. However, there are times and circumstances in the life of the Church when this promise makes less sense to us. For, if God has prepared a place for all of His persecuted children, why do so many Christians suffer and perish under the most brutal of persecutions?

Take, for example, the church shooting that took place in the village of Aduwan, in Kaduna State, Nigeria. On the night of February 23, 2013, Christians were gathered together at a home after a funeral service. In the dark of night, gunmen, presumably from a radical Muslim faction, opened fire on the gathering and attacked the village with gunfire for three hours. In the midst of the attack, Martha Blessed, a Christian mother, was shot and wounded while trying to protect her six-month old son, Alexander Blessed. Yet little Alexander died from the attack.[11]

It is hard to claim that we can properly sympathize with Martha Blessed. Weeks, and even months after the attack had happened, the kind of sorrow she must have felt over the loss of her son is too deep for verbal expression. And does not this kind of suffering, which is amongst the worst of sufferings, prompt us, as believers, to ask serious questions regarding the protection of God over our loved

---

[10] Along these lines, it is interesting that Jonathan Edwards' missionary post in the "wilderness" (as one might call it) of Stockbridge, which he held from 1751-57, allowed him to produce some of his most valuable theological works.

[11] Nigerian Correspondent, "Five Lives Lost in Attack on Christian Area of Northern Nigeria: Suspected Muslim Fulani Gunmen Target Funeral Where Christians were Gathered," *Morning Star News*, March 19, 2013, n.p. [cited February 17, 2014]. Online: http://morningstarnews.org/2013/03/five-lives-lost-in-attack-on-christian-area-of-northern-nigeria/.

ones? That is, if God has prepared places of protection for us in the wilderness,[12] then where was God's prepared place of protection for little Alexander?

These kinds of questions are extremely sensitive ones. They are also extremely difficult, for they involve the inscrutable will and foreknowledge of God. Yet one thing that grants us much hope when we come to such questions, with tears in our eyes, is the remembrance of the sorrows of Christ Jesus. He was, to be sure, protected by His Father when He was a Child. The dragon was not allowed to slay the Boy, Jesus. Yet when Christ grew up, and went to Calvary, why was there no prepared place of protection for Him?

> *Another sign was seen in heaven. Behold, a great red dragon, having seven heads and ten horns, and on his heads seven crowns. His tail drew one third of the stars of the sky, and threw them to the earth. The dragon stood before the woman who was about to give birth, so that when she gave birth <u>he might devour her Child</u>.* (Revelation 12:3–4)

Yes, the dragon was not allowed to devour the Christ Child. But did he not devour Christ at Calvary? Did not the dragon sink his sharp teeth into Christ at Calvary? How can this be? Why did not the Father prepare a place of protection for His beloved Son when He went to Calvary?

The Gospel is that the Father allowed His Son to be slain by the dragon, at Calvary, for the satisfaction of His wrath concerning our sins. That is, when the dragon thrust his claws (using iron Roman spikes) into Christ Jesus, at the Cross, it was our sins that caused such a horrific death. We all, like sheep, have gone astray. Each has turned to his own way. And so the Lord laid upon Him, the Lamb of God, the sins of us all. He took the dragon's blows in our stead, for our sins.

Yet did the dragon really *"devour"* Christ? Our Lord Jesus died, to be sure. He did not swoon, but died. He, the sinless Son of God,

---

[12] Interestingly, in ibid., a local pastor of Aduwan reports that God did provide a place of protection for many of the Christians who were under attack: "One miraculous thing is that the rocky hills on the eastern part of this village became a place of refuge for those who escaped from the attack....Even children who had never climbed these hills before suddenly were able to escape by climbing the hills at night."

took death for us, in His human flesh. Still, it was foreknown by the Father that death could never really *"devour"* His eternal Son. The grave was not strong enough to *"devour"* Him. Instead, on the third day, He rose from the grave and conquered sin, death, and the dragon, all in one victorious move. As Robert Lowry's famous Easter hymn celebrates, "He arose! He arose! Hallelujah, Christ arose!"

A Heavenly Place

She gave birth to a Son, a male Child, who is to rule all the nations with a rod of iron. Her Child was <u>caught up to God, and to His throne</u>. (Revelation 12:5)

The Father has, indeed, *"prepared"* a *"place"* of protection for us (Revelation 12:6). But the ultimate fulfillment of this grand truth is not an earthly one. It is, rather, a heavenly one. In the wilderness, in this present world, we find ourselves constantly crying out for the protective place of God's providential care for us. Yet, as saints in Christ, our victory song is sung not of the earthly places of protection that He has prepared for us, but of the heavenly refuge that Christ has gone ahead of us to prepare for us:

In My Father's house are many [abodes]. If it were not so, I would have told you. I am going <u>to prepare a place for you</u>. If I go and <u>prepare a place for you</u>, I will come again, and will receive you to Myself; that where I am, you may be there also. (John 14:2–3)

And,

These all died in faith, not having received the promises, but having seen them and embraced them from afar, and having confessed that they were strangers and pilgrims on the earth. For those who say such things make it clear that they are seeking a country of their own. If indeed they had been thinking of that country from which they went out, they would have had enough time to return. But now they desire a better country, that is, a heavenly one. Therefore God is not ashamed of them, to be called their God, for He has <u>prepared a city for them</u>. (Hebrews 11:13–16)

We live in a world in which we, as Christians, are hated and hunted by a fierce, fiery-red dragon. He hates Christian childbearing. He hates Christian children. And it is only as we suffer under his attacks, with persevering faith in God, that we, through our suffering, defeat him.

We also live in a world in which the dragon is devouring millions upon millions of precious, preborn children every year. He is slaughtering them, both chemically and surgically, with a cruel, blood-soaked, relentless slaughter. There is, right now, no legal, unassailable "place" of protection for them in the majority of the world's nations. Rather, the dragon's insatiable appetite for the blood of little babies in the womb is, currently, being fed both by the ideological lies of the world's universities and by the political policies of gross injustice that dominate the United Nations. Our world, under the dragon's rule, has on its hands the blood of a silent, global Holocaust of immeasurable proportions. The most helpless of human beings, whose little frames and little heartbeats constitute the very pinnacle of God's creation, are being massacred on a global altar, to a global, foreign god.

Still, this is the victory of the little martyrs who have been slain in the womb: like their Lord, they, too, have been *"caught up to God"* (Revelation 12:5),[13] but they through their own martyrdoms. They have overcome the dragon *"because of the Lamb's blood, and because of the word of their testimony"* (v. 11), and thus our God and Savior, Jesus Christ, has prepared a heavenly place of protection for them. They are numbered with those *"who came out of the great tribulation"* (7:14), and their blood is counted as part of *"the blood of prophets and of saints"* (18:24). There, in Heaven, they *"are before the throne of God"* and *"serve Him day and night in His temple"* (7:15). Their place in Heaven is a protected one, for *"<u>outside</u> are the dogs, the sorcerers, the sexually immoral, the murderers, the idolaters, and everyone who loves and practices falsehood"* (22:15). The little babies of the Abortion Holocaust, then, shall be found, in Heaven, to be a vast multitude of worshippers, who have been predestined by God to worship the Lamb, triumphantly and everlastingly, in victorious, radiant robes of righteousness. They shall

---

[13] Christ's glorious ascension, however, remains historically unique, and proclaims the exclusive nature of Christ's glorious divinity. For Christ alone ascended in His glorious, resurrected body, by His own power.

wear their victors' crowns, as the prized sons and daughters of Jesus Christ, sealed by the Holy Spirit, to the glory of God the Father.

    This, then, is *our* victory, which we already possess, and which no one can snatch from us: that Christ Jesus, who was slain for our sins, has conquered the dragon by rising from the dead. Having been snatched up to the Throne of God, our Father, and exalted to the right hand of the Father, He is preparing a place of everlasting safety and everlasting protection for us. There, in Heaven, we shall be like children, praising our Prince and King with shouts of "Alleluia!" and everlasting joy. And there, in Heaven, we shall share our meals together in perfect peace. While we eat of the bread of Heaven and taste of the fruits of Heaven, we shall listen, with attentiveness, to the glad, victorious retelling of the great history of when the fiery-red dragon of old was slain by a little baby Boy, who came to reside in the virgin's womb—who had a divine heartbeat in the virgin's womb—and who grew up to rule the nations with an iron scepter. Amen.

Divine Heartbeat

Conclusion:
They are "Still Speaking"

God's Word, in Hebrews 11:1, defines "faith" as *"the substance of things hoped for, the evidence of things not seen"* (NKJV). Faith, then, is the substance of unseen things that are seen. By faith, we can see the unseen realities of the Kingdom of Heaven.

However, in verse 4 of Hebrews 11, faith is also the substance of unheard voices that are heard. That is, not only, by faith, can we see the unseen realities of Heaven, but also, by faith, we are enabled to hear the unheard voices of Heaven. The world has neither eyes to see, nor ears to hear such things. Yet the glory of biblical faith is that it gives us eyes to see what God sees, and ears to hear what God hears. By faith, we hear the "silent" voices of Heaven speaking audibly—audibly, that is, to our hearts:

> *By faith Abel offered to God a more excellent sacrifice than Cain, through which he obtained witness that he was righteous, God testifying of his gifts; and through it he being dead <u>still speaks</u>.* (Hebrews 11:4)

Some Christians say that Abel's sacrifice was more acceptable than Cain's sacrifice because Abel offered a blood sacrifice, which prefigures Christ, while Cain did not. This certainly was providential. However, it is an insufficient explanation for the conundrum as to why God was pleased with Abel's sacrifice, and yet displeased with the sacrifice of Cain. What the text in Genesis 4:1-5 makes clear is that while Cain brought merely *"some fruit of the ground"* (that is, just an average, "not my best" type of offering), Abel brought *"the firstborn of his flock and of their fat,"* which was his *best portion*. That is, Abel's faith had substance to it. Contrary to Cain's hypocritical faith, Abel's faith was a true and living faith, and thus he offered his best to God.

In this act, Abel was declared to be righteous. His act did not make him righteous. He was not spiritually regenerated by his works. However, his act did provide justifying evidence of his faith. His faith was a living faith, not a dead faith, and so his act *proved* his righteous faith. This is in agreement with both Paul and James:

> *...for not the hearers of the law are just in the sight of God, but <u>the doers of the law will be justified</u>.* (Romans 2:13)

And,

You see then that a man is <u>justified by works</u>, <u>and not by faith only</u>. (James 2:24)

Again, this is not "justification by works," in the sense of "being saved by one's good works." For, all good works, done prior to faith, are ruined by our rebellious pride, and thus are seen as *"filthy rags"* in God's sight (Isaiah 64:6). We are saved, are spiritually regenerated, and are justified, by faith alone (Romans 4:1-5; Galatians 2:16; Ephesians 2:8-9). Nevertheless, if faith is living and authentic (and not dead and phony), it shall have the substance of works that proceed forth from it, like streams of water from a fountain, or like fruit from a tree. This living and authentic faith, as evidenced by works, is thus *"justified"* before God as a truly substantial faith (James 2:21, 25).

Abel's faith was a substantial faith. It was the substance of unseen things that are seen. It was also the substance of *unheard voices that are heard*. That is, Abel, though he was murdered (and thus silenced) by his brother Cain, is, by faith, still speaking today!

"The <u>voice</u> of your brother's blood <u>cries out to Me from the ground</u>." (Genesis 4:10)

And,

...and through it he being dead <u>still speaks</u>. (Hebrews 11:4)

To the world, this is absurd. If we, as Christians, tell the world that we hear Abel speaking to us, right now, at this very moment, the world will say that we have gone insane. The world does not hear Abel speaking. His voice is unheard to them. But by faith—by the substance of faith—we hear the unheard voices of Heaven.

Satan did his utmost to silence Abel, through violence and murder, and this is Satan's way. Whenever a true prophet speaks for God, Satan does his best to silence him. This is what Satan attempted in the case of Abel. He used Cain to murder Abel. He rejoiced greatly because he assumed that he had silenced Abel. But God, and not

Satan, always wins, in the end. By faith, Abel is not silenced! By faith, Abel is still speaking!

This was the same in the case of the prophet Micaiah, Son of Imlah (1 Kings 22:1-28). Micaiah was the only prophet who was brave enough to speak the truth to wicked King Ahab. While all of the other prophets (all 400 of them!) prophesied military victory for Ahab, Micaiah alone spoke the truth to Ahab and prophesied his military defeat. Therefore, Ahab sought to silence Micaiah by casting him into prison. And, politically speaking, Ahab did, in fact, silence him. But by faith, through Scripture, Micaiah still speaks!

Zechariah, Son of Jehoiada, tried to warn ungrateful King Joash about his detestable idolatry (2 Chronicles 24:20-22). But wicked King Joash would not listen to Zechariah's rebuke, so he gave the order to have him stoned to death between the Temple and the altar (Matthew 23:35). He silenced righteous Zechariah by murdering him. But by faith, through Scripture, Zechariah still speaks!

The same goes for the Four Major Prophets of the Old Testament. Isaiah, the Suffering Prophet, was, most likely, martyred by his own people, perhaps having been sawn in two. Jeremiah, the Weeping Prophet, was thrown, by permission of the treacherous King Zedekiah, into a muddy well in order to have him silenced. The Priestly Prophet, Ezekiel, was bound with ropes and confined to house arrest. The Apocalyptic Prophet, Daniel, was cast into the lion's den by his political enemies. In all of these nefarious ways, the Prophets' enemies thought that they had silenced them, but by faith, the Prophets are still speaking, ever so powerfully, even today!

Then, climactically, one of the most endearing passages of Scripture comes to us through the great Champion of Faith, the Apostle Paul, writing to Timothy, his son in the faith, and telling him about his upcoming martyrdom. "They have thrown me in the dungeon. They are going to kill me," Paul, in essence, warns Timothy. But then, in a burst of victorious faith, he writes:

> ...*I suffer trouble as an evildoer, <u>even to the point of chains</u>; but <u>the Word of God is not chained</u>!* (2 Timothy 2:9)

The Apostle's words have proved true. His chains could not silence him. The Word of God went out from him, and to this very day, the Apostle's voice speaks to Jew and Gentile alike, all around the globe!

Faith is the substance of unseen things that are seen, yes, but also *of unheard voices that are heard*. When Satan tries to silence the elect, God makes sure that the elect still speak, by faith. There is nothing—neither threats, nor persecutions, nor martyrdoms—that can silence the faithful voices of God's precious children.

Ed McCully is "Still Preaching"

The present author and his wife once stood in a museum amidst a photographic gallery of great American evangelists and missionaries of the past. They marveled at each of the photographs. They saw enlarged photos of evangelists from the era of the American Big Tent Revivals. They also saw a photo of a man standing beside his horse-drawn cart, with the cart doors flung open and the wooden shelves inside filled with Bibles and Gospel tracts. This evangelist to the American frontiersmen had obviously spent his days, heroically, in the hard, laborious work of the mission of the Gospel. Photographs such as these make a Christian's faith wax bold.

However, as the present author and his wife came to the end of the photographic gallery (being already in awe of these photos), they arrived at one of the last black-and-white photo enlargements, and it, in particular, caused them to freeze in their tracks. They looked up at an enlarged photo of five young men standing beside their wives and children. The children of the young Christian couples were small—most of them were toddlers and infants. The husbands looked vibrant, with joyful grins on their faces. The wives were young, modest, obviously pious, and yet had eyes glowing with hope.

It was then, in a moment of shocking surprise, that the present author and his wife noticed two names, printed under the photograph, which pierced them to the heart: "JIM ELLIOT… ELISABETH ELLIOT." These were the five missionary men, standing so vibrantly with their families, who would, shortly after the photograph was taken, go on to be martyred, quite brutally, by the very tribe of people in Ecuador whom they were trying to reach.[1]

---

[1] The five martyrs were Jim Elliot, Pete Fleming, Ed McCully, Nate Saint, and Roger Youderian. Their martyrdoms took place on January 8, 1956.

Conclusion: They Are Still Speaking

Many Christians alive today know about Jim Elliot. Elisabeth Elliot, Jim's widow, has made the story of her husband's life, faith, mission, and martyrdom well known. Through her books, she has done a heavenly work in preserving the memory of the life and legacy of Jim Elliot for the Church.

However, most Christians alive today are not as familiar with the story of another man who was in the photograph. His name was Ed McCully. He was one of Jim Elliot's closest friends.

It was during the present author's first pastorate that a retired, aged missionary (who had discharged his missionary calling by evangelizing Native Americans at the bottom of the Grand Canyon) told him about Ed McCully. He said to him, "Pastor, I used to know Ed McCully. We used to be friends in our college days. When I first learned of his death, I wept greatly. Pastor, you need to know that Ed McCully was a preacher! Pastor, you would not believe the way that Ed McCully could preach!"

So it was that the present author and his wife stood there, motionless, and in tears, in front of that black-and-white photograph of the five martyrs of Ecuador, standing with their families, including Ed McCully's wife and children.[2] The present author looked up at Ed McCully's picture and immediately remembered what the retired missionary had told him about Ed McCully's preaching gifts. He thus prayed to God, silently, and with tears of anguish: "Lord, Ed McCully was a great preacher. He could have preached a thousand great sermons to a thousand large crowds. So if Ed McCully was such a great preacher, why did you take him, Lord, when he was so young?"

According to Hebrews 11:4, Ed McCully, is, by faith, *still preaching*. He is preaching even as you, dear Reader, are reading about his martyrdom. He is preaching to us, Christ's Church, and his sermon to us is that the Gospel of Jesus Christ is of such infinite value that a man can lose his life, and thus be separated—by a murderous death—from his wife and children, and yet such a tremendous sacrifice for Christ is still worth it. *"Jesus Christ is that glorious!"* This is what Ed McCully is *still preaching* to those of us who have ears to hear him.

---

[2] At the time of Ed's martyrdom, his wife, Marilou, was pregnant with her third son. She never remarried, but worked first as a missionary in Ecuador, and then as a hospital bookkeeper in America. She died on April 24, 2004.

The Slaughtered Children are "Still Speaking"

Faith is the substance of unseen things that are seen, yes, but also *of unheard voices that are heard*. Satan works maliciously in order to silence the apostles, prophets, evangelists, and preacher-teachers of God, but by faith, they still speak. As John Chrysostom, himself a valiant martyr, once said, "For no speech avails so much, as that [of a] man's suffering."[3]

And if this is true—that those who suffer the most (for the sake of righteousness) speak the loudest—then, by faith, we ought to listen to the Anointed One, the Christ, who is *still speaking* to us in Hebrews 12:24:

> ...*[and we have come] to Jesus the Mediator of the new covenant, and to the blood of sprinkling that speaks better things than that of Abel.*

Who has suffered more than our Lord Jesus? Whose blood is able to speak more loudly than the blood of Jesus? If the voice of Jesus' blood, shed for the forgiveness of sins, speaks the loudest in this world, then we must plead that blood over our guilty world. For, are not all of us, in one way or another—whether directly, or indirectly, and whether by sins of commission or by sins of omission—guilty of selfishness regarding the Abortion Holocaust? Have we not all failed the preborn children, even we who love them and have pledged our lives to defend them, by elevating self-interest above their own plight? Therefore, should we not plead the blood of Jesus, the blood of grace and forgiveness that is *still speaking* even more loudly than the blood of Abel, over ourselves, our Churches, our nations, and our world? Perhaps God, in His wrath, shall remember mercy, and shall visit our land with the gifts of true repentance and true faith, and thus true healing.

Let us remember, then, that the "silent" voices of the little babies in the womb—including their "silent" screams when they are

---

[3] John Chrysostom, *The Homilies of John Chrysostom, Archbishop of Constantinople, on the Epistle to the Hebrews* 22.3 (NPNF¹ 14.466). The original quote has Chrysostom describing Abel's suffering, but the present author has added the parenthetical phrase to make it a more proverbial one. Taking the context of the quote into consideration, he thinks that Chrysostom would humbly permit this proverbialization of his words.

so murderously aborted—are, by faith, *still speaking* to us. As a vast army of martyrs, these precious children are still speaking to us of the love of God that is revealed to us in Christ Jesus. That is, through their martyrdoms, the preborn children of the world are speaking the Gospel to us. They are calling those who are currently dead in their sins—spiritually dead—to repent of their wicked crimes against God, to believe upon the Name of Christ Jesus (He who is God in the flesh), and to trade in their costly pride for the humble and free gift of salvation (the gift which comes only by faith in the Son of God). They are inviting people who have been living their lives outside of the Christian faith to turn away from their idols, and to return to their loving Creator, the Christ who has loved them all the way to the Cross. Their voices are beckoning lost people to deny themselves, take up their crosses, and follow the Jesus of Scripture.

The martyrs of the Abortion Holocaust are also calling those of us who believe—who are already Christians—to live more sacrificially for our neighbors. Their blood is summoning us to give a truly sacrificial witness to the Gospel. And the promise of their future resurrection from the grave, which shall be doxological, is beckoning us towards a more *God-centered* Abortion Abolitionism.

In the end, however, the voice that *still speaks* above all others (that is, the voice that speaks with the greatest authority) on the Abortion Holocaust is the gentle, quiet whisper of our Father, who is in Heaven. Neither with wind, nor with earthquake, nor with fire, but with a gentle whisper, the Father *still speaks*. He *still speaks*, as He always does, through His Word, and never apart from His Word.

In the Bible, we hear Him, the Father, *still speaking* of how He once wove together the body of His only-begotten Son in the womb. He reminds us that He once carefully carved His own Son's fingerprints in the womb, and that He once joyfully counted the exact number of delicate hairs that He had so skillfully set in place on His Son's preborn head. The Father *still speaks* to us, through Scripture, of how He once loved to listen to the sound of Jesus' heartbeat in the womb. In doing so, He *still whispers* to us, through Scripture, the things of the sacred mysteries of the glory that Christ Jesus shared with Him before the foundation of the world. And within those sacred mysteries, we learn to hear the Father's own heartbeat, which is a divine heartbeat of eternal, thrice-holy, Trinitarian love.

Divine Heartbeat

APPENDIX:
Abortion Condemned by the Church Fathers

"You shall not murder a child by abortion, nor kill [a child who] has been born." *The Didache* 2.2 (c. AD 60-150), the present author's translation.

"You shall not murder a child by abortion, nor, again, kill [a child who] has been born." *The Epistle of Barnabas* 19 (c. AD 70-132), the present author's translation.

"[Christians] marry like all [others], [and] bear children, but they do not throw away their offspring."[1] *The Epistle to Diognetus* 5.6 (c. AD 125-225), the present author's translation.

"…we say that those women who use drugs to bring on abortion commit murder, and will have to give an account to God for the abortion." Athenagoras, *Embassy for the Christians* 35 (AD 177), *ANF* 2.147.

"In our case, murder being once for all forbidden, we may not destroy even the fœtus [i.e. baby] in the womb, while as yet the human being derives blood from other parts of the body for its sustenance. To hinder a birth is merely a speedier man-killing; nor does it matter whether you take away a life that is born, or destroy one that is coming to the birth." Tertullian, *The Apology* 9 (c. AD 197-204), *ANF* 3.25.

"The womb of his wife was smitten by a blow of his heel; and in the miscarriage that soon followed, the offspring was brought forth, the fruit of a father's murder." Cyprian, *The Epistles of Cyprian* 48 (AD 251), *ANF* 5.326.

"The woman who purposely destroys her unborn child is guilty of murder." Basil of Caesarea, *The Letters of Basil* 188.2 (AD 374), *NPNF²* 8.225.

"Some, when they find themselves with child through their sin, use drugs to procure abortion, and when (as often happens) they die with their offspring, they enter the lower world laden with the guilt not only of adultery against Christ but also of suicide and child murder." Jerome, *The Letters of St. Jerome* 22.13.2 (AD 384), *NPNF²* 6.27.

---

[1] This, most likely, is a reference to the ancient Roman practice of infanticide by way of exposure. However, it certainly applies, albeit indirectly, to abortion.

Select Person Index

Alcorn, Randy: 16n27, 107-08, 222n8
Athanasius of Alexandria: 8n6, 13n15, 140n8, 260-61
Augustine of Hippo: 36n13
Bach, Johann Sebastian: 25-27
Baxter, Richard: xiv, 34n9, 38, 53n9, 216
Bounds, E.M.: x
Calvin, John: 37-38, 174-75
Carmichael, Amy: 98n10, 141n11
Chrysostom, John: xiv, 9, 36, 43n29, 45n1, 47n4, 61n13, 97, 272, 276
Comstock, Anthony: 73n11
Gibbons, Linda: 102, 108
Ham, Ken: 14n18
Henry, Matthew: 167
Hippolytus: 35-36
Irenaeus: 35n11, 152n16, 220nn.2-5, 221n6
Knox, John: 94n3
Luther, Martin: viii, x, 36-37, 39, 210n9
Martyr, Justin: 20n32
Ming-dao, Wong: 174n28
More, Hannah: 23n35
Owen, John: 38
Pink, Arthur: 38
Piper, John: 105n17
Schaeffer, Francis: ix
Tertullian: 18n31, 47n4, 152n17, 222-23, 274
Trewhella, Matt: 40n27
Tyndale, William: 4n4, 139, 173n27, 210
Wagner, Mary: 102-03, 108
Wesley, Susanna: 40
Wilberforce, William: ixn1, xiv, 23, 105, 125n11

About the Author

When grace abounds to the chief of sinners, Christians learn to boast in the Cross of Jesus Christ. Awed by the grace of God and the majesty of the Cross, Timothy Fan serves, pastorally, to remind Christ's people that they are God's image bearers, His craftsmanship, created in Christ Jesus for good works, and are, therefore, very precious to Him.

Raised in a Southern Baptist church in Denver, Colorado, Timothy studied chemistry in college and completed his seminary training at an Evangelical seminary, majoring in biblical studies. He has ministered as a teaching and senior pastor in churches in Utah, New Jersey, Pennsylvania, and Colorado. He presently serves as the founding pastor of Genesis Family Church in Westminster, Colorado.

Timothy's lifelong pursuits include savoring family life with his wife and children, training young men in whole-Bible preaching, speaking up for the preborn, being an advocate for global orphans, heralding the joys of Christian home education, and telling the Church about the rich spiritual legacy of an all-too-forgotten, ancient Christian pastor named John Chrysostom.

Soli Deo Gloria. Glory to God alone.

"For of Him, and through Him, and to Him, are all things. To Him be the glory forever! Amen." (Romans 11:36)

TO OBTAIN FREE MP3 AUDIO SERMONS BY PASTOR TIMOTHY FAN, PLEASE VISIT HIS NON-PROFIT MINISTRY WEBSITE AT:

www.godcentereduniverse.com

TO FIND MORE CHRISTIAN RESOURCES FROM AN ABORTION-ABOLITIONIST PERSPECTIVE, PLEASE VISIT:

www.gcupress.com

www.ingramcontent.com/pod-product-compliance
Lightning Source LLC
Chambersburg PA
CBHW032052090426
42744CB00005B/182